State and Local Government

State and Local Government

2007

Edited by Kevin B. Smith
University of Nebraska–Lincoln

CQ PRESS

A Division of Congressional Quarterly Inc., Washington, D.C.

CQ Press
1255 22nd Street, NW, Suite 400
Washington, DC 20037

Phone: 202-729-1900; toll-free, 1-866-4CQ-PRESS (1-866-427-7737)

Web: www.cqpress.com

Cover design by Auburn Associates, Inc., Baltimore, Maryland
Composition by Circle Graphics, Columbia, Maryland

♾ The paper used in this publication exceeds the requirements of the American National Standard for Information Sciences—Permanence of Paper for Printed Library Materials, ANSI Z39.48-1992.

Printed and bound in the United States of America

10 09 08 07 06   1 2 3 4 5

ISBN-10: 0-87289-297-2
ISBN-13: 978-0-87289-297-2
ISSN: 0888-8590

creating toll roads can relieve taxpayers
in ATT especially.

Contents

Preface

Change continues to be a central characteristic of state and local politics. For the past year or two, however, this has meant more than changing officeholders and policies. It has also meant changes in perspective. For example, in several states voters concerned about the effectiveness and financial stability of government voted for tax increases, more government spending or both. Hurricane Katrina demolished not only large sections of New Orleans and the Gulf Coast but also the reputations of executives at all levels of government, and it forced a reexamination of intergovernmental relations.

Both of these examples highlight how citizens and their representatives are reevaluating what government does, how it does it and how it should pay for it. For the past twenty years or so lower taxes were considered good, and less government regulation was considered even better. Recent activity in states and localities has called that conventional wisdom into question.

Some of these changes in attitude are being driven by the actions of the federal government, some by regional or local problems and some by issues beyond the control of any level of government. For example, energy policy at the state level during the past two decades has mostly been a tale of deregulating public utilities. Now states are scrambling to put together comprehensive energy policies to deal with rising fuel costs. Those with large agricultural bases—not always considered the firmest foundation for a state economy—are exploring the possibility of renewable fuels with gusto. Ethanol made from corn and biodiesel made from soybeans are currently hot topics in state legislatures and are leading policymakers to look at agricultural commodities in a whole new light.

State and local governments have dealt with a series of bruising battles over how evolution should (or should not) be taught in the classroom, and in the process have forced a reexamination of how education authorities should structure science and math curriculums. The threat of avian flu has pushed health and law enforcement agencies to take a long, hard look at their relationships with each other. A somewhat panicked recognition of the enormous financial obligations to retirement and pension benefits that now loom over governments has changed attitudes and perspectives on how public employees should be compensated. The list goes on. And on.

Highlighted in bold at the top of that list is Hurricane Katrina, surely the biggest tale about intergovernmental relations in a decade. Unfortunately, it is a story in which the most prominent plot lines revolve around incompetence, ineffectiveness and finger-pointing. The specific problems were bad enough: everything from the failure of the City of New Orleans to effectively plan—let alone implement—an evacuation of the city, to governors dithering over whether to allow the military to take charge, to federal officials ordering one hundred million tons of ice and sending much of it on a meandering journey to nowhere aboard a fleet of hastily hired trucks. Perhaps even more disturbing was the general problem: intergovernmental cooperation failed when it was most needed.

That failure has prompted an extensive self-evaluation by government at all levels. Whether this results in important lessons being learned will be put to the test the next time the federal system is confronted with disaster. What is indisputable, however, is that Katrina showed that local and state governments cannot count on the federal government to be the equivalent of an intergovernmental 9-1-1 service. At least initially, local and state governments are the first responders, and agencies at these levels are now reassessing how they can better work together when it really counts.

These shifts in perspective, and the events that prompted them, are detailed and explored in the readings throughout this book. Among the intended purposes of *State and Local Government* is to serve as an annual sounding on the health, direction and performance of states and localities. The readings show that not all is positive on these fronts, and they also show that state and local governments are willing to be flexible and to shift approaches if a problem or issue demands it.

Some of this shift in perspective is painful, especially when forced onto policymakers by outside events such as Hurricane Katrina, the avian flu or an energy crisis. Yet the ability to make such shifts also reflects the vibrancy and vitality of subnational governments. Undoubtedly, these are times when tough choices have to be made. Yet state and local governments are making them and surviving. Indeed, at least in some cases, they are thriving.

It is also important to note that among all this change, there are still some things that remain the same. Paramount among these is the central role that state and local governments continue to play in virtually all aspects of political, economic and social life in the United States. The readings in the 2007 edition of *State and Local Government* show that subnational governments remain closest to the day-to-day lives of citizens.

Thanks are owed to a number of people for making this volume possible: Charisse Kiino and the rest of the folks at CQ Press, numerous colleagues in the state and local politics parish of political science, and a number of grad students who drew the short straw and served as my research assistants as this volume was being put together. We hope that you find what follows informative and thought provoking.

State and Local Government

Federalism and Intergovernmental Relations

An ill wind recently blew through intergovernmental relations in the United States. In fact, it came ashore at more than one hundred miles per hour, devastated New Orleans, smashed communities from Texas to Mississippi and exposed serious weaknesses in the ability of local, state, and federal governments to work together.

Hurricane Katrina is certainly not the only story in federalism and intergovernmental relations from the past year or two. It is, however, the most important and the most instructive. Federal political systems mean that policy responsibilities and powers are, by design, divided between a central government and its regional counterparts. This arrangement of shared powers and overlapping policy responsibilities means effective government virtually requires effective intergovernmental relations. Katrina provided a classic example of ineffective intergovernmental relations: an unclear division of labor, a confused chain of command, poor coordination, communication breakdowns and a temptation—not always avoided—to assign blame instead of focusing on the problem at hand. As the hurricane made abundantly clear, when federalism doesn't work the results aren't pretty.

One of the few positive results of Katrina is a high-profile effort to examine how different levels of government can work together better. If the storm showed how intergovernmental relations should not function, perhaps it also contained lessons on how to do things right. To understand those lessons, to understand how to fashion more effective, coordinated responses to problems, it is necessary to first understand the nature of intergovernmental relationships. The connections among local, state, and federal authorities, as well as how responsibilities and power are divided among these authorities, are constantly evolving.

In recent years we have seen a steady erosion of New Federalism, the movement to devolve power from the federal government back to the states. In its place we have seen what has been termed Ad Hoc Federalism, or the idea that the federal government supports or opposes state and local autonomy based on political and fiscal convenience, rather than on the basis of a core philosophy of governance. Generally speaking, the federal government has been taking a larger role in a wide variety of issue areas—everything from disaster response, to insurance regulation, to public education. As Katrina showed, however, this larger role has not always translated into effective—or even accountable—governance.

NEW FEDERALISM BECOMES AD HOC FEDERALISM

Federalism is the central organizational characteristic of the American political system. In federal systems, national and regional governments share powers and are considered independent equals.[1] In other words, states are sovereign governments. They must obey the mandates of the U.S. Constitution, but other than that caveat, they are free to do as they wish. State governments primarily get their power from their citizens in the form of their own state constitutions. At least in theory, they are not dependent on the federal government for power, nor do they have any obligation to obey federal requests that are not mandated by the Constitution.

In practice, the federal system established by the U.S. Constitution left the federal and state governments to figure out for themselves who had to do what, and who had to foot the bill for doing it.[2] Initially, the federal and state governments tried to keep to themselves, pursuing a doctrine of dual federalism, or the idea that federal and state governments have separate and distinct jurisdictions and responsibilities. Dual federalism was dead by World War II, a victim of the need to exert centralized economic and social power to fight two world wars and deal with the Great Depression.

These needs, and the general acknowledgement that the state and federal governments had shared and overlapping interests in a wide range of policy areas, gave rise to cooperative federalism. The core of cooperative federalism is the idea that both levels of government must work together to address social and economic problems. The basic division of labor that emerged was for the federal government to identify the problem, establish a basic outline of how to respond to it and then turn over the responsibility of implementation to state and local governments along with some or all of the money to fund the response programs.

Cooperative federalism defined and described the basic relationship between state and federal governments for much of the twentieth century. This arrangement, though, always had critics who feared that the transfer of money at the heart of the relationship allowed the federal government to assert primacy over the states. The basic argument was that by becoming a central source of money for programs run by the states, the federal government would become a living embodiment of the golden rule: he who has the gold gets to make the rules.

This prophecy came to pass. The federal government began putting strings on its grants to states and localities, requiring them to pass and enforce certain laws or meet certain requirements as a condition of receiving the money. States and localities didn't like this much, but were faced with an uncomfortable choice. They could refuse to go along—as they were allowed to do as sovereign governments—but then they lost the money. Things got really bad as the federal government began passing unfunded mandates in the 1970s and 1980s, essentially ordering the states to establish programs and policies while providing either a fraction of their cost or no financial support at all.

Cooperative federalism spawned a backlash that coalesced into a sustained political agenda termed New Federalism, which took as its explicit goals the reversal of the flow of power from the states to the federal government and an end to the federal government's fiscal responsibilities to the states. President Ronald Reagan openly embraced New Federalism in the 1980s, cutting and consolidating grant programs. President Bill Clinton, like Reagan a former governor, also supported key New Federalism initiatives in the 1990s. These included radically transforming welfare policy by turning over much of the responsibility to the states and supporting passage of the Unfunded Mandate Reform Act, designed to stop the federal government from passing obligations on to the states without funding them.

When George W. Bush became president in 2001, it seemed as if New Federalism was about to hit a threshold moment. Bush was also a former governor, and his conservative political philosophy seemed naturally sympathetic to the notion of pushing power down from the federal government and toward the states and localities. Very early during his tenure as president, however, powerful forces aligned to slow, and even reverse, the trend of decentralization that had emerged during the previous two decades. A recession, the terrorist attacks of September 11, 2001 and drawn out guerilla conflicts in Afghanistan and Iraq created pressures on the federal government to take the central role. Political scientists and historians have long noted that power tends to flow toward the states during times of peace and prosperity and back toward the federal government during times of war and economic stress (this is sometimes called the cyclical theory of federalism). The reason for power accumulating at the federal level during such times is simple: the federal government is simply better positioned to coordinate and implement responses to problems whose causes and consequences are beyond the borders of the states.

Yet the fading of New Federalism is not simply a product of unforeseen national and international events. The Bush administration has pushed for federal primacy across a wide range of policy areas, many of which are traditionally the jurisdiction of state and local governments. Key domestic initiatives of the Bush administration have strengthened the federal government's hand at the expense of the states. The No Child Left Behind (NCLB) Act, for example, requires states and localities to set up expensive new programs that are not fully funded by the federal laws that require them.

NCLB is an example of the ad hoc nature of federal-state partnerships that have evolved under the Bush administration. Underlying cooperative federalism was a core philosophy of governance, a systematic notion of how federalism should work: the federal government will identify the problems, provide the resources (along with some constraints) and states and localities will actually address the problems. New Federalism had a different notion of how federalism should work, but one that was still relatively systematic: the federal government should allow the states to take more policymaking discretion and less money. Ad Hoc Federalism seems to lack any such consistency. NCLB restricted state policymaking discretion, and set up an expensive set of requirements that were not fully funded. In effect, the federal government chose to identify a problem, moreover one in a policy area long seen as the province of the states, then required the states to address that problem in a particular way, but did not fully back those requirements financially. This mix and match philosophy towards state-fed-

eral relations has sparked controversy. Conservative Republican lawmakers in such states as Utah, for example, have actually pursued legal action against a federal government controlled by conservative Republicans over the NCLB requirements.

This chapter contains a series of essays that highlight key areas of the most recent developments in state/local and federal relations. The essay by Jonathan Walters and Donald Kettl details the problems in intergovernmental relations exposed by Hurricane Katrina, and examines some of the lessons that need to be learned and applied to prevent similar failures in the future. The significant difficulties of coordinating federal, state and local governments are further highlighted in an essay by Jonathan Walters on the difficulties of how federal grants can be distributed most effectively. As the essay makes clear, it's not just having (or not having) federal money that counts for state and local governments. Sometimes the real problem is insuring that it's spent wisely.

Also included is a study of federal preemption of state laws by Joseph F. Zimmerman. Zimmerman's study shows that the federal government is acting less and less as a partner in a federal system, and more like the powerful head of a unitary system. While states inarguably remain important and influential policymaking actors, this research shows the federal government, in effect, taking over entire regulatory sectors of governance. Finally, the essay by Jack Penchoff shows another side of intergovernmental relations: interstate compacts. Intergovernmental relations covers not just vertical relationships, but also horizontal relationships. States do not simply deal with the federal government above them and local governments below. They cooperate with each other, forming contractual relationships in the form of interstate compacts. These relationships are a primary means to address regional and even national issues.

Notes

1. Kevin B. Smith, Alan Greenblatt, and John Buntin, *Governing States & Localities* (Washington, D.C.: CQ Press, 2004), 26.

2. The U.S. Constitution does lay down a basic set of responsibilities for federal and state governments. See Lee Epstein and Thomas G. Walker, *Constitutional Law for a Changing America: Institutional Powers and Constraints,* 5th ed. (Washington, D.C.: CQ Press, 2004), 323.

1

The Katrina Breakdown

Jonathan Walters and Donald Kettl

Coordination and communication problems between levels of government must be addressed before the next disaster strikes.

When Hurricane Katrina hit New Orleans, only one thing disintegrated as fast as the earthen levees that were supposed to protect the city, and that was the intergovernmental relationship that is supposed to connect local, state and federal officials before, during and after such a catastrophe.

In sifting through the debris of the disaster response, the first question is why intergovernmental cooperation broke down so completely. While it's hard even at this point to get an official accounting of exactly what happened, clearly there were significant communication and coordination problems at all levels of government. At the moment, much time and effort is being spent assigning culpability—for a lack of preparation, delayed decision making, bureaucratic tie-ups and political infighting—to individuals and agencies. But in the end, such investigations may produce little that is of widespread practical use.

What is more critical, and has significant implications for the future of emergency management in the United States, is the need to explicitly and thoroughly define governments' roles and responsibilities so that officials in other jurisdictions don't suffer the same sort of meltdown in the next natural or man-made disaster. The lurching tactical responses to the terrorist attacks of 2001 and this year's rash of major hurricanes only underline the truly fundamental issue: how to sort out who should do what—and how to make sure the public sector is ready to act when the unexpected but inevitable happens.

It won't be easy. Some in the federal government clearly feel that if they're going to be blamed for failures—failures that they ascribe at least in part to state and local officials—then they'd

From *Governing,* December 2005.

4

prefer a system where the federal government has the option of being much more preemptive in handling large-scale domestic disasters. States as a whole, though, are not going to go along with any emergency management plan that involves the feds declaring something like martial law. They would much prefer that existing protocols be continued and the Federal Emergency Management Agency regain its independence from the Department of Homeland Security and be led by experienced professionals rather than political appointees.

A GROWING FEDERAL ROLE

In fact, the history of disaster response and recovery in the United States has witnessed an ever-increasing federal role. On April 22, 1927, President Calvin Coolidge named a special cabinet-level committee headed by Commerce Secretary Herbert Hoover to deal with the massive flooding that was ravaging communities up and down the Mississippi River Valley that year. The scene, described in John M. Barry's highly topical chronicle, *Rising Tide: The Great Mississippi Flood of 1927 and How It Changed America,* arguably represents the beginning of the modern era of intergovernmental disaster response. (It also represents the first clear attempt to politicize federal disaster response, with Hoover consciously riding his performance during the disaster all the way to the White House.)

In 1950, the federal government began trying to formalize intergovernmental roles and responsibilities through the Federal Civil Defense Act, which defined the scope and type of assistance that the federal government would extend to states and localities after certain kinds of disasters or emergencies (although Congress had been offering financial aid to states and localities in a piecemeal fashion since the early 1800s). In 1979, President Jimmy Carter created the Federal Emergency Management Agency, largely in response to governors' complaints about the fragmented nature of federal disaster planning and assistance. And in 1988, Congress, passed the Robert T. Stafford Disaster Relief Act, which outlined the protocols for disaster declaration and what sort of intergovernmental response would follow.

From 1989 to 1992, a succession of disasters, including the Loma Prieta earthquake in California and hurricanes Hugo in South Carolina and Andrew in Florida put the whole issue of intergovernmental emergency response in

the public hot seat, notes Tom Birkland, director of the Center for Policy Research at the Rockefeller College of Public Affairs and Policy. In particular, the disasters highlighted the federal government's slow-footed and bureaucratic response in the wake of such catastrophic events. (To be sure, such events were also teaching state and local governments plenty about *their* emergency response capabilities). That, in turn, led to a major turn-around at FEMA, with the appointment of James Lee Witt, the first FEMA director to arrive on the job with actual state emergency management experience.

In general, two things were going on around the increasing federal role in emergency readiness and response, Birkland says. States and localities were getting hooked on federal money—especially for recovery. But American presidents were also discovering the political benefits of declaring disasters, which allowed them to liberally sprinkle significant amounts of cash around various states and localities in distress. "That spending grew considerably under the Clinton administration," says Birkland. "And it created the expectation of federal government largesse. Federal spending, however, was always meant to supplement and not supplant state and local spending."

LOCAL RESPONSE

But if the federal role in disaster response and recovery has increased—along with expectations of federal help—emergency management experts at all levels still agree on the basics of existing emergency response protocol: All emergencies are, initially at least, local—or local and state—events. "For the first 48 to 72 hours, it's understood that local and state first responders are principally responsible," says Bill Jenkins, director of the Homeland Security and Justice Issues Group, which is currently looking into the intergovernmental response to Katrina. "The feds come in as requested after that."

The extent to which the local-state-federal response ramps up depends on a host of factors, including the size of the incident and what plans and agreements are in place prior to any event. It also very much depends on the capacity of the governments involved. Some local and state governments have the ability to deal with disasters on their own and seem less inclined to ask for outside help. Others seem to hit the intergovernmental panic button more quickly. But whichever it is, say those on the front line of emergency response, how various governmental partners in emergency response and recovery are going to respond shouldn't be a surprise-filled adventure. Key players at every level of government should have a very good idea of what each will be expected to do or provide when a particular disaster hits.

Most important to the strength of the intergovernmental chain are solid relationships among those who might be called upon to work closely together in times of high stress. "You don't want to meet someone for the first time while you're standing around in the rubble," says Jarrod Bernstein, spokesman for the New York City Office of Emergency Management. "You want to meet them during drills and exercises." In New York, says Bernstein, the city has very tight relationships with state and federal officials in a variety of agencies. "They're involved in all our planning and all our drills. They have a seat at all the tabletop exercises we do."

During those exercises, says Bernstein, federal, state and local officials establish and agree on what their respective jobs will be when a "big one" hits. Last summer, for example, the city worked with FEMA, the U.S. Department of Health and Human Services, the Federal Bureau of Investigation and New York State health and emergency response officials on an exercise aimed at collecting 8 million doses of medicine and distributing them throughout the city in a 48-hour window. "What we were looking at is how we'd receive medical stockpiles from the federal government, break them down and push them out citywide. There is a built-in federal component to that plan," Bernstein says.

NO PLAN B

While pre-plans and dry runs are all well and good, they're not much use if not taken seriously, however. In 2004, FEMA and Louisiana's Office of Homeland Security and Emergency Preparedness, conducted a tabletop exercise, called Hurricane Pam, that simulated a Category 3 storm hitting and flooding New Orleans. It identified a huge gap in disaster planning: An estimated 100,000 people wouldn't be able to get out of the city without assistance. As is standard in emergency management practice, it is the locality's responsibility—at least initially—to evacuate residents, unless other partners are identified beforehand.

Critics of Mayor Ray Nagin say he failed to follow up aggressively on the finding. Last spring, the city floated the notion that it would rely primarily on the faith-based community to organize and mobilize caravans for those without cars or who needed special assistance getting out of the city. The faith-based community balked, however, citing liability issues. The city never came up with a Plan B.

Meanwhile, the Department of Homeland Security had great confidence in its 426-page "all-hazards" National Response Plan. Unveiled last January, it "establishes standardized training, organization and communications procedures for multi-jurisdictional interaction; clearly identifies authority and leadership responsibilities; enables incident response to be handled at the lowest possible organizational and jurisdictional level; ensures the seamless integration of the federal government when an incident exceeds state or local capabilities; and provides the means to swiftly deliver federal support in response to catastrophic incidents."

Katrina was its first test. And in the wake of the Category 4 storm and subsequent flooding, the city's vital resources—communications, transportation, supplies and manpower—were quickly overwhelmed. But DHS Secretary Michael Chertoff waited until 24 hours after the levees were breached to designate the hurricane as an "incident of national significance—requiring an extensive and well-coordinated response by federal, state, local tribal and nongovernmental authorities to save lives, minimize damage and provide the basis for long-term community and economic recovery."

The nation—indeed the world—bore painful witness to its failure. "There are mechanisms and protocols set up as part of the National Response Plan, and those were not followed," says John R. Harrald, director of the Institute for Crisis, Disaster and Risk Management at George Washington University. Harrald notes that under the response plan, one of the first things that's supposed to happen is the rapid activation of a joint operations center to coordinate the intergovernmental response. In Louisiana, that didn't happen quickly enough, he says.

CALLING IN THE TROOPS

As a result of Katrina, and to a lesser extent hurricanes Rita and Wilma, the general citizenry and elected leaders at all levels of government, as well as emergency responders up and down the chain of command, are demanding a comprehensive review of how local, state and federal governments work (or don't work) together.

Part of that discussion has to include what to do when a state or local government's ability to prepare, respond or to ask for help is either impaired or wiped out altogether. "The question is what do you do when state and local capacity fails for one reason or another, either because they're overwhelmed or they're incompetent," says GWU's Harrald. "Do we have a system that allows us to scale up adequately or do we need a system where we can bring the military in sooner but that doesn't give away state and local control?"

Bill Leighty, Virginia Governor Mark Warner's chief of staff, who volunteered to spend two weeks in Louisiana helping manage the state response to Katrina, says he thinks there needs to be a serious intergovernmental discussion about when, for example, it might be appropriate to involve the military more directly in a domestic crisis. It is a position born of watching FEMA in action, versus what he saw of the military while he was in New Orleans. FEMA's bureaucratic approach to every item it provided or action it took was, at times, brutally exasperating, says Leighty. "But when you tell the 82nd Airborne, 'Secure New Orleans,' they come in and they know exactly what to do and it gets done."

Even some long-time New Orleans residents, who watched helplessly as looters rampaged through parts of the city, say they wouldn't have minded at all if the military had stepped in to restore order. "There are times when people are overwhelmed," says Frank Cilluffo, director of the Homeland Security Policy Institute at George Washington University, "and they don't care what color uniform is involved in coming to the rescue—red, blue or green."

However, both Kathleen Babineaux Blanco, the Democratic governor of Louisiana, and Haley Barbour, the Republican governor of Mississippi, strenuously objected to requests from the White House to give the Pentagon command over their states' National Guard troops. And President George W. Bush's suggestion of a quick resort to the military in future disasters stunned many observers, including those in his own party. In a television address from New Orleans, he argued that only the armed forces were "capable of massive logistical operations on a moment's notice."

But governors were aghast at the idea that the military would become America's first responders. In a *USA Today* poll, 36 of 38 governors (including brother Jeb Bush) opposed the plan. Michigan Governor Jennifer

Granholm put it bluntly: "Whether a governor is a Republican or Democrat, I would expect the response would be, 'Hell no.'" For one blogger, the worry was "How long before a creek flooding in a small town in Idaho will activate the 82d Airborne Division?"

Bush grabbed the military option partly because of the poor performance of state and local governments. Indeed, everyone breathed a sigh of relief when Coast Guard Admiral Thad Allen arrived to assume command.

Part of the explanation also lies in public opinion polls. A Pew Research Center survey just after the storm revealed that nearly half of those surveyed believed state and local governments had done a fair or poor job—and there was no partisan difference on that conclusion. That meant the smart political play for Bush, although he didn't fare much better in the poll, was to suggest that the military might have to do what state and local governments could not.

That idea, of course, could scarcely be further from the strategy the Republicans had spent a generation building. The Richard Nixon-Ronald Reagan model of new federalism revolved around giving the states more autonomy and less money. But faced with the need to do something—and lacking any alternative—Bush reached back to Lyndon Johnson's Great Society philosophy of an expanded role for the federal government.

But Bush's plan to push the military into a first-response role was clearly less a broad policy strategy than a tactic to find a safe haven in the post-Katrina blame game. That became clear in November, when he announced his avian flu initiative. In that plan, he penciled in a heavy role for state and local public health officials.

CONTROL AND CONTENTION

Some believe there is a middle ground when it comes to issues of authority and autonomy. James A. Stever, director of the Center for Integrated Homeland Security and Crisis Management at the University of Cincinnati, says he and colleagues had forwarded a paper to the former head of Homeland Security, Tom Ridge, outlining the concept of "homeland restoration districts." The idea is to have established criteria for when a more robust federal disaster response might be appropriate. Recovery districts would allow for ad hoc federal takeovers of specific geographic areas when appropriate, says Stever, rather than creating some new, overriding national response protocol that calls for broad federal preemption of local and state authority.

But sifting through such ideas—and the others that are sure to surface—is going to mean rekindling the sort of conversation about intergovernmental coordination and cooperation that Washington hasn't seen in a long time. Whether the current Congress and administration will be willing to conduct that conversation isn't clear. State and local officials, for their part, have been called in by Congress to testify on how the intergovernmental response to disasters ought to go. But such sessions have frequently had the familiar ring of both state and local tensions over who controls federal funding, as well as a little tin-cup rattling.

For example, in testimony before the House Homeland Security Committee, David Wallace, mayor of Sugar Land, Texas, argued that the first lesson learned in the wake of Katrina is that local governments should have more control over how federal homeland security first-responder money should be spent. "There was a real concern from the beginning that an over-reliance by the federal government on a state-based distribution system for first responder resources and training would be slow and result in serious delays in funding reaching high-threat, high-risk population areas." Wallace concluded his testimony with a request for federal funding for what he describes as Regional Logistics Centers, designed to bring local regional resources to bear in the immediate aftermath of disasters.

Nor is it only touchy issues of funding and control related to readiness and response that need discussing, points out Paul Posner, who spent years as a GAO intergovernmental affairs analyst. "There's other knotty issues that cause a lot of intergovernmental friction, like federal insurance policies, local building codes and state land use policies." These are key issues that Posner points out all influence how vulnerable certain places are to disasters in the first place.

From hurricanes and pandemics and to earthquakes and terrorism, the United States is grappling with the prospect of a host of cataclysmic events. Taken individually, most communities face a small chance of being hit, but experts agree that its not a matter of "if" but "when" another large-scale disaster will occur somewhere in the United States. As Katrina so powerfully illustrated, a fragmented intergovernmental response can be disastrous.

2

Stressed Responders

Jonathan Walters

From *Governing*,
January 2006.

Federal disaster money
doesn't help much unless
governments get together
on how to use it.

When it comes to homeland security and disaster preparedness and response, the current buzzwords are
"coordination," "cooperation" and "interoperability."
Actually, those have pretty much been the buzzwords for the past
two decades, born of hard experience: That is, discovering in the
midst of a crisis that police can't talk to firefighters, who can't talk to
emergency medical personnel, who can't talk to state fish and wildlife
or forestry people, or any feds whatsoever. Or—even more basic—
discovering in the midst of a disaster that one fire company's hose
couplings don't connect up to those of a neighboring jurisdiction.

And so the country is now engaged in a often-ignored but crucial debate: How do you distribute federal grant money for homeland security in a way that avoids fragmentation and encourages
cooperation?

Localities have long argued that because they bear the initial
brunt of emergency response, they are entitled to more control over
how federal money is spent. The U.S. Conference of Mayors argues
that Congress should ditch the current "state-based system for distribution of federal first responder assistance" and hand the money
directly to local governments. State officials respond that the money
has to be distributed to localities in ways that will ensure coordination and reduce duplication, and that states are the only ones who
play that role.

In fact, the argument goes far beyond the issue of homeland
security. Control of federal grant money has been a point of contention between states and localities ever since the invention of
federal aid, whether the money is for economic development, environmental protection or social services. Locals always argue their

status as the providers of first resort; states always argue that flinging money at disparate localities virtually guarantees a fragmented system.

Which is why a third approach is worth considering as the emergency response debate heats up. It is an approach supported by a growing cadre of emergency response officials who are actually serious about cooperation, coordination and interoperability. They argue that all significant disasters are, in fact, not local in nature but regional. Therefore, they say, any solid preparedness and response plan should not be organized along local lines but by region, taking in multiple localities and states.

One of the more dogged proponents of this third way is James H. Schwartz, chief of the Fire Department in Arlington County, Virginia. Schwartz was incident commander at the Pentagon on 9/11, and his agency's response on that day is now widely considered a model of rapid and effective intergovernmental action.

Schwartz doesn't argue that states should be stripped of their role as keeper of the purse strings. Rather, he says, states should leverage federal money to move entrenched local interests out of their compartmentalized worlds. Emergency response regions should be designated, and all

players within those regions brought together—law enforcement, fire, EMS, health, housing and social services—to figure out what threats the region might be vulnerable to. Inter-agency teams would then develop plans for responding to such threats.

In fact, there's an existing model for how to do this. It is the Metropolitan Medical Response System, created to pull together all the groups that would be required to step up in the event of a biological, chemical or radiological incident. It is administered by the Department of Homeland Security and operates in 124 metropolitan areas. Under MMRS, everyone from cops to doctors can be included in response plans.

"I've always said that I don't want any more money," says Arlington's Schwartz. "What I want is that the money we do have be spent more carefully and according to a system that's created by a meaningful conversation among all levels of government."

It's amazing that such a common-sense approach to a crucial area of public policy doesn't come naturally to those in charge of emergency response money. But it's not too late to force the issue. The conversation that Schwartz advocates is long overdue.

3

Congressional Preemption: Removal of State Regulatory Powers

Joseph F. Zimmerman

Congress pushes aside the states in order to claim the power to regulate.

From *PS: Political Science and Politics,* July 2005.

The balance of national and state powers has undergone continuous readjustment since 1790, without a constitutional amendment by means of numerous congressional preemption statutes superseding completely or partially certain regulatory powers of the states and thereby effectuating a major transformation in the federal system. Congress since 1978 has increased its regulation of subnational governments as polities by enacting preemption statutes containing mandates and restraints (Zimmerman 1994) while simultaneously enacting other statutes providing for extensive deregulation of the banking and communications industries and complete economic deregulation of the air, bus, and rail transportation companies.

Courts, including the United States Supreme Court, generally have interpreted broadly Congress's delegated powers, particularly the power to regulate "commerce … among the several states." The Supreme Court in *Elrod v. Ashcroft* (537 U.S. 186), in 2003, for example, upheld the constitutionality of the *Sonny Bono Copyright Term Extension Act of 1998* (112 Stat. 2827) against the charge that Congress abused its constitutional authority to offer copyright protection to authors "for limited times" by extending such protection from 20 to 70 years after the death of an author and to 95 years from the publication of works created for or by corporations. The Walt Disney Company was a prime beneficiary of the act.

A complete preemption statute may not deny states a role in the regulatory field as Congress recognized they could play helpful roles including enforcement of such a statute. The *United States Grain Standards Act of 1968* (82 Stat. 769), for example, allows the administrator of the Federal Grain Inspection Service to delegate authority to state agencies to perform official inspection and weighing. And the *Age Discrimination in Employment Amendments of 1986* (100 Stat. 3342) authorizes the Equal Employment Opportunity Commission to sign cooperative enforcement agreements with state or local fair-employment agencies.

PREEMPTION STATUTES ENACTMENT PACE

The Constitution's Framers apparently assumed Congress would employ the various delegated powers shortly after the fundamental document was ratified by the states. Congress in 1790 enacted two complete preemption statutes—*Copyright Act* (1 Stat. 124) and Patent Act (1 Stat. 109)—and subsequently enacted a total of only 29 such statutes by 1900. Many preemption statutes, including recent ones, were spurred by inventions and technological developments. Congress's reaction to inventions was not always rapid. *An Act to Regulate Interstate Commerce* (24 Stat. 379), creating the Interstate Commerce Commission to regulate railroad fares and tariffs, was not enacted until 1887. The Commission was abolished in 1996 (109 Stat. 803) because its most important functions were removed by economic deregulation preemption statutes and its remaining functions were transferred to other departments and agencies.

In the twentieth century Congress increasingly relied upon conditional grants-in-aid to encourage states to implement its policies until 1965 when heavy reliance began to be placed upon preemption statutes which were enacted at the following pace: 14 (1900–1909), 22 (1910–1919), 17 (1920–1929), 31 (1930–1939), 16 (1940–1949), 24 (1950–1959), 47 (1960–1969), 102 (1970–1979), 93 (1980–1989), 83 (1990–1999), and 42 (2000–2004) (Zimmerman and Lawrence 1992; Zimmerman 2005). A total of 520 such statutes have been enacted with several subsequently repealed. A significant number of these statutes were designed to eliminate interstate trade barriers (Zimmerman 2004). It should be noted that a few preemption statutes contain a sunset clause which Congress may extend. The *Internet Tax Freedom Act of 1998* (112 Stat. 2681) expired in 2003, but was renewed and extended in 2004 (117 Stat. 2615) for three years.

Congress at its discretion may broaden the coverage of a partial preemption statute, as it did in 1991 when it amended the *Employee Retirement Income Security Act of 1974* to include within its coverage telephone and electric cooperative welfare plans (105 Stat. 446). The act was amended again in 2000 "to clarify the application to a church plan that is a welfare plan to State insurance laws that require or solely relate to licensing, solvency, insolvency, or the status of such a plan as a single employer plan" (114 Stat. 499).

Commencing in 1965, Congress initiated a major federalism revolution as regulatory laws were enacted with increased frequency in a wide range of fields previously not preempted and a new type of preemption statute—minimum standards—was employed. Many statutes contain mandates requiring subnational governments to initiate specified expensive actions. Certain preemption statutes, primarily minimum standards preemptions, authorize grants-in-aid to assist subnational governments in financing their regulatory responsibilities. A small number of statutes contain restraints forbidding these governments to initiate a specific action, thereby necessitating a more expensive alternative, as illustrated by the *Ocean Dumping Ban Act of 1988* (102 Stat. 4139) which prevented New York City and other municipalities from continuing to dump sewage sludge in the Atlantic Ocean and necessitated the more expensive shipment of the sludge by dedicated trains to disposal sites in Texas (Zimmerman 1994). Fourteen preemption statutes devolve executive powers upon governors, thereby upsetting the constitutional balance of gubernatorial and legislative powers in each state.

The sharp increase in the number of post-1965 preemption statutes is a response to: (1) the failure of states by means of interstate cooperation to solve many multistate problems, including air and water pollution; (2) the ineffectiveness of conditional grants-in-aid in eliminating national problems; (3) the general failure of states to enact harmonious regulatory policies; (4) lobbying by industries, such as the motor vehicle industry, burdened with increasing nonharmonious state regulatory policies; (5) effective lobbying by public interest groups, particularly those representing civil liberties and environmental issues; (6) the election of members of Congress lacking state and local government experience; and (7) activism by certain members of Congress seeking to establish a leadership record in solving major problems as part of their respective strategy of winning the presidency in a future election. The pace of enactment of such statutes slowed somewhat after the Republican party assumed control of Congress in 1995, with 76 enacted by 2004.

INTEREST GROUP LOBBYING

A positive correlation exists between the increased number of preemption statutes enacted by Congress and the growing influence of private and public interest groups, which naturally transferred part of their attention from state capitols to the national capitol as Congress became more deeply involved in traditional state and local governmental functions. Groups unable to achieve fully or partially their goals by lobbying state legislatures and governors redirected resources to influence Congress, the president, and national bureaucrats with varying degrees of success.

How can states protect their regulatory authority against potential congressional preemption? Chief Justice John Marshall of the United States Supreme Court in *Gibbons v. Ogden* provided an answer in 1824, relative to the interstate commerce clause, when he opined: "The wisdom and the discretion of Congress, their identity with the people, and the influence which their constituents possess at elections, are, in this, as in many other instances, as that, for example of declaring war, the sole restraint on which they have relied to secure them from its abuse" (22 U.S. 1 at 197).

Herbert Wechsler in 1953 employed this thesis to develop the political safeguard of federalism theory, holding that states can engage in the national political process to help elect members of Congress who will protect the states' reserved regulatory powers. Justice Harry A. Blackman of the Supreme Court endorsed this theory in 1985 in *Garcia v. San Antonio Metropolitan Transit Authority* (469 U.S. 528 at 556) when he wrote "the principal and basic limits on the federal commerce power is inherent in all state participation in federal government action." He urged states to seek protection of their regulatory powers not in the courts, but in the political branch of government, i.e., the Congress.

Subnational government officers often lobby Congress for relief from burdensome mandates. The 104th Congress responded by enacting the *Unfunded Mandates Reform Act of 1995* (109 Stat. 48) establishing new congressional procedures for enactment of mandates. The next year Congress provided relief from expensive directives contained in the *Safe Drinking Water Amendments*

of 1986 (110 Stat. 1613) which threatened numerous small local governments with the choice of bankruptcy or abandonment of their drinking water supply system.

Each of the following four sections contains a brief description of the roles played by interest groups in the enactment of a devolution or a preemption statute.

Insurance Industry Regulation

Congress took no action to regulate the business of insurance and the Supreme Court in 1868 in *Paul v. Virginia* (75 Stat. 168) opined such business did not involve interstate commerce and therefore was exempt from congressional regulation. Subsequent nonharmonious state regulation of insurance companies led to a major court challenge. The Supreme Court in 1944 reversed its earlier decision and held that the business of insurance involves interstate commerce and was subject to congressional regulation (322 U.S. 533). The potential loss of substantial amounts of revenue derived from such regulation induced states to lobby Congress to reverse the Court's decision. Congress responded by enacting the *McCarran-Ferguson Act of 1945* (59 Stat. 33) devolving authority to states to regulate the business of insurance. Continuation of disharmonious state regulatory powers encouraged the insurance industry to lobby Congress successfully to provide relief in 1999 (113 Stat. 1415, 1419) in the form of the establishment of national minimum standards in 13 areas and threatened to establish a national licensing system for insurance agents if 26 states did not establish a harmonious licensing system by 2002. A national licensing system was avoided when 35 states were certified as having a harmonious licensing system.

Water Quality

Citizens, growing increasingly concerned with environmental pollution, organized national associations which, by 1965, persuaded Congress to enact its first environmental regulatory act, the *Water Quality Act* (79 Stat. 903), now known as the *Clean Water Act*. Farm organizations were successful in ensuring the act would be relatively weak. Water quality today in many areas is poor because Congress did not address the animal manure problem. A 2004 report revealed animals in one Maryland-Pennsylvania watershed produce annually 77 million gallons of liquid manure and more than 58,000 tons of solid manure which are discharged into the Chesapeake Bay (Jarrett 2004, 22).

Motor Vehicle Safety Equipment

The motor vehicle industry in the mid-1960s changed its view relative to governmental regulation as it feared public demands for specific motor vehicle safety equipment would result in state legislatures enacting nonharmonious safety equipment requirements. Absent preemption the industry would be faced with the prospect it would have to manufacture vehicles with specific safety features for sale in each state to comply with the different regulatory standards. The industry lobbied Congress to enact the *National Traffic and Motor Vehicle Safety Act of 1966* (80 Stat. 719) which completely preempted state regulatory power over motor vehicle safety equipment with the exceptions of motor vehicles operated by a state or local government which met higher safety standards.

Air Quality Act

State legislatures commenced to regulate emissions from motor vehicles in the 1960s. This regulation concerned the motor vehicle industry, which feared a different engine emission control system would have to be manufactured to meet the different emissions standards in each state. The industry and its allies—glass, plastics, rubber, and steel industries—encouraged Congress to include a provision in the *Air Quality Act of 1967* (81 Stat. 485), now known as the *Clean Air Act,* totally preempting state regulatory authority over motor vehicle emissions. California had stricter standards than the proposed federal ones and successfully lobbied Congress for an exception from the preemption provision, thereby necessitating the industry to build two engine emissions control systems for several years until new emission control systems were developed enabling all new vehicles to meet the California standards.

Motor Truck Size and Weight

The trucking industry and the Teamsters Union simultaneously lobbied Congress successfully to remove state authority to establish maximum truck sizes and weights by enacting the *Surface Transportation Assistance Act of 1982* (96 Stat. 2097) allowing heavy trucks, including tandem and triple trailers, to operate on interstate highways, certain federally aided primary routes (designated by the secretary of transportation), and local "access" routes to service stations, motels, restaurants, and terminals. The act's purpose was to eliminate the patchwork quilt of conflicting state truck-size and weight limits

which often required a driver to detach one or two trailers prior to entering a state. The act, however, contains no criteria for determining whether older interstate and federally aided primary highways were capable of accommodating the larger and heavier trucks safely or identifying the local roads that are *bona fide* "access" routes.

State highway officers protested that the traffic congestion and substandard design and condition of many highways with interstate designations constructed prior to the enactment of the *National Defense and Interstate Highway Act of 1956* (70 Stat. 374) could not accommodate safely larger and heavier trucks including tandem-trailer trucks. Congress responded to state lobbying by enacting the *Tandem Truck Safety Act of 1984* (98 Stat. 2829–830) and the *Motor Carrier Safety Act of 1984* (98 Stat. 2829–832).

The first act established a procedure allowing a governor, after consulting concerned local governments, to notify the secretary of transportation that a specific segment(s) of an interstate highway can not accommodate safely large trucks and also permitting state officers to place reasonable restrictions on use of "access" roads by heavy trucks. The second act directs the secretary to promulgate rules and regulations establishing minimum safety standards for commercial motor vehicles, establish a safety panel to advise the secretary relative to whether state laws or regulations are incompatible with regulations promulgated by the secretary, and authorizes any person, in addition to a state, to petition the secretary for issuance of a waiver from his/her determination that a state law or regulation is preempted.

FEDERALISM THEORY

Theory has not kept pace with developments in the federal system. The theory of dual federalism is a simple one explaining a complete separation of national and state powers. The theory of cooperative federalism builds upon this theory by emphasizing the cooperative nature of national-state relations. Dissatisfaction with the explanatory values of these theories, commencing in the 1960s, led to a myriad of new terms. William H. Stewart (1984, 4) identified 497 figurative descriptors. Neither the two current theories nor the descriptors adequately explain the impact of complete, partial, contingent, and innovative preemption statutes on the current nature of the federal system.

An example of an innovative statute is the *Riegle-Neal Interstate Banking and Branching Efficiency Act of 1994* (108 Stat. 2338) which respects the long history of the dual banking system by including several exemptions and savings provisions excluding state statutes from preemption. The act also contains an "opt-in" section permitting interstate branching through *de novo* branches provided the state law "applies equally to all banks; and expressly permits out-of-state banks to establish *de novo* branches" (108 Stat. 1352). In addition, the act has an "opt-out" section (108 Stat. 2343) allowing a state legislature to prohibit interstate branching within the state otherwise authorized by the act.

There are three broad spheres of power: a national-controlling sphere, a state-controlling sphere, and a shared national-state-local sphere. The boundaries of the spheres change as Congress places more or less emphasis upon its three intergovernmental roles—facilitator, inhibitor, and initiator. A comprehensive non-equilibrium federalism theory must include elements of *imperium in imperio;* cooperative interplane interactions; informal congressional preemption in the form of conditional grants-in-aid, tax credits, and tax sanctions; and contingent, complete, partial preemption statutes (Zimmerman 2005).

CONCLUSIONS

Several original features of the federal system are observable today with states performing essential roles in an extremely complex and rapidly changing governance system as Congress displaces completely or partially their regulatory powers in an increasing number of fields. Congress in effect has become a unitary government in completely preempted regulatory fields and finances in part its policies in several other fields by imposing burdensome mandates on subnational governments.

Preemption statutes have produced fundamental changes in the nature of the federal system, yet it has not been converted into a unitary system. States retain numerous important regulatory powers that often are employed effectively in partially preempted fields. New York State Attorney General Eliot Spitzer, for example,

embarrassed the United States Securities and Exchange Commission by employing a 1921 state law (chap. 649) as the basis for successful fraud suits against the 10 largest Wall Street brokerage firms. The firms' salespersons had urged clients to purchase specified stocks knowing they were a poor investment so the firms could rake in the lucrative investment banking business and associated fees of companies preparing new stock issues. The firms paid $1.4 billion in fines to the State of New York and were forced to change their practices.

In sum, growing globalization of the economy, international trade agreements, interest group lobbying, and technological developments ensure Congress will play an increasingly dominant role in domestic governance by enacting preemption statutes particularly in the fields of banking, communications, financial services, and taxation. The federal system today is in a perpetual state of locomotion describable as kaleidoscopic rather than linear in nature.

References

Jarrett, Jan. 2004. "It's Time to Wake Up and Smell the Manure." *Bay Journal,* September 14, 22.

Stewart, William H. 1984. *Concepts of Federalism.* Lanham, MD: University Press of America.

Wechsler, Herbert. 1953. "The Political Safeguards of Federalism: The Role of the States in the Composition and Selection of the National Government." *Columbia Law Review* 54: 543–60.

Zimmerman, Joseph F. 2005. *Congressional Preemption: Regulatory Federalism.* Albany: State University of New York Press.

———. 2004. *Interstate Economic Relations.* Albany: State University of New York Press.

———. 1994. *Federally Induced Costs Affecting State and Local Governments.* Washington, D.C.: United States Advisory Commission on Intergovernmental Relations.

Zimmerman, Joseph F., and Sharon Lawrence. 1992. *Federal Statutory Preemption of State and Local Authority: History, Inventory, and Issues.* Washington, D.C.: United States Advisory Commission on Intergovernmental Relations.

4

States have used interstate compacts for more than 200 years to help settle disputes and face challenges together.

From *Statenews,*
August 2005.

Compacts Are Contracts

Jack Penchoff

Interstate compacts have played a role in state government since 1783 when the British signed the Treaty of Paris, officially recognizing the United States as a sovereign nation.

Many of those early compacts were extensions of agreements the Colonies made under British rule. And most were designed to settle boundary disputes.

More than 200 years later, compacts still play an important role as a tool of cooperation between states. That is why Delaware Gov. Ruth Ann Minner, CSG president, views the National Center for Interstate Compacts (NCIC), established by CSG in 2004, as part of her vision to promote multistate cooperation and problem solving.

"There are a lot of state compacts that citizens don't know about," she said. "In fact, some governors and legislators don't know about them."

Minner believes compacts are the principal mechanism for helping states address issues on the regional and national level.

"There is a growing need for our states to act together to address policy issues that may transcend our boundaries, or that are threatened by federal pre-emption," she said.

200 INTERSTATE COMPACTS

Some 200 compacts have been enacted nationwide to help states address multistate issues such as pollution, water rights, emergency management and child welfare.

Compacts, essentially contracts between states, can be comprised of as few as two states, such as the Delaware River and Bay Authority

16

Compact between New Jersey and Delaware, or as many as 50 states, such as the Interstate Compact on Juveniles.

Some compacts are steeped in the history of the United States. In 1785, for example, Maryland and Virginia hammered out an agreement about waterway rights on the Potomac River. The compact was negotiated at George Washington's Mount Vernon estate at what historians call the Mount Vernon Conference. The Maryland-Virginia Compact established regulatory authority between two states.

This was the first compact that wasn't about a boundary dispute.

One of the most famous compacts was signed in 1921 and established the Port Authority of New York and New Jersey. The compact ended nearly two centuries of bickering between the two states over navigation rights in their shared harbor. The dispute was so heated in the 19th century that police from the two states once exchanged gunfire in the middle of the Hudson River.

COMPACTS EVOLVE

The purposes of compacts have evolved since 1783 as the governing of states has grown more complex. Between 1783 and 1920, only 36 compacts were enacted, and most of those settled boundary disputes. Over the past 85 years, however, states have enacted more than 160 compacts.

Not only are new compacts being established, but also old ones are being updated. For example, Gov. Minner supports current efforts to revise the Interstate Compact on the Placement of Children.

Drafted in the late 1950s and first enacted in 1960, the compact "addresses the special needs of children in interstate situations, specifically when placed across state lines for adoptive or foster care," according to Minner.

All 50 states, the District of Columbia and the Virgin Islands are party to the compact, which is expected to be revised this year.

> *"There is a growing need for our states to act together to address policy issues that may transcend our boundaries, or that are threatened by federal pre-emption."*
>
> —Delaware Gov. Ruth Ann Minner

The National Center for Interstate Compacts is working with the American Public Human Services Association, which administers the compact, to strengthen it with provisions such as sharing data among states.

Such revisions should help states provide for more efficient adoptions and foster care placements.

"Say in a family with three children, both parents are killed and the closest living relative lives in another state," Minner said. "With this compact, it will be easier for states to work together in placing those children with out-of-state relatives."

A new compact currently winding its way through state capitols is the Interstate Compact for Juveniles. As of mid-July, 27 states had enacted this new compact and seven others were considering it. The new compact is an updated version of a 50-year-old national agreement that allows adjudicated youth to transfer their supervision between states.

"This new compact contains much needed enforcement mechanisms and ensures accountability among the states," Minner said. "Approximately 50,000 youth are subject to this agreement."

LOOKING AHEAD

The NCIC is also looking ahead at how new compacts may help states in other areas.

Working with the National Association of State Treasurers and the National Association of Unclaimed Property Administrators, CSG affiliates, NCIC is looking at potential plans that would return more than $12 billion worth of U.S. Savings Bonds that remain unclaimed in the U.S. Treasury.

Another problem confronting states, said Minner, is society's mobility. Between 1995 and 2000, for example, 11 million Americans moved across state lines, creating a problem with state election registration databases.

CSG and its affiliates, the National Association of State Election Directors along with the National Association of Secretaries of State, are examining the issue and the potential for a compact addressing the interstate sharing of voter registration information. "It would ensure that citizens are registered and vote in the appropriate jurisdiction and eliminate intentional voter fraud," said Minner.

COMPACT EDUCATION

Minner has been familiar with Interstate Compacts for more than 30 years. "My involvement with compacts began in the mid '70s when I was in the legislature," said Minner.

Working with the National Association of State Treasurers and the National Association of Unclaimed Property Administrators, CSG affiliates, NCIC is looking at potential plans that would return more than $12 billion worth of U.S. Savings Bonds that remain unclaimed in the U.S. Treasury.

During her years in the legislature, she served on a transportation committee that worked with a compact among motor vehicle administrators. "Because of that, I became interested and started looking at compacts."

However, she notes that many state officials are not aware of compacts and the roles they play in state governments in responding to shared problems.

The initial goal of NCIC is to raise awareness among state officials about interstate compacts.

"Our first task is education," said Minner. "Compacts are contracts between states. We are responsible to each other and we should do what we can to help each other."

PART

II

Elections and Political Environment

Politicians typically do not want to support instituting or raising taxes for fear of antagonizing voters. Voters took matters
into their own hands, however, in 2005 . . . by voting to hike
their taxes and increase government spending. Eleven proposals to
increase taxes, up spending, or do both were on state ballots in 2005
and voters approved them all.

Voters typically are also attracted to "outsider" politicians who
come to office with fame and a broad popular base, no taint of a
political career and a promise to shake things up. But tell that to
California governor Arnold Schwarzenegger. He wasn't on the ballot in 2005, but the central policy initiatives of his administration
sure were. And they bombed.

Voters of late do not seem to be interested in "typical."

Thirty years ago California voters kicked off the ballot initiative
era by passing Proposition 13, which signaled the start of a tax revolt
that swept across the country. Ever since, it has been rare for a politician to openly call for increased taxes, at least rare for any politician who wants to stay in office. In 2005, however, there seemed
to be at least some indications that the antitax, antispend well was
running dry with the electorate.

Consider some of the spending measures that were on the ballot. In Ohio voters approved a proposal to borrow $2 billion to pro-
mote economic development (in 2003 they rejected a more modest
$500 million proposal to do the exact same thing). New York
backed a proposal to borrow $2.9 billion to invest in transporta-
tion infrastructure. Texas also supported a billion dollar proposal
to relocate railroad tracks. Governors in all three states (all Republicans) backed the measures. Voters in Washington State rejected a

proposal to overturn a fuel-tax increase imposed by the state legislature.[1] Colorado voters actually voted to let the state government keep an estimated $3.7 billion that otherwise would have been returned to them.[2]

What the heck was going on?

Well, one possibility is that it was just an unusual election cycle. It's not like voters everywhere were begging for higher taxes and more government spending. The tax and spend ballot initiatives that were approved were generally narrowly targeted, or addressed specific financial problems faced by state governments. Nonetheless, the notion that voters have become more supportive of tax and spend anything is an important signal from electoral participants. Voters seemed to be willing put their money where their votes were. Perhaps they have become increasingly uneasy about the ability of government to finance the programs and services they demand, and are now more willing to look beyond antitax and antispend rhetoric.

It will take a lot more than an election cycle or two to assess which of these perspectives is more accurate. Nonetheless, a restive electorate in an off-year electoral cycle raises some interesting implications for elections at all levels of government in the next year or two.

DIRECT DEMOCRACY: NOT POLITICS AS USUAL

Roughly half the states allow some form of direct democracy, in which citizens get to make major policy decisions themselves rather than electing representatives to make those decisions on their behalf. The most common method is the ballot initiative, which puts proposed laws to a popular vote.

The 2005 election cycle—as has been usual and typical ever since the phenomenal success of Proposition 13—showed a wide variety of groups stepping up to use ballot initiatives to bypass the legislature in order to make policy. Less usual and typical were who some of these groups were, and the results that the voters delivered.

Schwarzenegger, seeking mostly to exert more centralized control over state spending, backed a series of ballot measures in California that would seem at first blush to invite broad popular support: limiting state spending, reining in expensive public pensions, making it easier to get rid of poorly performing teachers and using a nonpartisan panel of judges to take the lead in

redistricting legislative boundaries. There was an explicit political gamble here: if the proposals passed, Schwarzenegger gained an upper hand over the legislature, which had been resisting some of his proposals.

Schwarzenegger lost the gamble. Suffering from declining popularity ratings, he not only found himself dealing with a recalcitrant legislature, but also an angry and energized set of public employee unions who took their case to the public during the initiative fight. The public did not side with the action hero turned state executive. They stuck with the teachers, and with higher spending.

A more important signal that voters have reached some sort of antitax, antispend threshold is the voter-approved rollback of Colorado's Taxpayer's Bill of Rights (TABOR). TABOR is recognized as a high-profile achievement of, and a model for, the antitax movement. It is a constitutional amendment (passed by voters as a ballot initiative) that imposes strict tax limitations on state government. These limitations were so strict they prevented state government from addressing the financial stress on many state programs that had been imposed by several years of recession. In 2005 Colorado voters were presented with Referendum C, which proposed letting the state keep billions that would otherwise have been returned to the taxpayers under the provisions of TABOR. In a bitterly fought contest, Referendum C narrowly passed.

Two essays in this section detail the story of Schwarzenegger's, and TABOR's, setbacks. The essay by Daniel Weintraub highlights the potential political fallout—especially in terms of the shifting power balance between the executive and the legislature in California. Chris Frates's essay provides an analysis of the campaign for Referendum C in Colorado, and also its companion initiative, Referendum D. What both stories share is the common theme of a changing political environment for state elections, one in which voters can no longer be relied upon to rally behind tried and true antitax, antispend proposals, and one in which the traditional supporters of lower taxes and lower spending—Republicans in general, and conservative Republicans in particular—showed a tendency to split ranks to support what they perceived as legitimate financial needs.

One other essay continues the general theme of a changing political environment in the states. Dan Seligson's piece takes a look at Democratic governors in overwhelmingly Republican states (Wyoming, Arizona and Kansas), and explains why the GOP is having a hard time ousting red state Democrats from the top job in state politics.

ALL POLITICS IS LOCAL

While three of the essays in this section tell the story of a shift in voter sentiments and a changing political environment, two others show that some things in politics remain constant. Count among these the truth in the old aphorism that "all politics is local." The study by Benjamin Highton looks at how the availability of voting machines can affect voter turnout. This study highlights how all elections, even presidential elections, rely on a very local infrastructure. How that infrastructure is supplied—or not supplied—may help determine the outcome of an election.

David Mark's essay takes a look at retail politics. Although big time political races conjure up images of spin doctors, big media buys, and campaign consultants, it turns out that down at the state level actually meeting and talking to voters still matters. Even for the big offices. Running in the Montana gubernatorial race in 2004, Democratic candidate Brian Schweitzer estimates he pressed the flesh with a quarter of the electorate. It's a political touch that paid off. He won. Turns out this old style, grassroots form of electioneering is far from dead. In less densely populated states especially it is alive and well, and an important determinant of who has won, and who will win, elective office.

Notes

1. Dennis Cauchon, "Spending Not Such a Bad Word to Voters," *USA Today,* November 11, 2005, www.usatoday.com/news/nation/2005-11-09-ballot-initiatives_x.htm.
2. Chris Frates, "Coloradans Reach Their Limit with TABOR," *State Legislatures* (January 2006): 24–26.

5

Schwarzenegger Rebuffed

Daniel Weintraub

Voters soundly defeated the California governor's ballot measures, and the Legislature may be stronger as a result.

Governor Arnold Schwarzenegger's year-long battle to wrest control of the state budget from the Legislature, move redistricting to an independent commission, and hem in California's powerful public employee unions fell flat on Election Day when four ballot measures he was backing were defeated, most by very wide margins.

Although many observers—including the governor himself—said the results were a message to legislators and the governor to solve the state's problems in the Capitol, not at the ballot box, the unambiguous vote seems more likely to empower the Legislature's Democratic majority to rebuff even more of Schwarzenegger's policy proposals. Unless the governor relents, the result would be a statehouse more gridlocked than the one Schwarzenegger was trying to blast past by going directly to the voters.

Still, with the former action movie star facing what looks to be a tough re-election fight in 2006, Schwarzenegger can be expected to be less confrontational this year than he was in 2005. He could hardly be more so.

A chastened but unapologetic Schwarzenegger said after the vote that he should have listened to his wife, Maria Shriver, who, he said, advised him not to press for the special election. But the governor said that even though he lost, the big gamble was in keeping with his style.

"I think that I operate with a different mentality than most people do, which is that I am very forceful and impatient," he said. "And I always have mapped out, my entire life, a program and a work schedule, and also a schedule of when I want to accomplish things. I always was successful with that, and with

From *State Legislatures*, January 2006.

tremendous determination and with a tremendous amount of will."

A year ago, he said, he figured he could enact his concept of reform by proposing an agenda, inviting lawmakers to meet him halfway, and taking it to the voters if they refused. But now he sees that in politics, it doesn't always pay to move quickly.

"Here in this Capitol, and on the job as governor—or I think any politician—I think you have to be more patient."

LESSONS LEARNED

Reaction among the governor's opponents was mixed.

"We won, they lost," said Gale Kaufman, a key strategist for the California Teachers Association, which spent more than $50 million on the campaign—even mortgaging its headquarters building—to defeat Schwarzenegger's agenda. The CTA and its labor partners in the newly formed Alliance for a Better California are expected to seek to defeat Schwarzenegger when he runs for reelection next year.

In the Legislature, Assembly Speaker Fabian Núñez, a former Los Angeles labor organizer who has feuded almost non-stop with the governor, was in no mood to make nice after the election.

"You can't just move on," Núñez said. "It just can't be one of those things where you sing 'Kumbaya' and you move on. Lessons have to be learned."

But on the other side of the Capitol, Senate Leader Don Perata was more magnanimous, saying he was urging his allies to "please forgive, and let's move on."

Perata said he felt as though 2005 was a wasted year because of the special election, and he said he wants no part of a strategy that would seek to stymie the governor for another year in hopes of hurting his reelection prospects.

Perata said he would seek agreement with the governor on a major bond measure to rebuild the state's aging highways, ports and levees, a plan to reduce the cost of housing by reducing regulation, a goal of hiring 100,000 new teachers, and a major education reform that would relieve the schools of what he sees as micromanagement from Sacramento.

"I don't want to spend next year doing what we did this year," Perata told reporters. "I'm getting too old to waste a year of my life."

THE BEGINNING OF THE END

It was a strange year indeed. Twelve months ago, Schwarzenegger was riding high, with his public approval rating at about 65 percent, a near record for California governors. He had been on the winning side of nearly every ballot measure he supported or opposed in the 2004 elections, and had helped re-elect George W. Bush as president with a last-minute appearance in Ohio.

But all of that began to unravel when Schwarzenegger broke a promise on future education funding he had made to the state's teachers union and education lobby, infuriating a powerful interest group that immediately launched television and radio attacks bringing his credibility into question. Although the governor eventually gave the schools $3 billion in new funding, that was still far short of what they said they were due, and their advertising campaign seemed to convince the voters that he had actually cut school spending rather than increase it.

Yet even as his approval rating was in a free-fall, eventually bottoming out at 36 percent in September, Schwarzenegger launched his assault on teacher tenure, public pensions and other sacred cows of the state's dominant Democrats.

Many of the proposals he put forward actually had significant early support among voters, who said they liked the idea of rolling back public employee pensions, limiting state spending, making it easier to fire teachers and giving judges the power to draw district lines.

But several of the measures Schwarzenegger was backing had drafting problems, forcing him to juggle his agenda even as he was gathering signatures to qualify the initiatives for the ballot. By the time he called a special election, which polls repeatedly showed the voters did not want, the governor had settled on three measures.

One would have extended teachers' probationary period from the current two years to five and made it easier for districts to fire incompetent instructors. It failed, 55 percent to 45 percent.

Another would have created a new state spending limit, tweaked the state's constitutional mandate for minimum education funding and given the governor the power to cut spending when a deficit was looming. Voters rejected it 62 percent to 38 percent.

A third initiative would have taken the job of drawing new district lines from the Legislature and given it to a panel of three retired judges, with a mandate to redistrict the state as soon as the 2006 elections. It lost, 60 percent to 40 percent.

Schwarzenegger also endorsed a fourth measure that would have required public employee unions to obtain the written permission of their members annually before deducting money from their paychecks for political purposes. The so-called "paycheck protection" initiative galvanized the public employee unions and became the focus of an effective advertising campaign featuring firefighters, teachers and nurses complaining that the governor was attacking them for problems he should have been solving in Sacramento. Although it led by a wide margin in early polls, it eventually failed by vote of 53 percent to 47 percent.

The only idea that seems likely to be revisited this year in the Legislature is redistricting. Both Núñez and Perata committed themselves during the campaign and shortly after to the idea of creating an independent commission to draw new district lines after the next census.

6

Coloradans Reach Their Limit with TABOR

Chris Frates

In one of the fiercest issue campaigns watched nationwide, Colorado voters chose to give money back to the financially strapped state.

I t is the national anti-tax movement's Foundation Stone—the Colorado constitution's Taxpayer's Bill of Rights (TABOR). This fall, big-government spenders sweet-talked voters into taking sledgehammers to The Rock. And by doing so, taxpayers chained themselves to more government spending and higher taxes.

Or so the faithful would say.

Their opponents would tell you that assessment is, to put it politely, bunk.

Supporters of November's ballot measures to let the state keep more money and authorize bonding said the measures were necessary to keep the state budget off life support.

The fight united Democrats and Republicans and put business and labor on the same team. It also split the Republican Party, damaged the governor's reputation with his conservative base and brought national anti-tax leaders like Grover Norquist and former U.S. House majority leader Dick Armey to town.

In short, it was like no other issue campaign the state has ever seen. And all the fuss was over two little letters, C and D.

Referendum C successfully asked voters to let the state keep an estimated $3.7 billion over the next five years that would have otherwise been returned to taxpayers under TABOR. Its companion measure, Referendum D, would have used some of that money to borrow $2.1 billion largely for transportation and school improvements, but was narrowly rejected.

Supporters said the money was needed to help the state recover from the more than $1 billion legislators had slashed from the budget over the past four years. A provision of TABOR limited the

From *State Legislatures,* January 2006.

25

state's ability to recover quickly from the economic downturn even as more revenue rolled in.

The TABOR revenue limit would have forced lawmakers to return surplus money to taxpayers while making even deeper cuts. Essentially, the state would have been running a surplus and a deficit simultaneously. For next year, that meant almost $500 million in additional cuts and $600 million in TABOR refunds, according to legislative economists.

BIPARTISAN DEAL

The problem pushed Democratic legislative leaders and Republican Governor Bill Owens to the bargaining table last winter where they banged out the details of what eventually became Referendums C and D.

Owens, a fiscal conservative that *National Review* once named the best governor in America, was an unlikely poster boy for the Vote Yes on C&D campaign. A strong TABOR supporter—he helped campaign for its passage in 1992—Owens was a darling of the conservative right whose name often made the rounds as a possible presidential contender in 2008.

After Democrats took control of the legislature in 2004 for the first time in four decades, Owens drafted a plan to right the state's sinking budget. The state, Owens reasoned, could not afford to refund money to taxpayers while slashing services.

For the first time since it passed 13 years ago, TABOR was about to become the problem, the governor said.

So Owens and Democratic leaders crafted a plan both sides could sell to their constituencies. They used a provision within TABOR that allows elected officials to ask voters whether the state can keep more money than the limit allows. Voters have approved hundreds of similar measures on the local level, often to fund needed projects. Now, state officials were asking all Coloradans to let them keep their money.

"I want to stress in the strongest possible terms what (the proposal) does not do," said Owens the day the deal was announced. "It doesn't change the structure or function of TABOR. The spending caps remain in place. Colorado's taxpayers retain the ability to vote on every tax increase."

Even so, it was not an easy sell.

IS IT A TAX INCREASE?

Opponents labeled the measures a permanent tax increase that could be avoided if lawmakers were willing to prioritize the state's needs and look for more government efficiency. Politicians manufactured the budget crises, critics argued, because it is easier to dip into taxpayers' pockets than make tough choices.

They also criticized supporters for not addressing Amendment 23, a constitutional amendment that requires annual increases in school funding. Referendums C and D, they said, did nothing to reel in spending.

The constitution, supporters said, prohibited them from putting an Amendment 23-related question on the ballot in an odd-numbered year.

The budget debate split the Republican Party and led to ferocious infighting. Gubernatorial candidates Marc Holtzman and Bob Beauprez joined state lawmakers and others who opposed the measures.

The lesser-known Holtzman hitched his fledgling campaign to the issue and pummeled Owens for supporting the measures and Beauprez for not opposing them rapidly enough. Holtzman starred in several anti-C&D ads, one of which was paid for in part by a $100,000 donation from his father.

Beauprez and others complained that Holtzman used the ad to skirt campaign finance laws that limit contributions to a gubernatorial candidate to $1,000. The secretary of state declined a request by the Beauprez campaign to rule on the matter.

SIDES LINE UP

Meanwhile, Owens was joined by a cadre of Republican leaders like University of Colorado President and former U.S. Senator Hank Brown and current and former state legislators. Most of the state's business leaders and prominent Republican donors also backed C&D.

On the left, Democrats were united on the measures. In fact, the state party voted formally to endorse them, which led the opposition to attack the measures as the work of liberal Democrats.

The Yes campaign counted among its supporters Republicans and Democrats, every daily newspaper in the state, wealthy business executives and union workers and more than 1,000 other groups, many of which had felt the sting of the budget pinch.

On the no side, Republicans partnered with traditionally conservative groups like the Colorado Club for Growth and the Independence Institute, a local think tank. National heavy hitters like Norquist's Americans for Tax Reform and Armey's Freedom-Works also came to play.

The battle sounded more like a candidate race than an issue campaign. It came complete with television attack ads, accusations and big money. The Yes side said they raised a total of about $7.5 million. Major opposition groups reported raising about $3.2 million through the end of October.

Not surprisingly, the campaign centered on numbers, which both sides tried to use to their advantage. For instance, supporters used a non-partisan legislative staff analysis to show that the measures would cost most taxpayers an average of $500 over the proposed five-year period.

Opponents, however, divided the estimated $3.7 billion cost by the number families to get a $3,200 price tag. But to receive the $3,200, a family would have to qualify for each of 17 special tax breaks, which no one does.

Proponents meanwhile argued that the measures were not a tax increase. And while Referendum C did not raise the tax rate, it did increase how much taxpayers pay each year.

BATTLE TO THE WIRE

Throughout the campaign, several polls showed the two sides neck-and-neck with neither side breaking 51 percent. Conventional wisdom says that ballot measures need an approval rating near 60 percent before campaigning begins in order to have a chance. Many predicted that the measures were doomed.

The Yes campaign worked to illustrate how more cuts to government programs would hurt the state. CU president Brown said state money for colleges and universities would dry up. Business leaders and others argued that without accessible higher education, the state would be left without educated workers. And crumbling roads and bridges would hurt the quality of life and the ability of businesses to move their goods. Perhaps most importantly, the state would no longer be economically competitive.

Critics called the arguments scare tactics dreamed up by "country club Republicans" and liberals who don't understand the pressures of the everyman. Opponents showed up at supporters' campaign rallies with a giant wooden horse to illustrate the "Trojan horse tax increase."

During dueling press conferences across the street from each other, emotions flared when the mother of a developmentally disabled man confronted Jon Caldara, chairman of the "Vote No; It's Your Dough" campaign, over his use of pigs to characterize state spending.

"Don't call us pigs," the mother told Caldara after he trotted out a huge swine, made from a propane tank and papier-mâché, to emphasize a report on wasteful government spending.

"I never have called you pigs. I called the people under that dome spending like pigs," replied Caldara, who also heads the Independence Institute.

At the height of the campaign, supporter Denver Mayor John Hickenlooper jumped out of an airplane to illustrate the state's falling revenue. Opponents aired a spot where a greedy politician ripped an envelope labeled "tax refund" out of the hands of a mother and stole an ice cream cone from a little girl.

When election night came, Coloradans narrowly approved Referendum C by about 41,000 votes and defeated D by almost 15,000 votes out of about 1.1 million cast. By approving C, voters told state leaders they wanted their money spent on the four areas outlined in the measure: primary and secondary education, health care, colleges and universities, and transportation. Supporters took D's rejection to mean that voters weren't comfortable with $2.1 billion of debt.

WATCHED NATIONWIDE

The vote has reverberations far beyond Colorado's budget situation. With the strictest revenue restriction in the country, Colorado has been a beacon for anti-tax activists. After the election, both sides were ready to spin the results.

Norquist, of Americans for Tax Reform, said his national movement had not been damaged by the outcome. The off-year election's lower voter turnout tilted in the supporter's favor because special interests are more likely to outnumber regular voters.

"The only loser on Nov. 1 were the taxpayers of Colorado and their children and grandchildren," he says. "Everyone else in the country is stronger and better off because of that vote."

Owens' fall from conservative grace will also help the anti-tax cause, Norquist says, because the governor will serve as an example to other politicians. Since advocating for the measures, Owens has been banished from presidential short lists, he says.

Norquist had also predicted that opponents would need to spend about $1 for every $10 the supporters spent to defeat the measures. He also said his group would not have to spend money in Colorado. Turns out, Americans for Tax Reform spent almost $150,000 on advertising and phone banks in the last two weeks of October.

David Bradley, a policy analyst for the Center on Budget and Policy Priorities, says the vote "sends a pretty strong signal to people considering it in other states that they better think twice about whether or not they actually want to pass TABOR and put it in their constitutions." After all, he says, Coloradans have lived with the amendment and know the consequences.

Still, the Colorado vote will only slow the anti-tax movement, not stop it, he says.

"This is a well coordinated, nationally funded movement that will continue to push for TABOR wherever they see there's an opportunity to do so," he says.

In 2006, a handful of states could see similar revenue limitations on their ballots including Kansas, Maine, Nevada, Ohio, Oklahoma, and Oregon, says Bradley, of the liberal think tank.

LAWMAKERS RELIEVED

Back in Colorado, lawmakers are relieved to be able to start restoring programs, but everyone realizes the budget is not awash in revenue. Owens' budget office estimates the state will see an extra $505 million over the next fiscal year. Of that, about $200 million will pay for required increases in K-12 education funding, Medicaid and prisons. Another $117 million will be used to repay the state's reserve fund and $66 million will be used to restore a property-tax credit for seniors. That will leave about $122 million to restore cuts to other programs.

"We've avoided the bullet, but it's going to be a conservative budget with very little in new spending other than what we committed to through Referendum C," Owens says.

With the divisive campaign over, both sides have already turned their attention to 2006. Republicans are working to reunite as a party to keep the governor's man-

Money Won't Go That Far

With an estimated $3.7 billion pouring into state coffers over the next five years, it might sound like lawmakers could hold a pig roast with all the pork to be had at the Capitol. But that impression would be flat wrong.

In fact, lawmakers of all stripes talk about crafting a sparing budget next year—they have no other choice.

Consider the numbers. Next fiscal year, lawmakers will keep $505 million more than they would have been allowed if the limits imposed by the Taxpayer's Bill of Rights had not been suspended, according to Governor Bill Owens's budget office. The money will be used to avoid $365 million in cuts that legislators would have been staring down if Referendum C had not passed.

"I think the voters need to know that we still have to be frugal," said Democratic Senate Majority Leader Ken Gordon the day after the election.

And there's not much room for squabbling over where the money will be spent. When voters passed Referendum C, they not only told officials how much money they could keep, but where they could spend it.

Almost all the $505 million coming in next fiscal year has to be evenly split among primary and secondary education, health care and higher education. Lawmakers have flexibility to spend $100 million of that money in those three areas and transportation.

The $100 million would have been used to repay the bonds Referendum D would have authorized had it passed. The $2.1 billion would have paid largely for improvements to transportation and schools.

One other likely point of controversy will be a request by Owens to spend $80 million more on roads this year than the law requires. Democrats have said it is not clear whether that request fits within the guidelines of Referendum C.

sion and take back control of the legislature. Democrats are fighting to keep control of a legislature it took them four decades to recapture and electing one of their own as governor after eight years.

And it is likely those contests will feature discussion on how state leaders handled the new money taxpayers entrusted to them.

7

Home State Blues: Republicans Face Tough Foes in Red State Democratic Governors

Dan Seligson

Democratic governors not only survive, they thrive, in Republican states.

From *Campaigns & Elections,* August 2005.

Democrats holding the top state office in Wyoming, Arizona and Kansas could be considered strangers in a strange land.

Their party brethren hold virtually no sway in legislatures; their voters were solidly in the Bush camp in the 2004 election.

Yet Kansas Gov. Katherine Sebelius, Wyoming Gov. David Freudenthal and Arizona Gov. Janet Napolitano appear poised for re-election in their respective Republican strongholds.

Sebelius continues to enjoy support in a state that picked Bush over Kerry by a 62 percent-to-36 percent margin. Freudenthal appears strong, as does Janet Napolitano, who garnered "very good" or "good" marks from 79 percent of state residents in an Arizona State School of Journalism/KAET-TV poll.

That could contrast with the blue state blues being experienced by their fellow party members and executives in the Midwest. As the three Democratic governors appear to be thriving on GOP turf, Michigan Gov. Jennifer Granholm and Illinois Gov. Rod Blagojevich are both slumping in polls and running close in hypothetical races against Republican opponents.

The relative strength of the red state Democrats and the current weak position of the two Midwest Democrats did not surprise Larry Sabato, political science professor at the University of Virginia. He publishes the Crystal Ball, a Web site that analyses and predicts political contests around the country.

"Unlike a Senate contest, which is all about ideology, a gubernatorial contest is all about competence," Sabato said. "It's about the nuts and bolts of governing—education, transportation, health care. Napolitano, Freudenthal and Sebelius were elected in part on personal qualities and in part because [the voters] wanted a change from the majority party. Right now all three are in pretty good shape."

Sebelius' popularity says nothing about the state of her party in the Sunflower State. Sightings of Democrats are rare in Topeka, where Republicans hold twice as many state House seats and three times as many state Senate seats as their rivals. But the state GOP is badly split between conservative and moderate factions, leaving an opening for a relatively fiscally conservative, socially middle of the road Democratic governor like Sebelius.

"Skillful Democrats can take advantage of divisions in the Republican party—between the Christian Right and the more business-oriented, socially liberal Republicans," said Allan Cigler, political science professor at the University of Kansas. "Her success is probably most related to the failures of the Republicans to get their act together on a number of issues. The defining battle is social conservatives versus the more moderate wing of the party. It's enabled her and a number of other Democrats to win the governorship."

And it might enable her to win a second term, as the GOP's top choice to run, U.S. Rep. Jerry Moran, R-Kansas, has expressed wariness in taking on Sebelius, Cigler said. Several other top tier candidates, including a bevy of state officials, have declined to challenge her.

It would seem odd then that the ideal answer to Republicans at odds over issues such as teaching evolution, school funding, tax rates and government intrusion would find their answers across the aisle. Yet, Kansans have elected Democrats to the governorship with some regularity. The National Governors Association lists an even split in Kansas governorships between 1967 and the present, with Democrats and Republicans each in office three times before Sebelius' election. At the same time, Kansas's voters have not sent a Democrat to the U.S. Senate since the 1930s.

In Wyoming, it is the fierce libertarian streak of the voters and Freudenthal's ability to distance himself from the national party that has positioned him for a promising re-election bid in 2006. With Vice President Dick Cheney the state's favorite son, Wyoming Republicans align themselves with the Bush administration. Democrats like Freudenthal can be free agents, loosely defined by their party label. In fact, Democrats held the governorship in the traditionally red state for a 20-year run, between 1975 and 1995.

University of Wyoming professor John King said Freudenthal was forceful in fighting the feds on issues such as the introduction of wolves into Yellowstone National Park and other issues where state residents fear intrusion. He stayed out of the 2004 presidential election, in which Wyoming voters gave Bush 69 percent of the vote to an anemic 29 percent for Kerry. Only neighboring Utah went for the president at a higher rate, giving Bush 72 percent of the vote.

Straying too close to the party line could have been harmful for the Wyoming governor, because stumping for Kerry in a state where Bush was virtually guaranteed to garner two-thirds of the popular vote, stumping for Kerry would have at least been ignored and at most been a reminder of the blue zone surrounding the governor's mansion in the decidedly red state.

"I can predict Wyoming will go Republican in the next 'X' number of presidential elections. But for state offices you do have a certain look at the individual rather than the straight party label," King said. "He espouses a very moderate policy agenda, and he protects Wyoming's interests from Washington, which are so much the politics of this area. Democrats need to do that here."

King said in the immediate future, no strong opposition looms for the incumbent, so long as his popularity holds up.

In Arizona, a state generally more favorable to Democrats than Wyoming and Kansas (President Bill Clinton squeaked out a win here in 1996), Napolitano remains popular with voters despite a lop-sided allotment of seats in favor of the GOP in the state legislature.

It is something Sabato attributes to the personal qualities of the incumbent as well as the interest of the voters—more than a quarter of whom are not registered as either Republican or Democrat.

Meanwhile, in the blue states, Michigan's Granholm represents something of a break in tradition. Republicans have held the top statewide elected post for 32 of the past 42 years while, until the election of Blagojevich in Illinois, Democrats had been unable to win the governorship since 1977.

And holding on to office could be challenging for both Democrats, recent polls would suggest. Blagojevich's approval rating this spring stood at 35 percent, according to a *Chicago Tribune*/WGN-TV poll—a 5 percent drop from the same mid-May poll conducted in 2004. Granholm fared slightly better in a late May poll, garnering a 53 percent approval rating, but still appearing vulnerable in a head-to-head battle with Republican U.S. Rep. Candice Miller, who trailed the incumbent by only 3 percent in the poll.

Republican candidates started tossing their names in the ring for the race early this year, with two Michigan state lawmakers chiding Granholm for the state's 7-plus percent unemployment rate—one of the highest in the nation—and budget difficulties from the year before. Political experts quoted in the *Associated Press* said the serious GOP opposition to the Democratic incumbent would likely become public in September when Republicans hold an annual leadership conference.

Blagojevich could face a run from a six-term congressman, U.S. Rep. Ray LaHood, R-Ill. The only governor of the five states mentioned with his majority party in both houses of the state legislature, Blagojevich reportedly faces criticism from Democrats for his support of a medical malpractice bill limiting damages as well as changes to state pension funds for future state workers.

The fates of all five Democrats—the popular alternatives to Republicans in Arizona, Wyoming and Kansas, and the struggling blue-state leaders in Michigan and Illinois—are hardly sealed more than a year out from the 2006 race.

On Sabato's Crystal Ball site, (www.centerforpolitics.org/crystalball), the University of Virginia pundit foresees wins by both Granholm and Blagojevich. But no serious competition has emerged yet. As for Freudenthal, Sebelius and Napolitano, holding on to current popularity will be crucial in the coming months.

"Right now, all three are in pretty good shape," Sabato said. "The candidates make the argument that they are a check against power, and voters are paying attention and getting the picture. In Michigan and Illinois, the early line is the incumbents will prevail, but it would not be a great shock if one of them lost. It would be a tremendous shock if they both lost."

8

Long Lines, Voting Machine Availability, and Turnout: The Case of Franklin County, Ohio in the 2004 Presidential Election

Benjamin Highton*

Do fewer voting machines mean fewer voters? This study suggests the answer is yes.

Perhaps the most visible of Ohio's problems were its long lines. Christopher McQuoid reached his polling place in Columbus at 4:30 p.m.... By 7:30, he was getting impatient. And when he finally voted at 9:30, there were 150 people in line behind him. "I was lucky.... I had the day off" [he said]. But how many people decided not to vote because of long lines, and was it enough to make a difference? No one has been able to say with authority (Dao, Fessenden, and Zeller 2004, 1).

Within polling places, does the scarcity of voting machines cause longer lines and thereby dissuade some people from voting? Are voting machines scarce in some areas because turnout would be low, irrespective of the availability of voting machines? In Ohio in the aftermath of the 2004 presidential election, the answers to these questions carried very real and significant political stakes. Consider the following from Franklin County, the second most populous county in the state.[1] In precincts where voting machines were plentiful (i.e., where there were fewer registrants per available voting machine), turnout was especially

*I appreciate input from SSRC Commission members Henry Brady, Martha Kropf, Walter R. Mebane Jr., and Michael Traugott with whom I collaborated on the SSRC's "Interim Report on Alleged Irregularities in the United States Presidential Election of 2 November 2004" (Brady et al. 2004). I also thank Benjamin Bishin for comments on the paper. The Social Science Research Council and its staff, including Jason McNichol, Dashiell Flynn, and Sarah Alexander, provided generous support for this work. The views expressed in this paper are not necessarily shared by other SSRC Commission members or the Social Science Research Council.

From *PS: Political Science and Politics*, January 2006.

high and John Kerry's share of the presidential vote was low. In contrast, in areas of machine scarcity (i.e., precincts with many registrants per available voting machine), turnout was lower and Kerry's vote share was higher. These relationships are shown in Figures 1A and 1B. Given the strong association between machine availability and the Kerry vote, if machine (un)availability was a cause of (low) turnout, then Kerry may very well have received fewer votes than he would have had more machines been available or had the distribution of available machines been less skewed toward precincts that were more supportive of George W. Bush.

While voting in a single county in a single election rarely draws national attention, what happened in Franklin County in 2004 did. The final vote in the Electoral College favored George W. Bush over John Kerry by 286 to 251. Had Kerry won Ohio, which he lost 49 to 51%, its 20 electoral votes would have given him a bare majority of the electoral vote and victory in the presidential election. None of these observations has gone unrecognized in the media and among interested observers, party leaders, and elected officials. Although no one has contended that a turnout reduction caused by the scarcity of voting machines in Franklin County alone cost Kerry

enough votes to give Bush the win and the presidential election, it was a primary point of contention in the election's aftermath. For example, the problems in Franklin County received substantial attention in front page articles in both the *Washington Post* (Powell and Slevin 2004) and the *New York Times* (Dao, Fessenden, and Zeller 2004).

Most notable are the events of early January 2005. On January 5, the Democratic staff of the House Judiciary Committee issued a report on "Preserving Democracy: What Went Wrong in Ohio." The report includes an analysis of voting machine allocations in Franklin County and contends that it "appears to be [one] of the pivotal factors concerning the vote and outcome in the entire election in Ohio" (29). On January 6, when Congress was scheduled to officially ratify Bush's reelection, there was a formal challenge to the counting of electoral votes for only the second time since 1877. Stephanie Tubbs Jones, a Democratic House member from Ohio, and Barbara Boxer, a Democratic Senator from California, objected to awarding Ohio's electoral votes to Bush, in part based on concerns about machine allocations, long lines, and turnout. As Senator Boxer said in the subsequent debate, "Why in the Columbus area alone did an

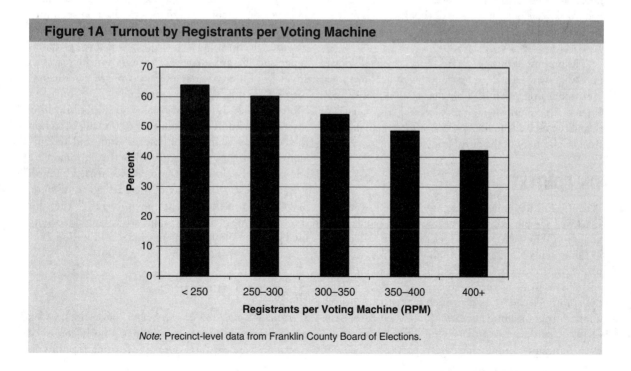

Figure 1A Turnout by Registrants per Voting Machine

Note: Precinct-level data from Franklin County Board of Elections.

Figure 1B Kerry Vote Share by Registrants per Voting Machine

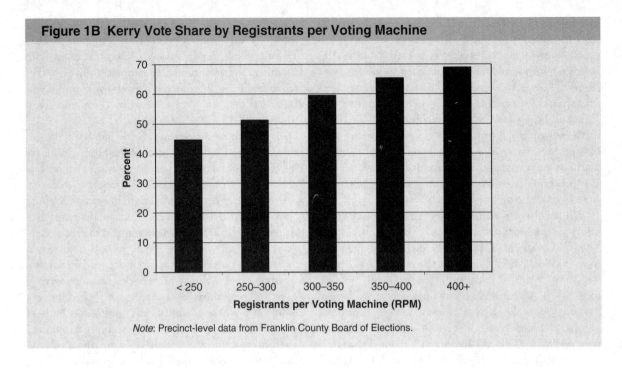

Note: Precinct-level data from Franklin County Board of Elections.

estimated 5,000 to 10,000 voters leave polling places out of frustration without having voted? How many more never bothered to vote after they heard this because they had to take care of their families or they had a job or they were sick or their legs ached after waiting for hours" (*Congressional Record* 2005, S41).[2]

The purpose of this paper is to answer these questions: (1) What was the effect of voting machine allocations on turnout in Franklin County in the 2004 presidential election? (2) How many more people would have voted had there been no machine shortages? (3) What were the partisan implications of the distribution of voting machines?

THE CONTEXT

With Ohio's Republican Secretary of State J. Kenneth Blackwell serving as co-chair of the Bush/Cheney campaign in Ohio, concerns about election administration in Ohio were often cast in partisan terms. Indeed, some of the controversy in Ohio could be linked to decisions and actions made by the secretary of state. But, in Ohio the county election boards, which make the decisions about voting machine allocations, are each composed of two Democrats and two Republicans. As a result, even though there may have been partisan effects of

machine scarcity, partisan motivations to cause them seem unlikely.[3]

In Franklin County, the county election board allocates voting machines to precincts based on the number of "active voters," which is determined by turnout in previous elections. As a consequence, if some precincts experience disproportionate registration increases in advance of a particular election or greater turnout surges, then it is likely that wait times will be longer on Election Day as the ratio of voters per machine increases. In addition, heading into the 2004 election there was a surge in registration statewide and an especially high turnout was expected as the national vote appeared very close and Ohio was identified by both presidential candidates as a key battleground state. These factors likely added to the problems. Writers for the *Washington Post* reported that while Franklin county used less then 3,000 voting machines on Election Day, it needed 5,000 (Powell and Slevin 2004).

RESEARCH DESIGN

Presumably, machine scarcity causes longer lines, which in turn lowers turnout, especially in a hotly contested election where the total number of voting machines is less than 60% of what is needed, as it was in Franklin County.[4] But, estimating the magnitude of the turnout drop along with the partisan implications requires more precise and systematic analysis. In order to assess whether machine availability caused lower turnout and cost Kerry votes in Franklin County, the first question to address is what turnout would have been had there been more voting machines in use. One obvious approach is to compare turnout in precincts with ample numbers of machines to turnout in precincts where machines were more scarce (i.e., Figure 1A). However, this correlation between machine availability and turnout will only reflect the causal effect of machine availability on turnout to the extent that other differences across the precincts are unrelated to turnout. Given that complaints about long lines tended to be from precincts that are disproportionately urban, minority, and poor, this seems unlikely to be the case. For example, one straightforward fact about turnout is that those with less education are less likely to vote, even among the registered (Jackson 1996). Because the poor and minorities are less educated, one would expect lower turnout in precincts where they comprise larger proportions of the population, irrespective of the number of available voting machines. This raises the question of whether the relationship between machine availability and turnout reflects the causal effect of machines on turnout or whether it reflects the fact that machines are scarce where turnout is lower. Of course both factors are probably at work. As Brady et al. (2004) wrote in a report on the 2004 presidential election for the Social Science Research Council:

> What would be the likely outcome if an analyst could control for other plausible factors related to turnout? Just as it is implausible to attribute all of the differences in turnout associated with varying registrant to machine ratios to machine availability, it seems equally implausible to argue that machine availability (and hence wait times) has no effect on turnout. Consequently ... we believe it reasonable to argue that long wait times in more Democratic districts suppressed turnout to some degree. (17)

Distinguishing the two phenomena requires the use of a measure or measures that take into account differences across precincts that are related to turnout, but that are causally independent of machine scarcity in 2004. The measure I use is precinct-level turnout in the 2002 Ohio gubernatorial election. Several considerations

make this variable especially attractive. First, because the election was only two years before the presidential election, there was unlikely to be much compositional change in the precincts between the two elections. Second, because it took place in a midterm election year, turnout was much lower, thereby making it less likely that machine allocations would matter much. Indeed, a check of local newspapers reveals no reports of long lines, machine scarcity, and other incidents like those present in 2004.[5] Although overall turnout was lower, there was a strong correlation across precincts. As Figure 2 shows, precincts that had comparatively high turnout in 2002 also had high turnout in 2004; those with low 2002 turnout tended to have low 2004 turnout (r=.85). Thus the question becomes: After taking into account turnout in 2002, did precincts with greater numbers of registrants per machine in 2004 have lower turnout than precincts where machines were more plentiful.

RESULTS

Reporting the results of a series of OLS regressions, Table 1 helps answer the question of whether there was a causal relationship between the number of registrants per available voting machine (RPM) and turnout in 2004. The first two columns are based on using a single variable, the number of registrants per voting machine, to measure the relationship between RPM and turnout. The first column (Model 1) reports the apparent effect of RPM on turnout without taking into account turnout in 2002. The results indicate an increase in RPM by 100 registrants is associated with substantially lower turnout of 10 percentage points. Model 2 adds turnout in 2002 as a control. Compared to its effect in Model 1, the apparent effect of RPM is reduced by more than half (65%). In Model 2, an increase of 100 in RPM is associated with lower turnout of 3.5 percentage points, a nontrivial effect to be sure, but significantly smaller than the estimate obtained without controlling for turnout in 2002.

Models 3 and 4 allow for the possibility that the rate at which turnout declines with increasing RPM is not constant. These models relax the linearity assumption by distinguishing five types of precincts based on RPM values (less then 250, 250–300, 300–350, 350–400, and 400+). The results for Model 3, which do not include the control for turnout in 2002, show that compared to precincts with less than 250 RPM,

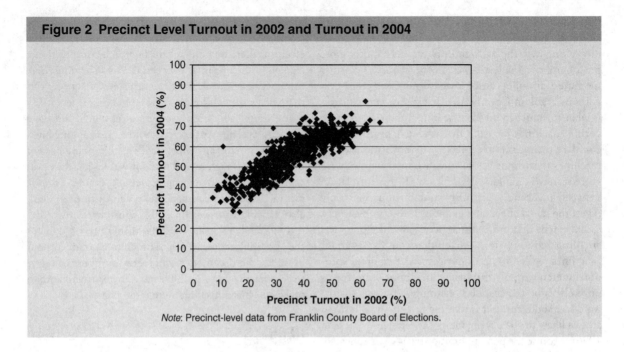

Figure 2 Precinct Level Turnout in 2002 and Turnout in 2004

Note: Precinct-level data from Franklin County Board of Elections.

turnout was about 10 percentage points (9.9) lower in precincts with 300–350 RPM and 22 points lower in precincts with over 400 RPM. But, after taking into account turnout in 2002, Model 4 shows that the 9.9 point gap drops 74% to 2.6, and the 21.8 percentage point difference drops 65% to 7.7.

Simply put, the results indicate that the simple relationship between RPM (whether measured in a linear fashion or otherwise) and turnout significantly overestimates the causal effect of RPM on turnout. More modest effects are apparent when an appropriate control variable is taken into account.

Table 1 Estimating the Effect of Machine Availability on 2004 Turnout in Franklin County, OH (Precinct Level)

Variable	Model 1	Model 2	Model 3	Model 4
Registrants per Machine (84–552)	−.100 (.004)	−.035 (.003)	n/a	n/a
Registrants per Machine				
0–250 (baseline)	n/a	n/a	—	—
250–300	n/a	n/a	−3.7 (.72)	−1.0 (.49)
300–350	n/a	n/a	−9.9 (.75)	−2.6 (.55)
350–400	n/a	n/a	−15.3 (.89)	−4.6 (.70)
400 +	n/a	n/a	−21.8 (1.05)	−7.7 (.85)
Turnout in 2002		.59 (.02)		.59 (.02)
Intercept	86.7 (1.22)	45.2 (1.56)	64.0 (.57)	36.8 (.97)
R^2	.45	.76	.46	.76

Notes: Dependent variable is precinct-level turnout of the registered in 2004. Models estimated with OLS. Standard errors in parentheses.
Source: Franklin County Board of Elections

Nonetheless, there are effects, and therefore the question of whether machine scarcity cost Kerry votes remains open. One way to answer this question is to use the coefficients in Table 1 to estimate how much higher turnout would have been (on a precinct-by-precinct basis) if there were no scarcity and to assume that the turnout gains would have translated into votes for Kerry and Bush in proportions equal to those based on the votes that were actually cast in the respective precincts.

Take a concrete example. If a precinct with over 400 RPM had more machines to bring the RPM down to less than 250, then turnout in the precinct would have been an estimated 7.7 percentage points higher (according to Model 4 in Table 1). If that precinct had 1,000 registered voters, then the 7.7 point increase translates into 77 additional voters. If those who actually voted in the precinct split their votes 60% [f]or Kerry and 38% for Bush (with 2% voting for other candidates), then the increase of 77 voters would be expected to include 46 for Kerry and 29 for Bush, with a net advantage of 17 for Kerry.

Conducting the analysis across all 788 precincts in Franklin County and then aggregating the results produces a predicted turnout increase (based on Model 4 in Table 1) of 21,786 voters if all precincts had RPMs of 250 or less. Of these additional voters, an estimated 13,691 would have voted for Kerry while 7,912 would have voted for Bush. Thus the estimated net benefit for Kerry would have been 5,779 votes. With a final statewide margin of about 120,000 votes for Bush, a net increase of 5,779 votes for Kerry would have diminished the margin, but would not have altered the election outcome.

Conclusion

The strong association between the availability of voting machines and turnout in Franklin County, Ohio in the 2004 presidential election was largely the result of factors unrelated to the causal effect of the availability of voting machines on turnout. That said, after controlling for other causes of turnout, the relationship does not disappear, suggesting that machine scarcity was a cause of lower turnout. The magnitude of the effect in terms of votes was about 22,000, which would have diminished George W. Bush's statewide margin by about 6,000 had there been no scarcity of voting machines on Election Day. Thus long lines at polling places in Franklin County

do not appear to have cost John Kerry the presidential election, but they do appear to have cost him votes.

Given that the Franklin County Board of Elections, like all Ohio county election boards, has four members, two Democrats and two Republicans, attributing the scarcity of voting machines and its consequent effects to partisan maneuvering is probably not warranted. Instead, the unusually close national election where the stakes were perceived to be especially high combined with Ohio's status as a key—perhaps *the* key—battleground state produced a much larger than usual number of citizens who would have liked to vote. This was apparent in advance of the election as registration rates surged in Franklin County and elsewhere. But, fully accommodating this desire would have required many more voting machines than the county had on hand. Michael R. Hackett, the deputy director of the Franklin County Board of Elections, explained the decision not to acquire more machines this way: "Does it make sense to purchase more machines just for one election? … I'll give you the answer: no" (quoted in Powell and Slevin 2004). While many would disagree with Hackett, his question and answer touch on two important points. Administering elections requires ample resources. Administering them well requires even more.

Notes

1. All the data analyzed in this paper are from the Franklin County Board of Elections, some of which was made available through Knapp (2004). All turnout rates are calculated as the percentage of registrants that voted.

2. Perhaps needless to point out, Columbus is the heart of Franklin County.

3. Consider the report written by the Democratic staff of the House Judiciary (House Judiciary Staff 2005). While it does not shy away from blaming Blackwell for a host of problems ("there were massive and unprecedented voter irregularities and anomalies in Ohio … caused by intentional misconduct and illegal behavior … involving [the] Secretary of State" (4)), when discussing the problem of long lines and machine availability in Franklin County, though, no blame is attributed to Blackwell.

4. The effects are likely greater for potential voters who have less free time, like the employed, and smaller

for those with more free time, like the retired. Because I use precinct-level data, analyzing the differential effects of scarcity based on individual characteristics like employment status are beyond the bounds of this paper.

5. To the extent that the composition of precincts changed between 2002 and 2004, turnout in 2002 will be an imperfect control variable and lead to overestimating the causal effect of machine availability on turnout. Thus the results reported in Table 1 should be viewed as upper-bound estimates of the effects of machine availability on turnout.

References

Brady, Henry E., Guy-Uriel Charles, Benjamin Highton, Martha Kropf, Walter R. Mebane Jr., and Michael Traugott. 2004. "Interim Report on Alleged Irregularities in the United States Presidential Election of 2 November 2004." Social Science Research Council. http://elections.ssrc.org/commission/research/Interim Report122204.pdf, accessed on 3/15/05.

Congressional Record. 2005. January 6.

Dao, James, Ford Fessenden, and Tom Zeller Jr. 2004. "Voting Problems in Ohio Spur Call for Overhaul," *New York Times,* December 24.

House Judiciary Democratic Staff. 2005. "Preserving Democracy: What Went Wrong in Ohio." January 5. www.house.gov/judiciary_democrats/ohiostatusrept 1505.pdf, accessed on 3/15/05.

Jackson, Robert A. 1996. "A Reassessment of Voter Mobilization." *Political Research Quarterly* 49 (June): 331–349.

Knapp, Joe. 2004. "Effect of Voting-Machine Allocations on the 2004 Election—Franklin County, Ohio." http://copperas.com/machinery/, accessed on 12/15/2004.

Powell, Michael, and Peter Slevin. 2004. "Several Factors Contributed to 'Lost' Voters in Ohio," *Washington Post,* December 15.

9

Retail Politics Alive and Well: Large Media Buys Have Limited Effectiveness in Small Population States

David Mark

Some candidates for major office still campaign the old-fashioned way: by kissing babies and pressing the flesh.

BOZEMAN, MONT.—After Brian Schweitzer's successful race for Montana governor in 2004, the Democrat mused that he had shaken the hands of nearly a quarter of the electorate on the campaign trail.

While that sounds like a bold claim, the new governor may in fact have accomplished the feat, or something close to it. According to the Montana Secretary of State's office, about 456,000 people cast votes in the November 2004 gubernatorial election, meaning Schweitzer would have had to shake hands with about 112,000 people.

In a state that places a high value on retail politics, the effort was time well spent. Montana, which has about 900,000 residents, and other small-population states are among the last bastions where big media such as television and radio advertising do not dominate the political landscape. People are often unwilling to show their loyalty at the ballot box if an office-seeker does not show up in person—and not just on the campaign trail.

"They expect to see their elected officials and know them. They expect to see them at the gym," said Matt McKenna, a veteran Democratic strategist who runs the Bozeman, Mont., office of the public affairs firm Strategies360.

Statewide candidates in Montana do not avoid television and other mass media efforts; it's just that personal contact almost always trumps pre-packaged efforts, said McKenna, a Montana native.

"It's a little different than getting a telemarketer call during dinner," he said. "People still appreciate that you are out here. People still expect that."

Campaign strategies in small population states such as Montana, Delaware and New Hampshire differ markedly from those employed

From *Campaigns & Elections,* September 2005.

in densely populated states where the most effective way to reach voters is through television and other mass media. In 2006, when U.S. Sen. Dianne Feinstein runs her re-election race in California and Sen. Bill Nelson of Florida ask constituents for another term in Washington, most voters will only see these Democrats—and their Republican opponents—in television commercials, direct mail pieces and on the Internet.

For states so vast and populations so large, the old-fashioned art of retail politics, meeting voters individually, has diminished in importance. In California, with about 33 million people, statewide candidates often make only fleeting campaign appearances in the largest cities, Los Angeles, San Francisco, San Diego and Sacramento. They will also occasionally show up at county fairs and other events in medium-sized television markets, such as Fresno or Bakersfield, but usually only to drum up media coverage that will be featured on that day's news.

Retail politics reigns in Delaware, a small state where elected officials are also friends and neighbors. Delaware is just 100 miles long and 35 miles wide, making it the second smallest state after Rhode Island. With its 830,000 or so residents, Delaware enjoys the usual stable of elected officials—two U.S. senators, one U.S. House member, governor, lieutenant governor and other state-wide officeholders. There are 41 members of the state House and 21 members of the state Senate, along with a city council in the three largest population municipalities, Wilmington (75,000 people), Newark and Dover (about 30,000 each).

With all these offices in such a small state, residents even vaguely involved in business and civic life are likely to know many, if not most, of their elected officials on a first-name basis. First State residents expect to see their elected representatives, including federal office-holders, back home for ribbon cuttings, Little League playoffs, barbecues and other such activities. In Delaware, candidates meet on a regular basis with fire-fighters, police,

teachers, civic association leaders along with civic, arts and public health groups.

Delaware's lack of its own television stations contributes to the importance of retail politics. Residents of Wilmington rely on television from Philadelphia, about 30 miles to the north, while folks in southern Delaware watch stations from Baltimore, about 120 miles to the west. Running television ads in markets where the majority of viewers cannot vote in the election at hand often makes for a poor use of resources. And even if candidates do want to run television commercials, the advertising rates of the big-city stations are often prohibitively expensive.

Ground zero for retail politics with national implications is New Hampshire, home of the first presidential primary. Presidential hopefuls visit New Hampshire early and often, sometimes starting within months of the last election. Former U.S. Sen. John Edwards of North Carolina, a 2004 presidential hopeful who ended up the Democratic vice-presidential nominee, has already made several visits to the Granite State this year in anticipation of another run for the White House in 2008.

In the year before the primary, the odds are good that on any given day a presidential candidate will be in the state. Because New Hampshire is a small state both geographically (it is the seventh smallest state with an area of 9,304 square miles) and population-wise (less than two million people) and because the candidates spend so much time there, voters have the opportunity to get to see the candidates face-to-face.

Presidential candidates routinely make the rounds of events that might seem to befit local politicians, including speeches to Rotary Clubs and in the homes of local Democrats.

New Hampshire also offers the opportunity to build a unique level of grass-roots support. The state House of Representatives has more than 400 members, the largest in the country. Individual state lawmakers have their own political contacts that can be helpful to presidential candidates.

Political Parties and Interest Groups

Political parties and special interest groups are in some ways the Rodney Dangerfields of democracy: They get no respect. Some might argue that their low reputations are thoroughly deserved. State legislatures often appear to be more arenas for partisan wrestling matches than institutions attending to the public interest. Special interest groups have a not wholly undeserved reputation for being focused on only one set of narrow concerns: their own. And, many agree, it all seems to be getting worse.

Take Wisconsin. The Dairy State always has had a reputation for squeaky-clean government, the sort of place where legislators accepting even modest gifts from a lobbyist (a drink, sports tickets) can create a "scandal." Not anymore. In the past couple of years the legislature has been roiled by a corruption and kickback controversy that really is a scandal, no quotation marks needed. Charges include using taxpayer money to support partisan campaigning and requiring lobbyists to make partisan donations in exchange for consideration of their legislative wishes. At least six legislators have seen their careers derailed by charges stemming from this payola scheme, and partisan bickering in the legislature has prevented strong corrective measures to repair its image. It did pass a bill that bans convicted felons from lobbying that, if anything, further sullied the state government's reputation, as voters asked why were convicted felons allowed such opportunities for influence in the first place?[1]

Increasing partisanship and the growing influence of special interests, often through means considered shady if not illegal, are common complaints about state politics these days. Wisconsin is far from the only state that provides at least some kernel of justification for these alarms. But are political parties and special interest groups really that bad?

The short answer is no. Political parties and special interest groups actually do good things for democracy and, as some of the readings in this section will detail, reflect conflict as much as cause it. Among the many services political parties and special interest groups provide state politics are mobilizing voters, packaging coherent policy proposals for public debate and generally connecting citizens to their government. The ultimate currency in representative democracy is votes, and political parties and special interest groups fight mighty hard to get themselves on the majority side of the electorate.

There's no doubt that those fights become intense and heated. It is debatable, though, whether they are any more intense and heated than they used to be. And while lobbying reform is a hot issue in many states, it's not clear that this trend is being driven by a sudden surge in questionable influence peddling.

POLITICAL PARTIES AND SPECIAL INTEREST GROUPS: DIFFERENCES AND SIMILARITIES

At what point does a political party stop being a political party and become a special interest group? For many people the distinction is a little blurry, and it's no wonder. As already noted, political parties and special interest groups do lots of the same things, including supporting each other. Both raise money, endorse candidates and try to get government to support their favored policies.

They are, however, fundamentally different. Here's how you tell them apart: Political parties run candidates for office under their own label, and they help organize the government. Special interest groups do not. Candidates might vie for the endorsement and campaign support of, say, the National Rifle Association, but they run as Republicans and Democrats, not as nominees of the NRA. Once in office elected officials organize government into the majority and minority parties, with the majority controlling the key leadership posts in the legislature. Even in nominally nonpartisan governments—which include most local governments and Nebraska's unicameral legislature—candidates often are not shy about declaring their partisan credentials and seeking party endorsements. In effect, informal party systems can exist even where they are formally prohibited. Political

parties are virtually impossible to keep out of politics. The same might be said of special interest groups. While they do not run their own candidates for office or organize government, they most definitely try to influence the decisions government makes.

The scramble to win elections, control the key offices and institutions of government, and influence the decisions of policymakers tends to create a negative image of political parties and special interest groups. In some cases, the skepticism, or even outright cynicism, is justified. Political parties do at times engage in a win-at-all-costs mentality, and special interest groups have been known to try to engage in checkbook democracy.

Yet there is a flip side to this that often gets left out of such judgments. First, political parties and special interest groups, most of the time, take care to stick to lawful activities—stories of graft, kickbacks, and other forms of outright corruption get so much attention because they represent the exception rather than the rule. Second, political parties and special interest groups represent the fundamental democratic rights of citizens in action.

As citizens, all Americans have a right to band together with people of similar interests and support a common cause. That, in a nutshell, is what political parties and special interest groups do. Many people are cynical about special interest groups, but make an exception for "their" groups. Mention "special interest" and most people do not think of teachers, police officers, or firefighters. Yet all have an organized lobbying presence in virtually all states and many localities. The point is that one person's narrow-minded, selfish special interest is another person's noble cause.

Most states regulate political parties pretty much like public utilities—they view them as providing a necessary public service and seek to ensure that that service does not unduly profit, benefit, or exclude certain people or groups. For example, many of these regulations are explicitly aimed at preventing such antidemocratic, antimajoritarian activities as "boss" control of political parties.[2]

Special interest groups are relatively lightly regulated. It is generally recognized by state law (not to mention the First Amendment of the U.S. Constitution) that individuals and organizations have a right to petition government and make their preferences known. The regulatory machinery is thus often aimed at registering and reporting rather than actually dictating what special interests can and cannot do.

RECENT TRENDS

Despite being different in many respects, political parties and special interest groups share an unfortunate reputation in many quarters. In this section a number of readings explore the reasons—real or imagined—behind the conflicts created by political parties and lobbyists, and also explore the steps that are (or are not) being taken to deal with the negative implications of this conflict. Alan Ehrenhalt explores the widespread perception of rising partisanship in state legislatures, and the increasing lack of civility it supposedly visits on the business of government. There is certainly some truth to the claim that party battles can make for brutal debate, but Ehrenhalt points out there's nothing new or shocking about that. There never was a golden age of bipartisanship in state legislatures; partisan politics has always been part and parcel of the business of democratic politics in the United States. Things might have gotten particularly unpleasant in the last decade or so, but some of the more extreme proposals to deal with the problem—such as doing away with parties altogether—are unlikely to do much good even if enacted. Fact is, people disagree on a lot, and getting rid of political parties won't make that go away.

A more reasonable program to take the edge off of partisanship is explored in the essay by Cynthia Kyle. The Michigan Political Leadership Program is designed to take people from opposite ends of the party spectrum and get them together to explore what they have in common, rather than to fight about what they disagree on.

More than a decade old, the program has scored important successes in promoting bipartisanship, helping to train a wide range of community leaders at all levels of government who know how, and are willing to, reach across the party aisle to promote good policy, and even to promote each other's political careers.

The essay by Morgan E. Felchner shows the importance of money to state political parties, and why they have little choice but to make tending their finances a central objective. The first article by Alan Greenblatt ("Lobby Decoration") provides a short overview of lobby reform laws being proposed and implemented in various state legislatures. It remains to be seen whether any of these laws will help shore up the image of special interest groups, or restore the sorely battered faith in good government in places like Wisconsin.

The second essay by Alan Greenblatt shows how special interests and political parties can become so intertwined they create internal conflicts. The Republican Party in Kansas is split between moderates and conservatives affiliated with the Christian Right. This has created an internal split on such issues as abortion rights and teaching evolution in public schools, and raised questions within the Republican Party about the influence of religious leaders on public policy.

Notes

1. "Nothing Scandalous," *Governing,* May 2005, 17–18 and "Lobbying Decoration" *Governing,* March 2005, 16–17.

2. Malcolm E. Jewell and Sarah M. Morehouse, *Political Parties and Elections in American States,* 4th ed. (Washington, D.C.: CQ Press, 2001), 76.

10

Theory of Partisan Relativity

Alan Ehrenhalt

The past decade has brought a marked increase in partisan unpleasantness in legislative bodies almost everywhere in the country.

Not many people noticed it at the time, but last year the Oregon Senate passed a bill that would have pretty much eliminated political parties from state government altogether. The governor, the attorney general and other state officials would run on a ballot without partisan identification. So would all the legislators. In all likelihood, party caucuses and party leadership would disappear from the Capitol in Salem. There would be no need for them.

The bill didn't get anywhere in the House, but the fact that such a sweeping measure passed one chamber—and by a 20–10 margin—offered at least a clue that something interesting was going on. A few weeks ago, the author of the legislation, state Senator Charlie Ringo, announced his unexpected retirement. He said he no longer wanted to serve in an institution poisoned by partisan bickering. "The blind allegiance to party," he said, "is killing us."

The departure of Ringo isn't likely to put out the fire over the issues he raised. *The Oregonian,* the newspaper with the largest circulation in the state, also has been on something of a rampage. "Fierce partisanship in recent years," the paper concluded in one of many editorials on the subject, "clearly has contributed to the legislature's failures." It cited the inability of the 2005 session to deal with crucial questions of health care, school funding and tax policy. *The Oregonian* is urging that a governmental reform commission appointed last year take a serious look at Ringo's fundamental idea: Crack down on partisanship by simply writing parties out of the electoral equation.

One could write this fervor off as characteristic Oregon quirkiness, if something along similar lines weren't going on right across

From *Governing,* March 2006.

the border, in Washington State. There, the crusader has been State Treasurer Mike Murphy. Last year, he asked the legislature to make his own office nonpartisan. Management of the state's money, he argued, has no logical or useful connection to political party agendas. The legislature turned him down. It also rejected a bill to make county sheriffs nonpartisan officials. But the ideas aren't going away. *The Seattle Times* is agitating for nonpartisan county councils. "It's time for politicians to rid themselves of the party label," the paper's editorial page editor opined last year. "If you think of an issue that ended in partisanship, then you also think of an issue where county government has failed."

Similar sentiments are beginning to stir, if somewhat less dramatically, in California and Colorado. In the Observer section of this month's magazine, Alan Greenblatt recounts how two California legislators, consistently rebuffed in efforts to establish a more civil and bipartisan climate, are seeking to bypass the legislative process and create a citizens' commission aimed at reaching the same goals. Meanwhile, in Colorado, two dozen first-term legislators have formed a bipartisan caucus designed in response to what they see as growing public resentment at partisan excess. "The voting populace," one of the members said recently, "is so tired of partisan bickering."

As you may have noticed by now, all of these states have something in common: They are in the West. Out beyond the Rockies, political parties have never had a very good reputation. It was California that pioneered in the use of the direct primary to weaken state party bosses; Washington that first experimented with a primary ballot that didn't have partisan labels on it; Oregon that made famous the voter initiative process.

All those things happened in the early years of the 20th century. Now, in the early years of the 21st, one might plausibly contend that a similar regional revolt is underway— that the visceral Western resentment against "Eastern" party bosses, autocratic leadership and government in general is simply making one of its periodic comebacks.

It may be a plausible argument, but I don't think it will

There's a commonly held perception that civility once prevailed and partisan excesses were kept in check.

prove to be accurate. I think what's starting to happen in the West isn't so much a regional eccentricity but rather a broader form of dissent that will, as have many other political and governmental ideas, gradually work its way east across the mountains. The truth is that the past decade has brought a marked increase in partisan unpleasantness in legislative bodies almost everywhere in the country. Many theories have been advanced to explain what has caused it—district maps that produce too many safe one-party seats; negative campaign ads that leave candidates bearing long-term grudges; interest groups that demand partisan rigidity as a price for support—but the existence of the phenomenon itself is difficult to dispute.

The frustrations have probably been greatest—among legislators and voters alike—in states that used to consider themselves relatively free of the problem. These include not only Washington and Oregon but also Midwestern states such as Wisconsin and Minnesota, where good-government traditions were once thought sufficient to preclude the most egregious partisan abuses.

In Wisconsin, where the pressures of partisan competition in recent years led to illegal fund-raising, indictments of leaders in both parties, and a widespread public distrust of the entire governmental process, the atmosphere of personal hostility has left quite a few senior members lamenting that the collegial institution they once served in has essentially ceased to exist. "What has changed in the last 20 years," one veteran told a reporter recently, "is that the people on each side of the aisle don't just fight about policy. They don't like each other very much as individuals. People are actually told they shouldn't mingle socially with the other side." Last year, the Democratic leader of the Assembly complained that the Republican Speaker refused to talk to him or even look at him. The Speaker retorted that the Democrat was "crazy" and "a very bitter person."

Common to most of the current complaints about partisan excess is a notion that there was a Golden Age of bipartisanship, a time in the not too distant past when opposing forces disagreed respectfully, came together when necessary for the common good, and established close personal friendships outside the confines of the chamber. Legislators all over the country like to talk about this. But when was the Golden Age, exactly? That's a little harder to pin down.

In Oregon, there's a pretty clear consensus about when the Golden Age was: It was in the early 1970s, when the revered Tom McCall was governor and the state passed landmark bills controlling pollution and preserving rural land from the ravages of sprawl. "The late 1960s and early 1970s," longtime newspaper editor Doug Bates wrote last year, "have been transmogrified into such a misty, mystical time in state lore that frustrated Oregonians waste too much time longing for a new Tom McCall to lead us from the dismal swamp of mediocrity." The answer, Bates insisted, wasn't another McCall—it was the re-creation of a legislature willing to rise above partisanship.

In every legislative body that I know of, there's a commonly held perception that civility once prevailed and partisan excesses were kept in check. But if you strapped yourself into a time machine and traveled back to the Oregon legislature of 1969 or 1971, I can almost guarantee that you'd find some legislators expressing the same nostalgic laments for a still earlier period—probably around the time they first took the oath of office.

As far back as you might wish to go in American political history, you'll see essentially the same thing: politicians of one generation complaining that the civility and public spirit of the previous years have disappeared in an orgy of partisanship; and, further back, a different set of politicians from the previous generation making a similar complaint.

Jeffery Jenkins, a Northwestern University political scientist who studies the history of partisanship, argues that, however powerful nostalgia may be, vicious party infighting has been a constant in public life all the way back to the days when Thomas Jefferson denounced Patrick Henry as having "an avaricious and rotten heart," and urged loyal Jeffersonians to "devoutly pray for his death."

Jenkins does offer one caveat: He says that the period from 1945 to 1965 really was a bit less partisan, with consensus politics prevailing in Congress and most of the states. But this was a historical aberration, and it came at a high price: tightly knit legislative oligarchies that excluded blacks and Republicans in the South and largely ignored urban interests in the Midwest. Politics was less partisan in those years for a very good reason: Much of the country was operating under a one-party system. If you look back to that time, you find most experts proclaiming that the cure for legislative failure was more partisanship, not less. More partisanship is what we got; it just doesn't look very pretty now that we have it.

In the end, one has to say that Charlie Ringo is right: There has been an epidemic of partisanship in the past decade, and we will all be better off if we can make it subside. But that probably doesn't mean trying to ban it from legislatures altogether. Two hundred years of American history suggest that this isn't a realistic option.

As my witness on that point, I call upon George Washington, a politician who didn't like parties very much but ultimately found a way to live with them. Partisanship, he wrote, is "a fire not to be quenched. It demands a uniform vigilance to prevent its bursting into a flame, lest, instead of warming, it should consume."

11

Partisan Buster

Cynthia Kyle

The Michigan Political Leadership Program makes it easier for state lawmakers to have good relationships with others across the aisle.

Beer's in the bathtub. Soft drinks are chilling. Homemade brownies, chocolate chip cookies from a bakery, Cheetos and potato chips tumble over the hotel suite's dining table.

The sofa's packed with people, knee to knee and nose to nose in the heady conversations of school board budgeting, bipartisan coalitions and the nitty-gritty of campaign fundraising.

A newly elected African American school board member is bumping elbows with a suburban city clerk intent on learning more about voter diversity.

Mid-floor in this tiny campus hotel room, a political consultant is holding court alongside a reporter who periodically exclaims "that's incredible" to an explanation of why all public colleges should be private.

These are members of the 2004 class of the Michigan Political Leadership Program (MPLP), a training program launched in 1992 to combat strictly partisan politics in a term-limited state.

"One of my proudest moments in life was creating MPLP," says Bob Mitchell, a legislative staffer, Democratic congressional candidate, consultant and now founder of Trans-Elect New Transmission Development Co. based in Reston, Va. He and a small group in Lansing, Mich., wrote a business plan and raised $750,000 to give life to MPLP.

From MPLP's ranks have emerged 100 past and present elected community leaders. Among them are school board members, 10 members of state government and now a speaker of the House of Representatives.

This Friday night, like Fridays once a month from February through October, the 2005 MPLP Fellows are coming together to dine, debate and learn more about themselves and each other.

From *State Legislatures,* February 2006.

Political affiliations along with conservative-liberal labels will be shed in common tales of winning and losing elections, their hopes and dreams for a better world, and the good food they've brought to share.

"I truly love that program," says John Helmholdt, a political fundraiser with roots in the Republican Party and a 2004 MPLP graduate. He's organized two political action committees of up-and-comers in Grand Rapids, his hometown. "They're starting to get in line to become part of this program."

Just after dinner tonight, members of the Class of 2005 are huddled in small groups in a Marriott Courtyard conference room in Grand Rapids.

The fellows are intent on tonight's assignment: They are to envision themselves as an incumbent member of the Michigan Legislature, running in a district that is entirely new territory.

The district is buffeted by the global economy, and voters are restless, the printed assignment cautions. "Recent polling shows that 65 percent of all registered voters think the state is on the wrong track. How do you get re-elected despite these challenges?"

The fellows must ask themselves why they're running, how they will launch campaigns, contact voters, raise money and keep track of every task. They're plotting media buys and filling in campaign calendars.

One group barely breaks concentration even as guests enter the room. The group is searching for a "hot topic" that will touch the voters in an exercise they hope to take with them into real-life, hands-on campaigns they likely will face outside this venue.

Later this night, Fellows designated as hosts will welcome colleagues to a flood of snacks and after-hours debate that will spill with them into nearby bars and restaurants well into the night.

Early Saturday, after bacon, scrambled eggs, cereal and sweet rolls, they'll board a trolley to tour Grand Rapids, and witness housing, health care and entertainment development rising in the city's downtown.

Later, they'll be challenged by a "Budget Busters" exercise that will divide them into assigned political parties and ask them to bring the state's budget in balance against a vortex of declining revenue.

A SELECT GROUP

Each year since 1992, coincidentally when Michigan voters passed the most restrictive term limits in the nation,

24 political junkies and legislative hopefuls have been selected from across the state to take part—at no charge to themselves—in this unique multi-partisan learning environment. So far, some 300 people have gone through the program and 100 typically apply each year for the slots.

For each of the 10 monthly weekends, the MPLP fellows move from community to community throughout the state, meeting consultants, reporters, business leaders and fundraising specialists they hope to call on when they need help as candidates, newly elected officers or citizen activists.

"This is in-depth training," says 2005 Fellow Janice McCraner, a Republican and county commissioner. She typically drives four hours to MPLP weekends. "I haven't missed a session. After my first one, I was so enthralled. I'm amazed at the experts they can bring in."

Among 2005 fellows are a township planning commissioner who works in distance learning at the University of Michigan, a former state Senate aide who is with an association, the founder of a breast cancer-fighting foundation, a precinct delegate and a former Detroit police officer turned criminal investigator for a state environmental agency.

They are led by a man and a woman, one a Republican and one a Democrat, who challenge the 24 to craft campaign strategies, debate the finer points of media relations and get to know each other as people rather than as members of the other political party.

"It has allowed me to be more of a 21st century leader, not getting bogged down in the stereotypes of the past," says Lindsay Huddleston, a legal research analyst for Democratic Governor Jennifer Granholm. He took part in the class of 2004.

"Here was a program where for one weekend a month it was OK to say you love politics," he adds. "It was almost a support group."

A BOND FORMS

Members of each class talk of how surprised, and gratified, they are when fellows contribute money and support to their campaigns.

Detroit attorney James Heath, a 2005 Fellow, came within 20 votes of unseating an incumbent House member, and is considering a second run. He'll be armed with MPLP insights next time, he asserts. And, his classmates predict, he'll have 23 more volunteers—his MPLP colleagues.

Each term ends with an even larger show of support—a poignant fundraiser now so large it must be scheduled over two days at two ends of the state. Graduates compete to sell tickets, rise for a standing ovation, and laugh together in the crossfire of national political figures of opposing viewpoints.

The first year's reunion speakers were strategists Mary Matlin and James Carville, fresh from political combat for opposing political parties and just a year married.

"We picked people from both sides of the aisle," recalls Aaron Payment, now in his second year as tribal chairman of the Sault Ste. Marie Tribe of Chippewa Indians and member of MPLP's inaugural class in 1992.

Payment then directed the tribe's state and federal policy efforts and drove across half the state to attend the training. "You need a license to drive a car. You need a license to get married. You don't need a qualification to be a legislator," he says.

Now Payment serves as an MPLP presenter, introducing new classes of Fellows to his tribe and governance. "In many cases, I'm giving people their first exposure to Native American people," he says.

Former Republican National Committee Chair Ed Gillespie and former Democratic National Committee Chair Terry McAuliffe will square off March 2, 2006, in a banquet hall in the state's southeastern corner. Speakers and sponsors will then trek through the frosty dark to Grand Rapids for an early morning breakfast repeat.

Until then, MPLP fellows spend their weekends together—with a different roommate each session.

Fellows say universally that the program, now housed in Michigan State University's Institute for Public Policy and Social Research (IPPSR), fosters new relationships and greater understanding in an era of term limits.

"I really can't say enough good things about the program," says Barbara Goushaw, a political consultant in Berkley outside of Detroit.

She's half of the only MPLP marriage to date. She and her husband Fred Collins were Fellows in back-to-back years. "Politics brought us together," she says. They are also the group's only Libertarian Party members.

TERM LIMITS AS CATALYST

MPLP "has been a great icebreaker," says Craig DeRoche, a member of MPLP's inaugural class and now on its alumni board. He was 22 and working as an insurance claims adjuster when tapped.

Though he may have been a virtual unknown in Lansing, he built coalitions through MPLP and business connections before his state House term. He climbed from city council to House member, and then in the first year of his second term, to speaker of the House.

The suburban Detroit Republican moved swiftly. He installed a former policy analyst, rather than a staffer from the GOP caucus, as chief of staff and mixed business leaders with political leaders on his transition team.

DeRoche credits the savvy moves to "kind of a blend. My understanding of the political process, my life experience and MPLP."

It was term limits that helped bring DeRoche to Michigan's capital, but partisan politics that inspired MPLP's creation, Mitchell says.

"I always thought it was a travesty that we do so little in our country to prepare people to serve in public office," he says.

"There are plenty of campaign schools. The real job is what happens after you get elected, I saw example after example of people taking positions not based on being the best solutions but being what was good for politics. Because of term limits, the program is even more important."

In recent years, MPLP has gained a following as a training ground for elective politics, but its intent is far broader, insists Lynn Jondahl, former state House member and MPLP co-director from 1995 to 2002. "It's a valuable way for anyone who in the broadest sense wants to develop skills to work in the political world."

MPLP's current co-directors have considerable such experience.

James Agee is a former public school principal and superintendent who served in the state House and was the Democratic nominee for lieutenant governor in 1998.

Anne Mervenne, now a suburban Detroit lobbyist, worked 12 years in the administration of Republican Governor John Engler, directing the governor's Detroit office and advising the state's first lady. She was a legislative staff member and served as a county commissioner for four years.

Former Fellows have made the most of their training.

"Pan"—short for Patricia Anne-Godchaux was the first MPLP graduate elected to the House. She won a GOP seat in suburban Detroit and now co-directs a similar program, the Institute for Local Government, at the University of Michigan-Dearborn.

"I learned a lot about running a campaign. More important, I learned a lot about statewide issues," she says.

Republican Senator Wayne Kuipers, in 2002, was the first Fellow elected to the Senate. He also served in the House from 1999 to 2002. "It certainly helped me articulate what I was believing and feeling. We had to debate. We had to fight. We had to argue. We had to stand up for what we believe," he says.

MPLP directors try for a 12–12 split between the two political parties. Interaction is encouraged.

Ed Clemente, from the class of 1997, was the first Democrat elected to the state House from MPLP ranks. The House member from a suburban Detroit community formed a fast relationship with MPLP colleague and now fellow legislative rookie Representative Dick Ball, a Republican from the state's more rural midsection.

"It makes it easier up here (in the Legislature), especially with term limits, to have a pretty good relationship with someone on the other side of the aisle," says Clemente.

Ball, an optometrist, had served on his local school board and lost two elections for state House before he put MPLP training to work. "What I learned in MPLP really served me well," he says.

"There are people who are interested in running for office," says Doug Roberts, IPPSR director and former state treasurer during a Republican administration. "They go through the program and, lo and behold, they end up getting elected, and they can at least talk to each other."

Financed for the Future

There have been changes in the Michigan Political Leadership Program. National political consultants served as presenters in the early days.

"We decided against doing that," says Lynn Jondahl, former state House member and MPLP co-director from 1995 to 2002. State-based agency directors, media managers and fundraising consultants were called upon, instead. A series of forums—on broad topics like health care and higher education finance—have opened to the public as well as to fellows recently. The W. K. Kellogg Foundation of Battle Creek and Herbert H. and Grace A. Dow Foundation of Midland in Michigan have contributed grants.

A session on ethics was added. A transportation case study was the fruit of joint work with the Southeast Michigan Council of Governments.

An annual dinner was added as a way to help pay for an ongoing program. Governors have worked the dinner. MPLP fellows join lobbyists, students, nonprofit association leaders and supporters for what is now considered the state's largest multi-partisan event.

"It's a real fine mix of Michigan politics," says Jondahl.

12

Making Ends Meet: State Parties Struggle to Shore Up Their Finances

Morgan E. Felchner

Cash-strapped state parties need electoral victories to help balance the books.

For some Democratic state parties in the South, the sweep of red that occurred in the last election extends right onto their balance sheets. Troubled Democratic state party organizations, most notably in Florida, Arkansas and Oklahoma, are having money problems that are unlikely to be resolved unless the party itself scores some wins on Election Day 2006.

"The key ingredient is the identity of the governor in most states," said Larry Sabato, director of the Institute of Politics at the University of Virginia. "... If a state has an incumbent, popular Democratic governor, then the [Democratic] party in that state will fare well financially. If the governor is a Republican and popular, then the GOP will fare well."

The cash-strapped state parties are getting some help from Washington, D.C. Democratic National Committee (DNC) Chairman Howard Dean and his staff recently launched a national strategy to boost electoral prospects outside the party's traditional bases in the Northeast and on the West Coast. Twenty states have been the beneficiaries of this coordination plan so far.

"We intend to have an active effort in all 50 states with paid staff on the ground as soon as possible to help with congressional and local elections," Dean wrote in an early 2005 post on the DNC Web site.

The DNC is sending staff members to assess the financial needs of individual parties to determine what each one needs; after that, the committee hires people—whom the DNC pays—to work with the state parties. Some staffers from those organizations will attend organizing summits in Washington, D.C., to plan how to best use resources.

From *Campaigns & Elections,* August 2005.

51

"This is part of a big strategy to really empower state parties, make sure that the front lines of our campaigns have the resources they need to function," said Luis Miranda, director of regional and specialty media for the DNC. The committee hopes to have those staff members in place by the end of the year.

The state parties have received financial assistance from the DNC before. During the 2003–2004 election cycle, Florida received nearly $4.5 million, mostly for an open seat Senate race the Democrats lost narrowly, Arkansas received about $377,000 from the DNC and federally registered party committees, and Oklahoma Democrats got about $1.8 million. These were direct transfers to the parties, the program this year does not transfer funds directly, rather it pays the salaries of staff members for each party.

There is much work to be done in states where Democratic state parties are riddled with debt. The situation is particularly acute in Florida. Several newspapers in the state recently reported that the Florida Democratic Party did not pay Social Security and payroll taxes for its employees during the six months from April 1, 2003, through Sept. 30, 2003. The Internal Revenue Service put a lien on the party's property and bank accounts for almost $200,000, no small sum for a party already facing fund-raising shortfalls.

Karen Thurman, the current chair of the Florida Democratic Party, inherited the problems from her predecessors. She learned of the party's accounting deficiencies soon after she took the job earlier this year. The former five-term U.S. congresswoman from the Gainesville area who also served in the state legislature, said the financial discrepancies are being cleaned up.

"While serious mistakes—and regrettable mistakes in judgment—were made over an extended period of time, there was no willful intent by anyone to avoid paying taxes or to break the law," Thurman said at a press conference in late June. "And the party's taxes have been paid and the levy has been lifted."

The party's fund-raising prospects do not look particularly strong, because Democrats are the minority party in most legislative arenas. In addition to a GOP governor, Jeb Bush, Republicans hold commanding majorities in both houses of the legislature and the state's congressional delegation. As of press time Florida had not received help from the DNC.

Arkansas Democrats, too, are in dire straits. The party, which is fighting to win the governorship in 2006 to replace term-limited Republican Gov. Mike Huckabee, recently reported $50,000 in debt. According Federal Elections Commission reports due in May, the party took out a $150,000 line of credit, forcing them into the red.

Debt is not new to the party, former chair Ron Oliver also took out a line of credit for $100,000 when he was chairman.

Arkansas Democratic Party Chairman Jason Willett told the *Arkansas Democrat Gazette* this was all part of a strategy to eventually strengthen the party and return it to the black. The open governorship should help spur fund raising.

"Utilizing the business practice and the line of credit is nothing new to the state party here or to state parties all over the country," said Gabe Holmstrom, executive director of the Arkansas Democratic Party. "It is a business practice that we use and will continue to use."

The resources sent by the DNC should certainly help. State party officials expect to add as many as 15 staff members; of those, between eight and 10 could be covered by the national committee's allotment of $150,000.

"The coordination with the DNC is going to be extremely helpful and will help us lay the ground work to not only win back the governor's mansion in 2006 but to make Arkansas blue in 2008," Holmstrom said.

In Oklahoma, the Democratic Party is riddled with debt. Add that to the fact that the Sooner State has not supported a Democrat for president since Lyndon Baines Johnson in 1964, and future prospects are not really rosy.

However, the Oklahoma Democrats do have a major asset in Gov. Brad Henry, elected in 2002 and in reasonably good shape for re-election in 2006. Sabato said the governor could lead fund-raising efforts to help his state party brethren.

Lisa Pryor, the new chairwoman of the Oklahoma Democratic Party, inherited the financial woes when she took office in May. Initially estimates set the debt between $200,000 and $400,000. At a press conference Pryor said the debt accrued up until May 14th totaled under $500,000. She said much of the debt came from the 2004 coordinated campaign on behalf of state candidates and then-U.S. Rep. Brad Carson, who ultimately lost to Republican Tom Coburn.

In June she had to lay off all paid employees, and the party began operating with an all-volunteer staff. The DNC rode in to the rescue, providing funding for three paid staff positions.

"I am very appreciative of the support that the DNC is providing to the Oklahoma Democratic Party," she said.

As of press time these were the only paid staffers at the party, but Pryor anticipates the political organization will be back in the block shortly, and will be able to hire more people.

In addition to the help from the DNC Pryor announced a new debt-elimination strategy, which includes proving to potential donors that the state party in being run professionally, efficiently and in an account-able manner. "We have 1.2 million registered Democrats in the state, and I am literally inviting every registered Democrat to invest one dollar," Pryor said.

Pryor's plan also calls for Henry and Carson to act as marquee figures for the party and help raise funds. Even though Carson lost last year, he remains a respected fig-ure among Oklahoma Democrats, someone who could still run for political office in the coming years.

"By the end of the year we are going to be stronger than ever," she said.

Sabato said this may be a good strategy.

"Small donor fund-raising, both across the Internet and via events, may be [troubled parties] best bet."

Still, he added, candidates there might be forced to find other avenues of support.

"No doubt Brad Henry has found it more useful to construct his own organization, since his state party is so weak," he said. "... He's done so well working out-side his party that Henry is now a heavy favorite for reelection in 2006."

The DNC's Miranda said the parties are on the right track.

"Florida is doing fine, Oklahoma and Arkansas are doing fine," he said. "They are all doing great work out there putting the state parties back on track and making sure we are taking these resources and putting them to good use."

The state party's financial fortunes should improve now that Democrats are taking on a more national strat-egy, to win votes—and financial contributions—in all corners of the country, Miranda said.

"A lot of these states haven't seen people in a long time from the national party," he said.

13

Lobby Decoration

Alan Greenblatt

There are some tough-sounding new lobby laws. It remains to be seen how much they amount to.

From *Governing*, March 2006.

If there's one thing any smart lobbyist ought to know, it's not to celebrate too loud when you win a big one. But a bunch of Florida lobbyists forgot themselves, and as a result they are stuck with an inconvenient new law. The law, which requires anyone who lobbies to file quarterly reports about fees and activities, had been a top priority for state Senate President Tom Lee, but there was less enthusiasm about it in the House, and it failed to win a majority there. House leaders grew miffed, however, when lobbyists who were gathered outside the chamber cheered lustily at the bill's defeat. The measure got brought up again, with a strict gift ban added to it. Cynics said that was a ploy designed to make it impossible to pass, but it passed anyway.

The new law in Florida is one of a large crop that has been appearing in state capitols lately. Lobby regulation was a hot topic in many legislatures even before Congress got religion on the issue following Jack Abramoff's plea deal. These bills tend to pop up under similar circumstances—there's nothing like a good scandal to get reformers' juices flowing. (There was even an Abramoff-style private-jet golf outing that helped prompt the Florida measure.) In Tennessee, Governor Phil Bredesen convened a special session earlier this year to address lobbying practices in the face of an FBI sting operation that snared four legislators on bribery and corruption charges.

But a good scandal doesn't always lead to reform with real teeth. The Wisconsin legislature has been enmeshed in a seemingly endless payola scandal that has led to several convictions. The response? A new bill to ban convicted felons from lobbying. If that sounds like a rather narrow approach to the problem, it is. But it also sheds light on the difficulties of placing any meaningful controls on the entire lobbying enterprise.

Wisconsin couldn't respond to the current scandal with a tough new anti-gift law, for the simple reason that it already has one of the toughest in the country. That didn't prevent huge transfers of money between interest groups and legislators from taking place anyway. A court had ruled that the gift law's key phrase—that legislators could not accept "anything of value"—didn't apply to campaign contributions. That made it all but toothless. "I can't think of anything that has more value to a politician than a campaign contribution," says Mike McCabe, of the Wisconsin Democracy Campaign.

Lobbying is a billion-dollar activity in the states. It can't be banned, and so—as with attempts to restrict campaign spending—it will continue to generate excesses no matter what kind of restriction legislators put on the practice. Usually the restrictions aren't enforced too well anyway. More than half the legislatures regulate themselves, through ethics committees. And the legislatures that are watched by outside entities, not surprisingly, tend not to give the watchdogs much in the way of resources or subpoena power.

Some critics complain that the very ineffectiveness of laws meant to limit influence peddling is a large part of their post-scandal appeal. "I think they are something of a façade that lawmakers can point to," suggests Leah Rush, of the Center for Public Integrity. "They say, 'Look how ethical we are—we have laws.'"

14

Church and State

Alan Greenblatt

In Kansas politics, the Christian Right doesn't just pressure the establishment anymore. It is the establishment.

Joe Wright and Terry Fox walk around the Kansas capitol like they own the place. Hanging around before lunch one day outside the Senate chamber, the two men are offering up hugs and handshakes with the effortless familiarity of the most seasoned legislators and lobbyists. That's not what they are, though: They are Baptist ministers from Wichita. They are in the capitol to make it clear that, in the wake of their triumph in forcing a vote on a constitutional ban against gay marriage, they plan to keep using their influence on a variety of political issues to come.

For the most part, the legislators seem glad they are there. "Topeka, in my opinion, is a very dark place," says state Senator Peggy Palmer, "and these people bring some light into this building. They keep us on the right path and I appreciate their help."

Palmer has good reason to feel this way. She is a parishioner at Wright's Central Christian Church—as are two other sitting legislators—and Wright had encouraged her to make a run for the Senate last year against a veteran incumbent. Angered by the legislature's refusal to move the gay marriage issue onto the 2004 ballot, Wright, Fox and other Wichita pastors joined with allies throughout the state's religious community to register tens of thousands of new voters. They published voter guides and helped elect enough conservative legislators not only to force a referendum on gay marriage, which passed easily in April, but possibly to tip the balance of power within a long-feuding Kansas Republican Party toward the conservative side.

Honored-guest status at the legislature is gratifying for Joe Wright, who hasn't always been a popular figure there. He prompted a walkout back in 1996 when he opened that year's House session

From *Governing*, July 2005.

with a prayer in which he told the members, among other things, that they had "abused power and called it politics … polluted the air with profanity and pornography and called it freedom of expression."

As recently as last spring, when Wright and Fox started coming regularly to the capitol to lobby against gay marriage, senators called them "the Taliban" and "the two Ayatollahs from Wichita." But there is little name-calling now. "The thing legislators understand is the power of who's got the votes," Fox says. "When we first came up here, some were friendly, most were cordial at best, but after the success of the marriage amendment, they not only will see us, they'll buy our lunch anytime."

Last year, in his best-selling book *What's the Matter with Kansas?*, Thomas Frank posited the notion that lower- and middle-income people are essentially being hustled by the conservatives on social issues, enticed to vote against their economic self-interest by an agenda consisting of "God, gays and guns." Even though moral issues are hot during election years, Frank argues, little substantive change ever takes place. Republican legislators pass bills that benefit their business constituency, keeping the social issues on ice until they are needed for the next election. After more than two decades of lobbying, the conservatives have made little progress toward outlawing abortion, which they oppose, or toward the legalization of school prayer, which they favor.

That may be the case in Washington, D.C., where business groups have enjoyed a run of legislative successes this year, even as the idea of a constitutional ban on gay marriage appears all but forgotten. But it's not true in Kansas, or in other places where conservatives gained new strength at the polls in 2004.

Topeka, like several state capitals, has become a primary battleground in the "culture war" (a term both Fox and Wright embrace), the center of debate about restrictions on abortion, the teaching of alternatives to Darwinian evolution, and limits on the rights of gay people to marry, adopt or serve as foster parents.

The Christian Right isn't prevailing everywhere, but it is shaping the agenda in many states with a push to preserve or reimpose traditional values. This year, Kansas and neighboring Missouri have each considered legislation to restrict stem-cell research. Arkansas, Georgia and Mississippi have passed bills endorsing the religious scruples of pharmacists wary of handing out contraceptives and morning-after pills. When Kansas voters

approved a gay marriage ban in April, their state became the 14th to write one into its constitution through public referendum.

STRUGGLE FOR CONTROL

The momentum of that victory, Wright and Fox hope, will help them promote a broader agenda in the months to come. If they can do that, conservatives may reach a tipping point in their grasp for power. Kansas is dominated by Republicans, but in recent years, warring factions have fought for supremacy. In 2002, the split within Republican ranks allowed Democrat Kathleen Sebelius to win the governor's mansion.

The question is whether conservatives and Christian activists can push forward with their programs and candidates without offending the moderates who are still in office and whose votes they need to win general election battles. A big test will come next year. Sebelius is up for reelection, but so far no Republican with credentials to hold the party together has stepped forward for the challenge.

As things stand, though, Wright, Fox, Palmer and their allies have the momentum. They have taken over the state Republican apparatus and enjoy firm control of the Kansas House. There are too few Democrats in the legislature for Sebelius to enact any substantial policy agenda of her own and, while moderate Republicans remain a significant presence in the state Senate, they seem increasingly dispirited and inert, unable to generate the passion that conservatives easily summon up around key issues and election battles. "Moderates are not as organized or charged up," complains Val DeFever, a former member of the state board of education and a moderate herself. "Conservatives will stand out in the rain until they get their way, and that's the moderates' problem."

Moderate GOP ranks in both chambers of the legislature were severely depleted last year, with nearly two dozen of the moderates losing their seats over gay marriage and a proposed tax increase. If the party seems more unified today, it's the unity of one side taking control, conservatives finally riding into power on the backs of grassroots activists such as Terry Fox and Joe Wright, and the organizational acumen of U.S. Senator Sam Brownback and some of the new legislative leadership.

"They have the upper hand—they control the party," says Bob Tomlinson, a moderate ex-legislator who is now the state's assistant insurance commissioner. "But they earned it at the ballot box. They didn't steal it. If you're a moderate, you have to consider the possibility that maybe your message is not what the public wants to hear."

There are other states, of course, where events are not playing out as social conservatives would wish. In Colorado, Vermont and Minnesota, Republicans have watched their legislative majorities dissipate or disappear because too many voters have proved unhappy with the social issue agenda, supporting centrist Democrats over Republicans tied to the religious right. Even in the more conservative constituencies of South Dakota and Arizona, there's been tension within the GOP between those who are passionate about moral issues and business interests that wish legislators would devote their attention to bread-and-butter concerns such as taxes and transportation. "We've heard a number of complaints from business leaders," says Tom Clark, of the Denver Metro Chamber of Commerce, "that there was way too much talk about the Ten Commandments and prayer in schools and too little about the things that make Colorado competitive."

One way to explain these events is to argue that conservatives will inevitably encounter a backlash if they push their agenda too hard. But another explanation is that social conservatives in some of the other states just have not gained the sophistication they have achieved in Kansas.

INTELLIGENT DESIGN

Much of this year's legislative session in Topeka was spent discussing education finance, since the state was under court order to relieve regional disparities in school funding. But moral and social issues remained at or near the top of the agenda. In addition to gay marriage, legislators argued over Sunday blue laws, gambling and limits on wine production. Although Kansas has no gun control laws to speak of, a bill was passed this year preempting localities from crafting any such ordinances of their own. A proposal to toughen state regulation of abortion clinics passed overwhelmingly, although Sebelius was able to twist enough arms to muster a one-third House vote that sustained her veto.

The biggest fight of the year, however, may be one that is occurring outside the legislature. It is being played out as the state Board of Education takes up the question of teaching evolution.

Most members of the moderate Republican faction wince the minute the subject comes up. One of them, Representative Ed O'Malley, who comes from the affluent suburbs of Johnson County, cups his head in his hands as he describes the dozens of media outlets that descended on his state for the start of the evolution hearings this spring. "Why do they have to do that?" he asks.

Kansas is famous for having gone down this road before. After a conservative-dominated Board of Education voted to block the teaching of evolution in 1999, voters changed the makeup of the board in a victory for more liberal constituencies. The pendulum has now swung back. Conservatives were better organized in last year's Board of Education voting—they won a key Republican primary, and Democrats contested only one of the five seats that were up. So the creationists again hold a majority on the board. "The conservatives have six votes," laments Democratic board member Bill Wagnon. "They're going to do whatever they want to."

But the creationists have learned a political lesson from 1999. This time, they don't intend to push the evolution issue any further than they think popular opinion will allow. Rather than insisting on overtly religious dogma, they are arguing that mainstream scientific evidence lends credence to the idea that humans are the product of "intelligent design."

During this year's debate, in fact, skeptics about Darwin's theory are talking more about science than most scientists do. "My objective," says Steve Abrams, chairman of the education board and a social conservative, "is good science that's empirically based, measurable, testable and repeatable." Pastor Fox calls the evolution debate "the mother of all political battles," but even he speaks of the wisdom of not pushing the issue as hard as it was pushed six years ago.

Similarly, on abortion, conservatives are seeking to present their proposals as reasonable and their opponents as extremists. There have been two major fights over abortion in Kansas this year. One surrounded the legislative proposal to tighten state regulation of abortion clinics, which passed the House 87–36 but failed to survive the governor's veto. That bill's ultimate defeat, according to Fox, "shows that the pro-choice, liberal faction is not ready to give any ground at all on this cause, even at the cost of protecting lives. Even moderates will say the governor is way out of step."

Kansas's other abortion fight surrounds Attorney General Phill Kline's year-long investigation into rape and child abuse cases, which resulted in the subpoena of medical records from abortion clinics. The subpoenas have drawn national attention and complaints from Planned Parenthood and other organizations that say they are an intimidating intrusion on patient privacy.

Kline, a conservative loyalist and battle-scarred veteran of the internal warfare in the Kansas GOP, allows that there can be a reasonable argument about whether abortions should be allowed in certain circumstances, such as when a pregnant woman has been abandoned. But Kline, like Fox, insists the desire to preserve that right has led the pro-choice side to abandon all reason. "I think they lose this battle," Kline says. "Americans do not support child rape and do not think privacy concerns should shield child rapists."

450-POUND GORILLA

Abortion is the issue that sparked the modern conservative movement in Kansas. In 1974, U.S. Senator Bob Dole ran one of the first major campaigns to trade heavily on the issue, narrowly defeating an opponent who had performed a handful of abortions as a physician. Pictures of aborted fetuses were stuck on car windshields in church parking lots the Sunday before the election. Ever since then, the issue has been a crucial mobilizing force not only for religious conservatives within Kansas but for activists around the country.

During the 1991 "Summer of Mercy," thousands of abortion protesters descended on Wichita, leading to 2,700 arrests. In the aftermath of that event, abortion became a political presence even on subjects where one would not expect it. At a legislative hearing on the topic of transporting natural gas, a producer was asked his opinion about abortion, the suggestion being that pro-life legislators expected him to come down on the right side of the question even if his business before the state was unrelated. Today, says state Senator Phil Journey, abortion may no longer be the 800-pound gorilla of Kansas politics, "but it's about 450 or 500 pounds."

This year, after the House failed to override Sebelius' veto of the abortion clinic bill, Pastors Fox and Wright

worked the hallways outside the chamber, telling reporters that the governor and those who sided with her would soon find their punishment. "The vote taken today will be the driving force behind the governor's election in November 2006," said Fox. "It is these very issues that will motivate and energize conservatives like Governor Sebelius has never seen."

That's possible, of course. The state's church leadership is not only aroused but sophisticated, some 1,200 ministers in constant electronic communication about politics. Many of their parishioners are activists as well. "If we represent the numbers we do in this state and we pay taxes, we ought to have a voice like everybody else," says Jerry Johnston, a politically prominent conservative pastor in Johnson County.

Not all Kansans—not all Republicans—feel that is what the state's clergymen ought to be doing. "I'm uncomfortable with my preacher telling me how to vote, and mine doesn't," says Sheila Frahm, a former lieutenant governor and U.S. senator who lost her Senate seat in 1996 to Brownback's conservative challenge. "Our country was built on the separation of church and state," Frahm insists. She and other moderates admit, however, that their point of view is losing steam.

But the Christian Right now faces a challenge endemic to party politics. Can conservatives keep their most ardent supporters fired up and invested, while maintaining a stance temperate enough to occupy a leading role on a broad range of issues?

So far, the evidence seems to suggest that they can find that balance. On school funding this year, for example, the conservatives engineered a skillful legislative compromise that left little room for dissent from either the governor or the moderate Republican legislators who originally favored a different approach. The deal was later rejected by the state Supreme Court, but it did demonstrate that conservative activists knew to operate in a demanding legislative environment. As seen in the evolution battle, even the most militant preachers are learning to take a careful, incremental approach on highly charged issues.

STAYING TOGETHER

The image of newfound pragmatism may change, however, if the different wings of the party can't coalesce behind a challenger to run against Sebelius. Candidates who have broad appeal within the GOP have already backed away, although one, Congressman Jerry Moran, may still decide to run. Further blood may be shed if conservative Republican legislators make good their threats to run against incumbents from their own party in primaries next year. Some of them are determined to follow through, no matter how much intraparty bitterness the move might create. "I am a conservative," says state Senator Kay O'Connor, who may challenge Secretary of State Ron Thornburgh. "Does that mean I have to be quiet? That's not the American way, as far as I'm concerned."

It may not be the American way, but it's the winning way, warns Senator Phil Journey, a leading conservative strategist. He points out that many of the pivotal votes in any state election continue to be cast by moderate Republicans in Johnson County, the state's richest and most populous jurisdiction, who can easily be made uncomfortable by the militance of the conservative wing. Their disaffection provided a needed boost to Sebelius in her first run for governor—a scenario Journey hopes to avoid repeating next year. He has worked hard to build alliances with moderates—relationships that he admits are fragile and "a lot easier to destroy than they are to build. If we have conservative candidates running against moderate Republicans, all that will have been for naught."

PART

IV

Legislatures

I n a representative democracy, citizens dissatisfied with their government reserve the right to throw the bums out. Don't like your legislator? Don't like the legislature? Don't give 'em your vote. There. Problem solved. Well, that's the theory anyway.

For citizens in many states, though, throwing the bums out isn't an option, it's the law. Heck, even if you love the bum who represents you—even if you resent a dedicated, hardworking, selfless public servant like your legislator being called a bum—you may have little say in whether he or she stays in office or not. Hundreds of state legislators continue to be booted from office not because voters don't want them, but because their time's up. Over the past few years, the full impact of term limit laws passed in the previous fifteen or so years are coming home to roost, and the results are not always those expected, by either opponents or proponents.

Term limits, of course, are not the only big story when it comes to recent trends in state legislatures. The readings in this section will reflect some other developments shaking up the traditional world of state legislatures (notably, the rise of bloggers providing an aggressive alternative to statehouse press corps as sources of information about what legislators are doing and why). That said, it is clear that term limits continue to be the issue with the broadest and most significant impact on legislatures, forcing wholesale turnover and altering the balance of power in state governments.

WHAT LEGISLATURES (AND LEGISLATORS) DO

State legislatures do three basic things: they pass laws, they represent the people and they oversee public agencies in other branches of government. This sounds simple, but it involves a lot of work. A state legislature can deal with more than twenty thousand proposed laws in a single year. Even the most sedate state legislature deals with more than one thousand bills.[1] It is not easy to ensure that the interests of all citizens get represented while managing that volume of lawmaking. Consider that California has a population of about 35.9 million. The California state legislature consists of eighty members in the House and forty members in the Senate,[2] which works out to roughly three hundred thousand citizens for every state legislator. Have you ever tried to keep three hundred thousand people happy? Most legislators would say don't bother—it can't be done. Overseeing public agencies in other branches of government is no picnic either. Most college deans will tell you it is hard enough to keep track of a single department with fewer than twenty faculty members. Try keeping an eye on the 2.7 million people employed in public higher education, the 1 million cops enforcing state laws, the 430,000 state utility workers and the 714,000 corrections employees.[3]

You might say this sounds like a full-time job, but it isn't, at least not in many states. Even some huge states—Texas, for example—have part-time legislatures. Americans have long been suspicious of professional politicians, and at the state level a common way to avoid creating a professional class of elected representatives has been to make sure the legislature meets on a part-time basis and that legislators only get part-time pay. Even in states with full-time legislators, the term limits movement has tried to make sure legislators do not settle into careers as elected representatives. Politics is one of the few careers for which experience can be a job disqualification. It is this general mistrust of the political class that fueled the term limits movement that has led to a number of unintended consequences.

TERM LIMITS AND OTHER TRENDS

In one sense, the term limits movement may be old news. Term limits are largely a direct democracy phenomenon, confined mostly to states with the ballot initiative. Currently, fifteen states have term limits for legislators, and that's six less than a few years ago. Term limits in Idaho, Massachusetts, Oregon, Utah, Washington and Wyoming have either been overturned by state supreme courts or repealed outright by legislative action.[4]

Repealing or overturning term limit laws has upset some, but it also seems clear that there is less appetite for term limits among the voters, and even buyer's remorse among some of those who initially supported such proposals. Evidence of this comes not just from the state level, but also from the federal level. Several members of Congress who campaigned on pledges to abide by self-imposed term limits had second thoughts when those time limits were up. In fact, seven members of Congress—all of them conservative Republicans—ran for reelection in 2006 after promising not to.[5] There seems to be little voter backlash about breaking these term limit pledges, and those who made the promises justify their decisions to renege on the grounds they did not fully understand the importance of legislative experience and seniority to being an effective legislator.

It's all well and good for members of Congress to have such second thoughts; no law bars them from running again regardless of what campaign pledges were made in the past. Not so at the state level. The law is the law, and no amount of second thoughts or reservations prevented twenty of the forty-nine members of the Nebraska unicameral legislature from being term limited out in 2006. Similar high rates of turnover already have occurred in Arizona and Michigan.

Two of the readings in this section take a look at the fallout of term limits. Arizona senator Jake Flake was an early proponent of term limits, backing the proposal with his vote in 1992 in the hope that it would make state government more responsive, more effective and more efficient. More than a decade later, he has become an outright skeptic, viewing term limits as a destabilizing force that makes state government unresponsive, less effective, and less efficient. In the essay that follows he explains why.

Alan Greenblatt's essay takes a look at the winners and losers in the term limit arena. It turns out that neither advocates nor opponents were wholly accurate in their predictions of what term limits would do to state government. Opponents believed term limits would make lobbyists more powerful, yet in some ways they have made lobbying more difficult. Effective lobbying is built on personal relationships, and building those relationships when the legislature has a revolving door can be hard to do. Supporters of term limits thought they would make state legislatures more responsive to constituents and more effective. This does not seem to be the case.

Chronically inexperienced state legislators seem to not just spend a lot of time spinning wheels, but also reinventing them by failing to follow through on the initiatives of previous legislatures and ignoring hard-won lessons from debates that gripped their predecessors. The big winner here seems not to be legislators, but governors, who have naturally stepped into the vacuum created by diminished, term-limited legislatures.

Shake-up and change in state legislatures is also a focus of the essay by Christopher Swope, although the agent of change is not term limit laws but technology. As Swope details, bloggers have become an important presence in state legislatures, and have opened new information channels outside of the traditional statehouse press corps. Some view the blogs as low-quality journalism, as more gossip, pontificating and entertainment than analysis and objective reporting. Nonetheless, statehouse blogs are becoming an accepted feature of the political world, and some legislators are even getting in on the act.

The final essay is more about change that isn't happening—or at least not happening fast enough. The days are long gone when a female legislator was a novelty, but women do remain a disproportionate minority in all state legislatures. Only about 22 percent of state legislators are female (although this varies from state to state, with 10 percent in Alabama, and 33 percent in Arizona, Colorado and Washington).[6] Leah Oliver, of the National Conference of State Legislatures, interviews four senior female state legislators, quizzing them on the trials and challenges of serving in elective office.

Notes

1. Kevin B. Smith, Alan Greenblatt, and John Buntin, *Governing States and Localities* (Washington, D.C.: CQ Press, 2005), 178.

2. National Conference of State Legislatures, "Current Number of Legislators, Terms of Office and Next Election Year," www.ncsl.org/programs/legman/about/numoflegis.htm (accessed April 15, 2004).

3. *The Book of the Sates 2003* (Lexington, Ky.: Council of State Governments, 2003), 459.

4. National Conference of State Legislatures. 2006. "The Term Limited States," www.ncsl.org/programs/legman/about/states.htm#repeal (accessed April 12, 2006).

5. Andrea Stone. 2006. "Term-Limit Pledges Get Left Behind." *USA Today,* www.usatoday.com/news/washington/2006-04-12-term-limits_x.htm (accessed April 14, 2006).

6. National Conference of State Legislatures, "Women in State Legislatures in 2005," www.ncsl.org/programs/wln/2004electioninfo.htm (accessed April 12, 2006).

15

Effects of Term Limits in Arizona: Irreparable Damages

Sen. Jake Flake

A supporter of term limits changes his mind.

Sen. Flake was originally a supporter of term limits, but having it implemented for 12 years now, believes it is a fundamentally flawed approach to government. It would be better to repeal term limits or increase the length of the terms to a longer period of time.

It was election day, 1992, and a historic question faced me and millions of other Arizonans: whether to adopt a term limits measure that promised to return state government to the people. This seemingly simple, painless prescription to our state's political ills struck me as a common sense idea. I voted for it without hesitation.

Along with 74 percent of those who cast ballots that day, I thought that term limits would make state government more effective and efficient. I thought they would make our lawmakers more responsive to those they serve. I thought they would encourage fiscal responsibility and common sense public policies. However, I was wrong.

Nearly 12 years later, it's clear that term limits are not only an impediment to effective policymaking—they are one of the most destructive political forces in my state's history, purging the Legislature of its most experienced, respected, and effective lawmakers regardless of, and often against, their constituents' will.

The result is a sadly dysfunctional legislature whose inexperience renders it less capable of effectively addressing the state's pressing needs. Without question, the most detrimental effect of term limits is its forced removal of the most experienced lawmakers, denying the legislature of the institutional knowledge so critical to effective policy-making.

In Arizona's case, state lawmakers are prohibited from serving more than four consecutive terms in one legislative body, meaning

From *Spectrum: The Journal of State Government*, Winter 2005.

that the House or Senate's most senior legislators never have more than six consecutive years of experience entering their final term.

This constant replacement of experienced lawmakers with inexperienced, untried, and often overwhelmed new members has a devastating impact on the Legislature's effectiveness in several ways.

First, it makes lawmakers dependent on non-elected actors for information and guidance on complex policy issues. Before term limits, it was common for lawmakers to become so familiar with a particular policy area that they became a resource for other legislators and stakeholders. These members were often committee chairmen, whose mastery of their subject areas was beyond question, making them a formidable force for their constituents.

With some exceptions, this practice has virtually ceased. Today, staff, lobbyists, and executive agency representatives are recognized as the authorities to which lawmakers turn for instruction, making them less capable of making independent judgments and less effective representatives of their constituents.

Rather than make legislators more responsive to those they represent, as term limits proponents claimed they would do, term limits force lawmakers to rely on non-elected individuals and groups whose interests may or may not be in harmony with the priorities of a lawmaker's constituents. The result is often confusion, with inexperienced legislators unsure of whom to trust.

Another harmful effect of the inexperience bred by term limits is the declining quality of proposed legislation. Since each year brings a significant number of new members with no prior experience, proposals that have already been discarded and dismissed are frequently reintroduced by unknowing lawmakers.

Likewise, as relative novices, these less experienced members often introduce proposals that are simply unworkable. While the legislative process typically prevents such measures from moving forward, they nevertheless consume valuable time and resources and reflect poorly on the legislature in the eyes of the public.

Similarly, the time constraints imposed by term limits force new lawmakers to 'make their mark' quickly, often at the expense of good policy. The rush to quickly pass significant legislation encourages a focus on individual rather than collective accomplishments and discourages the thoughtful, long-term planning necessary to ensure a proposal has been properly reviewed and vetted.

Term limits also have a destructive influence on the interpersonal relationships that make effective policy-making possible. As an eight-year lawmaker, I have observed that legislative successes are often, if not always a result of productive working relationships. Term limits paralyze these relationships by constantly removing experienced members and replacing them with lawmakers who are unfamiliar with their fellow legislators, staff, stakeholders and other elected officials.

This unfamiliarity breeds mistrust and suspicion, and prevents productive friendships from being established across ideological or philosophical lines. The lack of longstanding relationships of trust means that lawmakers must rely on other indicators, usually political philosophies, to know with whom to work. The compromise and collaboration so essential to policy-making is lost to partisanship and politicking, as lawmakers, not knowing their colleagues, retreat into ideological camps that frustrate the political process.

Non-legislators such as constituents, lobbyists, agency directors, business and community leaders, and other elected officials, also have little incentive to invest time and energy into relationship building since in a relatively short time those relationships will no longer be useful in a legislative sense.

The impact of term limits on legislative leadership is pronounced. During the last several years in Arizona, term limits have removed one Senate president and two speakers of the House from their posts after just one term of service as their bodies' leaders. The new presidents and speakers enter these constitutionally significant positions with relatively little understanding of their roles [vis-à-vis] the executive and judicial branches, let alone how to successfully and effectively manage the legislative process.

By preventing experienced lawmakers from holding leadership positions for long periods of time, term limits make legislative leaders incapable of establishing the political clout necessary to effectively represent their membership. In negotiations, executive agencies, lobbyists and stakeholders often choose not to work with current leadership since they know that a new speaker and president will likely be in office soon.

These experience-related factors have weakened Arizona's term-limited state legislature, making it less powerful, less effective, and less capable of fulfilling its constitutionally mandated responsibilities. This is not only contrary to the intent of our state constitution; it is detrimental to our voters who depend on lawmakers for effective representation of their interests and concerns.

So what is to be done? Along with many of my colleagues and members of the public, I have been arguing for years that term limits should be repealed. They are undemocratic, unconstitutional (I believe), and prevent effective representation of our constituents' interests.

Many states that embraced term limits in the 1990s have since seen the folly of their choice and repealed the measure. Others, like Arizona, have not yet made a serious effort to overturn what is still a relatively popular reform.

In the latter case, how can elected lawmakers, especially those in leadership, effectively do their job in a term-limited system? As a term-limited legislative leader, I have three suggestions:

(1) Work quickly to establish relationships of trust with fellow lawmakers.

This concept is crucial if one wants to enjoy any degree of success in states with term limits. Since term-limited legislatures operate in a compressed time frame, with rank-and-file members and leadership forced to advance their agendas in a relatively short time, it is essential to build these productive relationships quickly enough to ensure that challenging policy moves can be made as efficiently as possible.

(2) Hire trustworthy, knowledgeable, dependable staff.

Since staff members often remain at the legislature longer than the elected representatives, they often have a better familiarity with the issues facing state lawmakers. Having a trustworthy staff is essential for a term-limited legislature losing institutional knowledge with every election cycle.

Legislative leaders should also strive for as much continuity as possible within their staffs. Except in extreme circumstances, wholesale removals of entire staffs should be avoided. Instead, new staff can be brought in gradually enough to allow for seamless transitions. The level of turnover caused by term limits is bad enough; turnover among staff should be kept to a minimum.

(3) Position lawmakers with real-world experience in positions that will allow them to use that knowledge to positively influence policy.

With policy experience at a premium, legislative leaders should aim to maximize the resources that their members offer. Lawmakers who are empowered to use their non-legislative experience in their legislative positions strengthen the institution and become an even greater asset for their constituents. While nothing can replace actual legislative experience, real-world knowledge can be an effective substitute.

Even if these measures are taken, the devastating effects of term limits remain. Legislative leaders can and should take steps to minimize their impact, but the damage done by term limits is often irreparable.

At stake here is much more than just allowing effective lawmakers to stay in office, but rather the future of the state legislature as an institution. By depriving not only the legislature, but the people it serves of their most experienced and effective representatives, term limits weaken the legislative branch, threatening the checks and balances so central to our republican form of government.

After 12 years in Arizona, it's become obvious that the most effective form of term limits is that which our country's founders instituted: an election.

16

The Truth About Term Limits

Alan Greenblatt

Term limit laws have created some clear winners and losers. Among the losers are the legislatures themselves.

Steven Rowe is a big proponent of early childhood interventions. He believes they can help reduce rates of mental illness, learning disability and, ultimately, criminal behavior. While serving as speaker of the Maine House six years ago, Rowe translated his ideals into a specific program, sponsoring legislation that expanded child care subsidies, provided tax breaks to businesses offering child care help to their workers and created a statewide home visitation network. When it came time for a vote, Rowe left his speaker's rostrum for the first time to argue for it, saying, "I have never felt more strongly about a bill."

With that kind of a push from the chamber's top leader, it's no wonder that his package passed by an overwhelming margin. It may have been Rowe's most important accomplishment as a legislator. It was also one of his last. After eight years in the House, including two as speaker, he was forced out of office by the state's term limits law. Rowe is now Maine's attorney general—a good job, but one that doesn't give him much leverage over the program he created. His cosponsors on the child care law aren't in the legislature anymore, either. They have been term-limited out as well.

In the absence of Rowe and his child care allies, funding for the package has already been slashed by a third, with more cuts likely to come. Plenty of programs have lost funding in recent years as Maine, like so many states, has suffered from fiscal shortfalls. But Maine, along with other term limit states, is experiencing an added phenomenon: the orphaned program, vulnerable to reduction or elimination because of the forced retirement of its champions. "We're probably seeing more neglect because legislators aren't there to babysit their own legislation," says Renée Bukovchik Van

From *Governing.* January 2006.

Vechten, a political scientist at the University of Redlands, in California. "We're seeing laws that need updating, and that's the least sexy part of the job."

Every generation of legislators and leaders wants its own initiatives to brag about and, as a result, sometimes neglects programs closely identified with a preceding group. Under term limits, however, a generation can be as short as six years. Legislators become like people who inherit large, complicated appliances for which the owner's manual has been tossed aside. "The imposition of term limits [is] the most significant—and some would say drastic—institutional change in state government in the last two decades," write the editors of a forthcoming study by the National Conference of State Legislatures and the Council of State Governments.

It shouldn't come as a surprise that short-term legislators aren't prone to engage in long-term thinking. It's happening in all 15 of the states where term limits have gone into effect. In Arkansas several years ago, members of the legislature negotiated a solid waste fee to underwrite future environmental cleanups. After they all left office, a new group, not appreciating what the money had been set aside for—or probably not even knowing—dipped into it, disbursing the funds into a newly favored program of their own.

Even during Maine's recent downturn, the legislature continued to innovate in the fields of health and social service. In 2003, the state created the Dirigo program, which seeks to provide universal health insurance coverage through subsidies to employer-based plans. But new legislators are already arguing about the complex law they inherited. A few months ago, some of them accused Governor John Baldacci's administration of pulling a fast one by imposing assessments on insurance companies. They hadn't been around when these particular charges had been negotiated through a long, drawn-out process—in the legislature itself. "That's a major issue that was fought over just two years ago," says Sharon

In the absence of former Speaker Steven Rowe and his child care allies, some of Maine's early childhood programs have been slashed by one-third.

Treat, a former Senate leader and sponsor of the program, now term-limited out. "You would have thought there would have been some awareness."

EXECUTIVE CLOUT

Not all the arguments made against term limits at their inception in the 1990s have proven valid. One of the most common predictions—that with the members serving so briefly, all power would accrue to lobbyists hoarding the institutional and policy knowledge—appears to have been off the mark. Term limits have been a mixed bag for lobbyists, who must introduce themselves to a new, skeptical set of legislators every couple of years, rather than rely on cozy relations with a few key chairmen. Nor is there much evidence that legislative staff have taken advantage of member turnover to impose their own views on inexperienced legislators. In many states, the rate of staff turnover matches or exceeds that of members.

In other ways, though, the revolving-door system created by term limits has reduced the influence of the legislature itself. In particular, it has lost influence to the executive branch. One southern legislator-turned-lobbyist, who prefers not to be identified, says that he sometimes bypasses his state's legislature altogether, taking his clients' business directly to agency officials—the people who actually know how to operate the machinery of government. "There are some legislators who know as much as agency people do, but they're few and far between and they'll be gone very quickly," he says. "Agency heads are the true winners. They can outwait and outlast anyone and everyone on the playing field and they have consolidated their power."

Some governors have complained that lack of experience and expertise among legislators leaves them without strong negotiating partners. "A lot of these issues have to be dealt with in consecutive legislatures," says Angus King, a former governor of Maine who initially supported term limits but came to disdain them after burning through four different speakers, including Rowe, during his eight years in office. "They're very complex and if you always have to go back to square one, you never get anywhere."

Still, almost everyone involved in the legislative process sees governors as big winners under term limits. In addition to their constitutional authority to sign and veto bills, governors in term-limited states control many top-level state jobs that legislators facing short stints will soon want. Whether it is a question of job ambitions, a shortage of information or sheer inexperience, the reality seems to be that legislators do a far less effective job of competing with governors for power once term limits take effect.

According to the Public Policy Institute of California, that state's term-limited legislators make just half as many changes to the governor's budget as they did in the old days, representing many billions of dollars in legislative discretion that is no longer exercised. The NCSL/CSG study found similar budgetary effects in other term-limited states, including Colorado and Maine. "The crumbling of legislative power is clear across states," says Thad Kousser, a political scientist at the University of California, San Diego, and author of a book on term limits. "There's no more clear finding in the research than a shift in power where the legislature is becoming a less than equal branch of government."

EARLY DECISION

Kousser compares term-limited legislatures to airport terminals. Someone is always coming, someone else is going, and then there are the people who can't seem to find their way to the ticket counter. The state that best illustrates the who's-on-first confusion caused by term limits may be Florida, where House members last July picked Dean Cannon to serve as their future speaker. At the time, Cannon had served in the legislature all of six months. His term as speaker won't begin until 2010. But each freshman class in the Florida House has taken up the practice of choosing the person who will lead them once the class reaches its final two years in office.

One might assume that picking a House Speaker five years in advance reflects a healthy long-term perspective. In Florida, however, it reflects just the opposite: an almost manic habit of making premature decisions on the part of impatient members who know that the clock started ticking for them the day they were

Florida's Dean Cannon: After six months in the legislature, he became speaker-elect-elect-elect.

first sworn in. As absurd as it sounds, Florida's speakers-to-be in line ahead of Cannon are already being treated to some extent like lame ducks—even before they have a chance to take office. Influence in Florida is continually shifting to the next class coming through the pipeline. "With regard to Dean Cannon, he's a good friend of mine," says a House colleague, Baxter Troutman, "but for him to be speaker-elect-elect-elect—man, he gets inundated now because of the perception that he's going to have so much power handed to him."

Obviously the thinking in picking new speakers or Senate presidents well ahead of time is to give them some practical instruction before they take over the reins. As Sharon Treat, the former Maine Senate leader, points out, there are plenty of managerial challenges involved in running a chamber even before turning to the business of mastering issues, setting an agenda and getting a caucus to sign off on it. Other states have tried different approaches to the succession question. After burning through several speakers in its first few years following the arrival of term limits, the California Assembly gave the job to Fabian Nunez as a freshman, so there'd be at least a few years of stability at the top.

In some states, legislatures that recognize their weakness against the executive have tried to consolidate power in the hands of their leaders as a counterweight. Leadership, even when fleeting, still has its advantages. Leadership PACs have become the foremost source of campaign funds in some term-limited states, and leadership staff are the main in-house sources of information on process and policy for many confused legislators.

The Arkansas House has done away with its old seniority system—an obsolete concept anyway in a body whose members can serve only six years—and allows its speakers to pick committee rosters and chairs. Republican leaders in Michigan, who control both legislative chambers, have made a concerted effort to appeal early and often to newcomers, from the time they first express a tentative interest in running until they finally show up at Lansing. The argument is that by sticking together they can more effectively offset the power of Democratic Governor Jennifer Granholm.

Similarly, legislative leaders in Ohio, widely credited with

The Long and the Short
Length of time current House speakers have served in the legislature (years of consecutive service)

States With Term Limits		States Without Term Limits	
States With Term Limits		Wyoming	11
		North Dakota	13
California	3	Rhode Island	13
Michigan	3	South Carolina	13
Arkansas	5	Iowa	14
Colorado	5	Kansas	14
Ohio	5	Connecticut	15
Missouri	6	North Carolina	15
Florida	7	West Virginia	17
Maine	7	Idaho	18
Montana	7	Virginia	18
South Dakota	7	Maryland	19
Arizona	11	Wisconsin	19
Oklahoma	11	Indiana	20
Nevada	13*	Delaware	25
Louisiana	20*	Mississippi	26
Nebraska	N/A	Alabama	27
States Without Term Limits		Massachusetts	27
		Minnesota	27
New Hampshire	1	Pennsylvania	27
New Jersey	6	Hawaii	29
Alaska	7	Kentucky	29
Oregon	7	New York	29
Georgia	9	New Mexico	31
Vermont	9	Tennessee	31
Utah	11	Illinois	35
Washington	11	Texas	37

*Louisiana and Nevada have legislative term limits, but lawmakers have not yet been prevented from running for reelection because of them.
Sources: Project Vote Smart, National Conference of State Legislatures.

University, who wrote a book about governors and legislatures as contending powers. "If the legislature and the governor are controlled by the same party, the legislature pretty much gives the governor whatever he wants—they view themselves as members of his team."

In many states, the committee process has suffered perhaps the greatest blows under term limits. There's necessarily less depth of knowledge, and the old idea that a bill should be fully crafted and in shape to become law the minute it passes out of committee has, in many instances, become a thing of the past. Instead, bills are kept continually moving, replete with the mistakes of inexperience, in the full expectation that they will be amended on the floor or in the other body. That way, more legislators get the chance to make their marks during the short time they have in office. No one wants to kill a bill and set a colleague back a year, when she may have only six years in office. "They're afraid to antagonize each other, so they're willing to pass legislation out of their committee when it's not fully cooked," says Paul Gladfelty, who lobbies for corporations in California.

Double and triple committee referrals, once rare in California, have become routine. It's the opposite of specialization—legislators want a piece of all the action, not wanting to miss out on anything important during their brief moment of power. The fact that committees are no longer viewed as authoritative in their jurisdictional areas further strengthens the hand of other players, notably executive branch officials.

CHANGING MESSAGES

If early predictions of lobbyists seizing power under term limits have turned out to be misplaced, the fact is that that many term-limited legislators still come into office worried about the issue. Quite a few are at least initially suspicious of lobbyists of all stripes. "We are noticing that a lot of the freshman members come in with preconceived ideas about lobbyists," says Bart McSpadden, a lobbyist in Oklahoma, "that they are all slick and wealthy and everything is carried out behind the scenes and under the table."

Whatever lobbyists have gained in legislatures through the power of institutional memory, they seem to have lost with the decline of enduring relationships. Clearly, they can take advantage of the knowledge deficit that exists in term-limited legislatures, but building the contacts that

having done the best job of preserving their power under term limits in relation to the executive, have done so by involving junior members more fully in their decision-making process—for example, going over budgets practically line by line in caucus meetings.

Still, it's not like the old days, when speakers in many states held sway for more than a decade, far outlasting governors. "If leaders are there a short time, the idea of taking on the responsibility of preserving and protecting the institution is eroded," says Alan Rosenthal, of Rutgers allow them to take such advantage has become a more time-consuming and expensive proposition. The stereotypical golf-buddy lobbyist who wields influence through personal friendship has clearly lost out under the term limits system.

In some ways, this has led to a diffusion of lobbying power, affording a wider range of lobbyists an equal opportunity to make a first impression on new legislators. On the other hand, the new system puts a premium on the ability to orchestrate those first impressions, and the consensus among lobbyists is that it's difficult for small practitioners to compete against bigger firms with the resources and personnel to introduce themselves and their issues on an ongoing basis to continual waves of new members.

"You not only have to get to know these people," says Marcie McNelis, of the lobbying firm MultiState Associates, "but you have to educate them on the issues from scratch." Part of the business of getting to know a legislator, of course, comes through fundraising, which has become even more critical since term limits have created so many more open seats. Here, too, the bigger, more institutionalized lobbying firms have an advantage over the smaller outfits and the old-fashioned solo gladhanders.

However term limits may be playing out, it's hard to find a lobbyist of any stripe who likes them. "I don't know one lobbyist who thinks it's a good thing," says Rick Farmer, who has written about term limits as an academic and now works for the Oklahoma House. "If term limits are such a good thing for lobbyists, why do so many lobbyists hate them?"

It's not just the lobbyists. Talk to people who work in any state capitol where term limits exist—members, staff and reporters as well as lobbyists—and you will encounter the nearly universal opinion that term limits are obstacles to careful legislation and effective oversight. Travel a bit farther from the capitol, though, and you get a different point of view: Most people on the outside still like term limits. Legislatures in Idaho and Utah have repealed their limits, but for the most part legislators have been unwilling to argue for repeal in the face of popular will as expressed by ballot initiative.

Baxter Troutman, the Florida representative, sponsored successful legislation last year to extend the state's limits to 12 years per chamber. That measure now goes before voters in November, but similar attempts haven't fared too well elsewhere. Ballot measures to extend limits were soundly defeated in Arkansas and Montana in 2004, while California voters had two years earlier rejected an attempt to let term-limited legislators run again if they could collect enough petition signatures in their districts.

No matter how strenuously legislators and lobbyists may argue that term limits have made elected representatives less powerful, and left constituents with a weaker voice in governmental affairs, people outside of government aren't ready to buy that. The main effects of term limits are procedural, and it's difficult to make a convincing case that they've made any one particular policy worse, let alone imperiled the quality of life in any state that observes them. It's impossible to prove that term limits have led to higher taxes, declining services or deeper fiscal shortfalls. And the notion that term limits make legislatures less powerful is, after all, one reason why many people supported them to begin with. "The public voted initially for term limits because they don't like politicians and political institutions," says Rosenthal, the Rutgers political scientist. "That disfavor has continued." As a result, the public has gotten what it asked for, if not what it deserves.

17

Instant Influence

Christopher Swope

A new generation of Web scribes is shaking up state capitol politics.

Unlike newspaper and TV reporters, Internet bloggers are not allowed on the floor of the Texas House of Representatives. That's why Eileen Smith usually sits upstairs in the public galleries, the "cheap seats," she likes to say, looking down on the action below. One evening in May, Smith rests her hands on her laptop as the House gets sucked into a marathon debate on a doomed bill to create school vouchers. She types away whenever she hears something quote-worthy. Which is to say, she types only when she comes upon an argument she finds absolutely ridiculous.

Here's how it plays the next morning on Smith's Web site, "In The Pink Texas." "DAMN, if they're not still talking vouchers," Smith writes. "They all looked much better a few hours ago. The reps are sweating, their hairdos are all messed up—now I get it ... floor debate is like sex to them."

She continues, tongue in cheek, with digs at Speaker Tom Craddick and Representative Kent Grusendorf. Smith jokingly calls Grusendorf, the voucher plan's sponsor, "Schoolmaster G."

"It looks like Schoolmaster G's going down. He's being beaten something awful.... And the Speaker? I've never seen him look like this. He's got this crooked semi-smile pasted on his face, like he doesn't know whether to laugh or cry or take someone's ass OUT."

If In The Pink sounds gossipy, snarky, and a bit risqué, get used to it. Political blogs, the grassroots media sensation of 2004, are now sprouting in statehouses and city halls across the country. Eileen Smith is the "Wonkette" of Austin. In just five months of blogging, she has built a devoted daily readership of more than 1,000 people—a small but influential niche of legislators, staffers, lobbyists and journalists—who enjoy her scorching instant analysis. "In The Pink

From *Governing,*
July 2005.

has become a must-read at the capitol," says Gary Susswein, state editor of the *Austin American-Statesman,* the city's big mainstream newspaper. "She's funny, irreverent, and she's not self-righteous. Everybody reads her."

The Texas legislature convenes only in alternate years. The last time lawmakers met, in 2003, nobody had even heard of blogs. This year, seemingly from out of nowhere, there is a sort of "fifth estate" in Austin, popped up on the Internet like bluebonnets in springtime. The Texas blogging corps includes political junkies, college students, the producers of a talk-radio show, mainstream journalists, a lobbyist, and a couple of state reps who blog directly from the House floor (*see sidebar*). Not only do most people in Texas political circles now know what statehouse blogs are; many read at least a couple of them as part of their daily media diet. It amounts to a sudden and remarkable change in the political culture. With so many independent voices launching small-scale ventures that specialize in satire and stinging commentary, the Texas capitol is beginning to look like an American legislature of two centuries ago, in which slashing editors took out after ideological enemies with venomous low-budget broadsheets.

A blog, if you don't know yet, is a Web site that reads something like a diary. Anybody with an Internet connection can set one up in five minutes, for free. Political bloggers usually write about the day's news, borrowing heavily from newspapers and other sources, and put their own spin on it. Some bloggers do their own reporting, too—or dig deeper into stories floating around in the mainstream media. Most famously, it was bloggers who last year attacked a CBS News report on President Bush's National Guard service, exposing the suspicious nature of memos cited by news anchor Dan Rather.

Texas bloggers haven't blown open any big scandals. But they do scoop the statehouse press corps from time to time. A few are winning over a sizable audience with their witty writing and their blunt, opinionated analysis. As one lobbyist puts it, bloggers "have the luxury of being able to call bull 'bull.'" This appeals especially to the under-35 crowd, who are the most hooked on blogs. One recent afternoon in Austin, in the office of a Republican House member, five young staffers were chattering about news on the Texas blogs that day.

Not everyone in Austin is so enamored with blogs. Some complain that bloggers play loose with facts. Others are disturbed by the anonymity: A couple of Texas blogs

Blogrolling

Aaron Peña's "A Capitol Blog" isn't the sexiest in Texas, but of all the statehouse web offerings, his is arguably most in the know. That's because Peña is a state legislator. He blogs all day long from his laptop on the floor of the House of Representatives.

Peña, a Democrat, started blogging in January as a way to stay in touch with his constituents. But he also broadcasts little insider tips he hears on the floor—what time a vote is coming up, for example—that make his blog a must-read for some of the lobbyists, staffers and journalists who care about such things. He was the first to announce that his colleague, Richard Raymond, would be running for Congress. "No, Richard has not announced," Peña reported in February, "but you can trust me on this one."

Peña, who is 46, doesn't seem like an obvious entrant into the blogging universe. Until recently, he didn't even use a computer. But he likes the intimacy that he says blogging makes possible. He uses his blog, for example, to explain in his own words why he votes the way he does on certain bills. "Constituents can get to know more about me than what they see in a press release," Peña says. "They get a sense of who I am, and what I'm thinking, on a personal level."

There are lines that Peña, as a legislator, can't cross. He has to think about what sorts of information are appropriate to pass along, and what he should keep to himself. "Trust is the most valued commodity on the floor," he says. "Legislators need to know that when they talk to me, I won't just go and put whatever they said on the blog."

In Peña's view, however, all legislators should be blogging. His desk mate, state Representative Joe Deshotel, began doing it in May after Peña cajoled him for months. Peña set up a group blog, called "Lone Star Rising," and encouraged Democrats and Republicans alike to use it as a public forum to discuss issues. In fact, however, most of them have stayed away. "I notice the hesitation," Peña says. "They don't want to open themselves up, for fear that people will attack them."

Nobody would accuse Aaron Peña of not opening up. "It's fun to read what's inside a lawmaker's head," says Karen Brooks, statehouse reporter with *The Dallas Morning News.* "Every time I see Peña, I call him 'Dear Diary.'"

—Christopher Swope

are ghostwritten, and most allow readers to post comments without attribution. There's little to stop a political operative from using blogs to spread rumors that the mainstream media, applying a more stringent ethical code, would not touch.

What bothers Kate Linkous is the blogs' incessant negativity. Linkous is a press aide for Lieutenant Governor David Dewhurst, a Republican whose substantial power in Austin makes him a frequent target for the liberal side of the blog spectrum. "We live in a cynical age and the blogs are pretty cynical," Linkous says. "The more critical they are, the more readers they get. There are no lines anymore between what's fair game and what is not. I personally don't give blogs a lot of credibility."

PAJAMA POSTINGS

In a way, blogging is nothing new to Eileen Smith. A former journalist, the 33-year-old Smith has entertained her friends and family for years with sarcastic e-mails lampooning politicians in the news. In 2000, she chased dot-com dreams to Austin, but after two months, her employer, a Web site called drkoop.com, laid her off and then went bust. Smith landed a government job at the capitol, as a staff aide for the House Appropriations Committee, and got her first inside look at Texas politics.

Last year, Smith decided to take one more shot at the Latest Internet Craze. Political blogs were whipping up a buzz nationally, even if only a handful of bloggers had figured out how to make money doing them. With her husband's support—and no business plan—Smith quit her job in January and launched "In The Pink Texas" in February. She picked the name in honor of the pink granite from which the state capitol is built. Smith's blog is splashed with pink headlines and links; her *nom du web* is "Pink Lady."

Smith is at home, in her pajamas, when she begins her first round of Web postings each day. She wakes up, reads all the big Texas newspapers, newsletters and other political blogs, then puts up an item or two by 8 a.m.,

> *"We live in a cynical age and the blogs are pretty cynical. The more critical they are, the more readers they get."*
>
> Kate Linkous, press aide for Lieutenant Governor David Dewhurst

just in time to catch early birds at work in the capitol.

Two or three days a week, she packs her laptop into her backpack and trudges up to the capitol to prowl for stories. She hits up friends and acquaintances, admittedly not the highest-placed sources, for gossip. And she "liveblogs" from the Senate gallery or from committee rooms, taking advantage of the wireless Internet access that covers most of the capitol complex. "To me, this is such a pure form of journalism," Smith says. "I don't have editors telling me what to write. And I don't have to kowtow to advertisers."

In The Pink is mainly a medium of entertainment. If readers pick up useful information along the way, Smith says, so much the better. In this way, she's not much different from the "Daily Show" or the Weekend Update on "Saturday Night Live." To keep readers glued to her Web site, Smith grabs funny or titillating photos from the Internet, and writes punch lines. Her posting on school vouchers ends with two pictures of Britney Spears—one from the pop star's prim bubble-gum days and another from her bustier leather-clad phase. "Look what vouchers did to Britney Spears," Smith writes. "First shot taken from Britney's days at public school. Second shot is post-voucher, taken after she started attending private school. Oops!"

Smith insists that In The Pink is nonpartisan. "I was trained in journalism and do have a code I stand by," she says. "I'm not a party puppet." You don't have to read her blog too closely, however, to deduce Smith's politics. She rips hardest at social conservatives for their efforts to ban gay marriage and crack down on late-term abortions.

In The Pink dresses down Democrats, too. But it slams Republicans more. Smith contends that has less to do with personal bias than with the fact that Republicans control the House, Senate and all statewide offices in Texas. Reading her blog, you get the sense that Smith doesn't so much want to stoke partisan hatred as simply to poke fun at the daily carnival that is a legislature in session, filled with powerful people, egomaniacs and social climbers. "One thing I try to do," she says, "is to take the people in power and make them into real human beings."

Of one Republican senator, she writes: "His big head doesn't match his body. And, you know, his ego's writing checks his body can't cash." On one Democratic representative, who switched his vote on a bill: "Your job is to flip like the little pancake that you are, *you little pussy cat.*" On the governor: "Apparently Gov. Rick Perry has awakened from his session-long nap just in time to realize that a $20 billion increase in state spending is too much."

Smith's sarcastic take on just about everything has landed her in a couple of controversies. In one case, she ridiculed an economic development award that *Site Selection* magazine gave Governor Perry. In The Pink claimed that Perry's economic development staff had a cozy relationship with the magazine; a state official dismissed Smith's characterization as "nutty." The dispute bubbled up into the pages of the *Austin American-Statesman.*

Smith may not have press credentials, but her view from up high in the galleries lends her creative license. The distance between her and lawmakers enables her to write unambiguously. Mainstream reporters, down on the House or Senate floor, are more clued in to nuance. They hear legislators grumbling over a difficult vote, and sometimes identify with them for the hard choices they must make. "All I see is their vote," Smith says. "I sympathize with them. But in the end, that's their vote. That's their record."

FILLING A VOID

Nowhere is the influence of blogs felt more than among the statehouse press corps. Mainstream reporters and bloggers have a weird relationship, one that is symbiotic and competitive at the same time. Texas bloggers owe the press corps a huge debt. After all, most of what they write is based on news that appears in the pages of daily papers and newsletters. Meanwhile, political journalists read the blogs closely. One reason is that reporters, like legislators, enjoy seeing their names in print. But they're also looking for tips to follow up on, or new angles on an old story. "Blogs are good for reporters," says Karen Brooks, a statehouse veteran now with *The Dallas Morning News.* "They're another way to keep up with the chatter."

The Texas blogs have yet to beat the mainstream press on a big story. Traditional reporters nevertheless see bloggers as competition. "They keep us on our toes,"

Brooks says. This is surely a good thing. Coverage of state politics has been waning in every state where a Hollywood actor is not governor. To be sure, the press corps in Austin is not as bare as those in smaller state capitals—the *Morning News* alone had seven reporters at the capitol this year. But those reporters can't be everywhere. Charles Kuffner, a Houston-based writer whose "Off The Kuff" blog is well read in Austin, thinks bloggers are filling a void. He says that he frequently goes to campaign events where no other media are present. "I may not have a big audience," Kuffner says, "but if I'm writing about a state House race, that's probably the only place where you'll find any coverage of it."

Blogs are forcing the dailies, which are fighting to gain younger readers anyway, to adapt. The *American-Statesman,* for example, launched its own statehouse blog this year, called "Postcards From The Lege." Five reporters contribute quick-hit items, typically drawn from their own reporting. The pieces are shorter than typical newspaper stories, and timed to please the obsessive reader who clicks "refresh" on his browser all day long. "A lot of these items didn't have a home [in the newspaper] before we started," says editor Gary Susswein. "They were things that only a few thousand people in the capitol care about, but most of our readers don't. They would've died in our notebooks."

Postcards is more serious, and less freewheeling, than In The Pink and the other independent blogs. "The entertainment value is low," says Gardner Selby, the *American-Statesman*'s chief political reporter, "but the information value is high." Stylistically, the paper has loosened its necktie a bit with the blog, but not much. A pair of editors vets every item. "We're still a newspaper, and we can't expose biases and opinions openly," Susswein says. When asked about In The Pink, he replies, "She can definitely go in directions we might not go in. She can tell it as she sees it. We don't want to get in the business of telling it exactly as the reporter sees it. That would undermine our credibility."

Blogs may pose a more direct challenge to political newsletters. Texas has three of them, the *Quorum Report, Capitol Inside,* and *Texas Weekly.* Each charges $250 for an annual subscription, and is aimed more or less at the same niche of insiders that the blogs reach for free. Currently, the blogs come nowhere close to the newsletters in terms of providing useful information for staffers or lobbyists. But that could change. It all depends on who decides to take up blogging—and what sort of information they're willing to share. "Blogs now have more gossip and entertainment value than the kind of stuff that would dominate the decision-making political conversation," says Harvey Kronberg, editor of the *Quorum Report*. Kronberg admits that he reads In The Pink, but he doesn't see Eileen Smith or her contemporaries as a threat. "Blogs don't have the range, the reach or the institutional memory. That's not to say someone won't come along who does."

Indeed, the notion of a "blog corps" is a very fluid one. Even as statehouse reporters come and go, newspapers as institutions remain more or less the same. That's not at all true with bloggers. A Texas legislator, staffer or lobbyist may start a new blog tomorrow. Likewise, Smith, Kuffner or one of the other current bloggers could decide that blogging is no longer worth their time. The next time the legislature convenes, blogophiles may have a whole different set of Web sites to bookmark—new blogs that will rise and fall on their power to entertain and inform.

One likely addition to the blogging mix in Texas is new voices from the political right. Most of the current blogs come at politics from the left. That's probably to be expected—not because bloggers tend to be Democrats but because those first drawn to blogging tend to be dissenters. Nationally, conservatives first took up blogging because they believed a liberal media ignored their views. In Texas politics, the reverse has happened.

David Benzion, one of the few conservative bloggers in Texas, agrees with this theory. Benzion is managing editor of the "Lone Star Times," a blog that he and Houston talk-radio host Dan Patrick started in January.

> "Blogs now have more gossip and entertainment value than the kind of stuff that would dominate the decision-making political conversation."
>
> Harvey Kronberg, Editor,
> *Quorum Report*

"If you're a 'progressive' in Texas, you feel like you're under siege," Benzion says. "You're living in George W. Bush's conservative Texas. Some people on the liberal side picked up blogging in state politics as a way to vent. There are probably some on the conservative side who would be blogging about state politics, but don't feel the need to because they're basically content."

Sometime soon, Eileen Smith knows, In The Pink will reach a crossroads. Smith started blogging just to have fun and see where it goes. Very quickly, it's gone further than she expected. Now she's starting to think about business models, advertising, income. Her husband has been patient with her foray into blogging so far, but Pink Lady can't run an amateur enterprise forever. "I can write," she says. "But I don't know how to make money at this."

It's doubtful anyone will ever get rich writing a statehouse blog. There simply aren't enough readers. What's more likely, as the medium evolves, is that blogs will go legit. When the Texas legislature holds its next regular session in 2007, Smith predicts, bloggers will have press credentials and roam the capitol freely just like mainstream reporters. Smith brings up this point enough in conversation to suggest that the former journalist in her craves this kind of validation.

But if In The Pink went legit, wouldn't that ruin the cavalier quality that makes it so much fun for its fans now? Up in the cheap seats, Smith takes a break from typing to reflect on that. "I'm on a porch, a loft. I'm not down there building relationships with legislators," she says. "I like the separation between me and them. I'm the observer. It would be harder for me to say the things I do if I were their friend."

18

Wise Women

Leah Oliver

Being a woman and a legislator present unique challenges and opportunities. Four seasoned lawmakers offer some sage advice.

SL: What Motivated You to Become a Legislator?

Texas Senator Leticia Van de Putte: I am a pharmacist. I was motivated because I was angry about health care policy. I couldn't understand why we would pay hundreds of thousands of dollars for a premature baby, but we wouldn't pay for the prenatal vitamins for the mom. And I couldn't understand why we had a comprehensive mandatory record-keeping policy for vaccinations and immunizations of cows in our state, but we didn't have one for children.

Indiana Senator Beverly Gard: I was in the right place at the right time. In 1975, I was approached by a group of community leaders to run for the city council. I was the first woman elected in over 20 years. When a vacancy came up in my senate district, I chose to run for it.

Maryland Delegate Adrienne Jones: In the mid-1980s, I served on the Democratic State Central Committee for Baltimore County. When there was a vacancy in my district because of the death of a delegate, I was selected by the committee to fill out the remainder of her term. I always have been a lover of politics and public policy. I believe women are natural public servants—it is in our blood.

Delaware Senator Dorinda "Dori" Connor: My late husband had served in the legislature for 28 years. A month after he passed away, I defeated two opponents in a special election. The motivation was to continue to serve the public.

SL: What Prepared You for Legislative Work and What Other Skills Are Helpful to Have?

Gard: Serving in local government for 13 years was a tremendous asset going into the Senate. I'd also been involved in party politics.

From *State Legislatures,*
July/August 2005.

Many of the skills you use to manage a household, raise children or have a husband, come to play in the legislature.

Van de Putte: My role as a health care professional and as a mom prepared me for the legislature. In my career, I listen to people every day and then try to improve their quality of life. In the legislature, we listen to people and then we help craft solutions that people can use to improve their quality of life. I think my skills as a mom have come in extremely handy, too.

Jones: In local government, you deal with all sorts of personalities, community groups, other elected officials, so it really prepares you to adapt that to work as a legislator. I serve on the Appropriations Committee and deal with budgets. When you're dealing with the state's funds you've got to make sure it's right.

Connor: Having been an educator, I try to look at my job as my classroom. In some ways my constituents and my colleagues are still students—just older. I give them information; I share the facts; I look for input; I want their opinion.

SL: How are Women Important to the Legislative Process?

Jones: Women are multi-talented. Women bring a very different perspective. We don't mind consulting others. I think we provide an added service to the legislature.

Connor: Women want to bring it all in, listen to all the answers. We will bring our personal issues to the floor and are not afraid to talk about them. Gentlemen tend to keep a lot of that close to the chest. That's why we are an important balance.

Van de Putte: The important decisions in families' lives always have been made by women. It makes a difference when women are at the table. Just like it makes a difference when you're dealing with housing policy and you've got somebody who's been homeless at the table or you're dealing in health care policy and you have somebody who's HIV positive at the table.

SL: What Advice Would You Give to a New Legislator About Taking on Traditionally Women's Issues or Traditionally Men's Issues?

Connor: When I approach pieces of legislation, I don't look at it as a male issue or a female issue. There are issues that are very important for all of us to look at. You

should get involved in the whole process because you're here representing both genders and all issues.

Gard: My advice to a new legislator, whether male or a female, would be to look at their strengths and work toward their strengths. If you become an expert in any specific area, people are going to look to you for advice. For a woman, being accepted might take some time. My background is biochemistry and I'm chair of the Senate Environmental Affairs Committee. When I first came into the legislature, I heard a male voice in the back row say, "What does a housewife from Greenfield, Indiana, know about environmental legislation?"

Van de Putte: I've never been on a health committee. I love technology, science, telecommunications, utilities and alternative fuels. Don't be afraid to venture out into something you may not know, but you love. You will be surprised at how much other legislators will respect you.

Jones: Be adept at one or two areas so you are in a better position to serve on a committee that covers the subject areas you know well. And don't be afraid to serve on a budget committee when your interests may be child welfare or health care because these issues need advocates for funding.

SL: What Wisdom or Caution Can You Share with New Women Legislators?

Gard: Move slowly. Don't try to transform the state. Start building relationships, start learning issues. Learn the rules. Get to know the personalities involved and the politics. Do not forget the people who put you there. Develop a strong relationship with your constituents— use town meetings, press releases, questionnaires.

Van de Putte: It's incredibly important to know when to engage, when not to push the point. Try not to be one of the boys. Don't be afraid to ask questions or advice of senior members. If you represent your district then nobody's going to fault you. Take a deep breath, have a sense of humor, learn the rules, be respectful of other people.

Jones: Don't think you have to put in a bill the first year. Learn the system. Ask questions. All legislators have egos. They love it when you ask them for advice. By asking questions, you're developing a relationship and they'll remember you as a person who is concerned about the process. Don't forget about who put you there, because you can be on committees and travel to various forums and it doesn't mean a thing to your constituents if you're not able to deliver back home.

Connor: Be willing to accept if you've made a mistake. Learn your subject matter. Be consistent. Dress appropriately. Earn trust from your constituency. Take advantage of workshops and learn all the rules. Be prepared to eat the bear or the bear will eat you. The last thing that I do is look in that rearview mirror and give myself a pep talk. You've got to show confidence right from the beginning.

The Women's Legislative Network

The Women's Legislative Network of NCSL is dedicated to promoting the participation, empowerment and leadership of women legislators. It is an active, vibrant respected organization that serves the needs of women legislators in the 50 states. All women legislators are members of the Women's Legislative Network by virtue of their election to office.

The Network sponsors events throughout the year to give women legislators an opportunity to learn, meet colleagues from other states and enhance their skills. It sponsors forums and workshops on topics important to women legislators; hosts events for women legislators at NCSL meetings; provides networking opportunities through legislative receptions; and works with other organizations to ensure that the best resources and services are available to women lawmakers.

To become involved, attend Network events, subscribe to the Network News or apply for a Network Executive Board or Advisory Council position. Corporations can support the Network by becoming Alliance members.

Many women legislators have found the Network to be an important source of information, support and advice.

"One of the best things I did shortly after I was elected was come to an NCSL conference and go to the Women's Network," says Delaware Senator Dori Connor. "I felt automatic camaraderie not only with women in my state, but across the country. One of the best things women can do is jump in and get involved and learn from what others are doing."

Call or e-mail Leah Oliver, Network coordinator, with questions at (303) 364-7700 or leah.oliver@ncsl.org.

SL: What Are the Lessons You Have Learned from Legislative Leaders, Both Male and Female?

Van de Putte: One of the lessons I learned from the speaker in 1991 when I was a freshman was always vote your district. Don't be afraid to go against the grain if it's good for your district, because that's who elected you.

Gard: Shortly after I came to the legislature I set a goal to be a committee chairman. So I watched others to see how they handled their committees in really effective ways. One in particular, Senator Pat Miller, is an exemplary chairman. I tried over the years to develop some of the skills that she has in being decisive, fair, having control of that committee. I think most women chairs tend to be more inclusive, develop relationships, and work toward consensus.

Connor: On our first day in the legislature, we all knew in a very short amount of time who we wanted to pattern and who we did not. Senator Myrna Bair, our former caucus leader and former head of the Women's Network, gave sage advice, "Do not be quick to declare your opinion on a piece of legislation." After you declare, you may have to change your mind. Remember to keep that open mind, keep that judgment to yourself until that last minute.

Jones: One lesson I learned from legislative leaders was don't be afraid to ask questions. It is OK to get up on the floor and say, "Can you explain what this bill does?" Another lesson is keep your word, if you're going to support a bill and tell your constituents or lobbyists that you are going to vote in favor of a bill, do not vote against it on the floor. Finally, share your bills—you don't have to have 15 bills. Share a couple with a new legislator, particularly bills you know will pass. It gives that new legislator the confidence to work on other legislation on their own.

SL: Why Do You Think Only 22 Percent of Legislators Are Women and Do You Think That Will Change?

Jones: One of the biggest hurdles is fund-raising. Women, for the most part, are more reluctant to ask for money than men. In addition, women have multi-obligations—family, community activities, church—that tend to delay them looking at public office. It will change when there is more sharing of family responsibilities by the husband/partner/children that will allow women to enter public life earlier.

Van de Putte: I think one of our strengths turns to be one of the weaknesses; we tend not to worry about who gets the credit as long as the work gets done. But when you're running for public office you tend not to have ballot success unless people make a direct connection between your positive works and your name. I think it's critical that women get rid of the "I'm not worthy" type of mentality. Understand that you need money to do the campaigning so that you can get to do the public policy.

Gard: I've been involved in trying to recruit women. For a woman to serve in the legislature, regardless of the age of her children, it is going to change the dynamics of her home life. It's a family effort, it involves every member of her family.

Connor: We now are starting to see more women in government relations and as lobbyists. That's made a big difference. A male lobbyist came to me and was very concerned that I seemed to be leaning in opposition to his thoughts. He put his hand on my shoulder and said, "Now you know your husband would be supporting me." I was taken aback and I looked at him said, "But my husband's not here now. We are different people and our thoughts are different." Women lobbyists aren't like that. We speak each other's language.

SL: What Is the Role of Diversity in the Legislative Process?

Jones: It's critical. We have legislators in their late 70s and legislators in their 30s and both groups give us a different perspective. We have legislators from different walks of life, not only by race, gender, religion and ethnicity, but political philosophy and economics, as well. Diversity brings forth different types of bills, which gives all of us a positive learning experience.

Gard: Most of our districts are becoming more diverse. My district certainly is. It has changed dramatically over the 16 years that I have represented it. I don't think that the membership of the legislature reflects the diverse nature of the constituency there. We have a long way to go.

SL: How Important Do You Feel It Is to Have a Mentor? Did You Have One? If So, How Did He or She Affect Your Career?

Van de Putte: My first mentor was a local elected official and life-long friend. He had served in the legislature before coming back to serve in county government. He made it a point in the early 1980s to begin appointing women to commissions and committees. I still go to him for advice. When you look for a mentor, make sure you find someone who's not just successful, but who embodies that sense of public service that we all strive for.

Connor: My mentor would be my late husband. He had an ability to find common ground, to be a listener. He was able to suck it up, walk away and let it go. He never used a foul word, never spoke badly about anyone.

Jones: My mentor was my state senator, Delores Kelley. She was very instrumental when I first came to the legislature in terms of dispelling misconceptions I had about being a legislator and showing me the ropes. My second mentor was my Appropriations Committee chairman, the late Pete Rawlings, who gave me the opportunity of serving as vice chair of a subcommittee, which enabled me to show my expertise. Serving on the Appropriations Committee was instrumental in me getting recognized by our current speaker to serve in my present capacity as speaker pro tem.

SL: How Can Women Legislators Support Each Other?

Van de Putte: Several years ago, we had a whole package of bipartisan women's health initiatives. But we could not get the bills set for the House floor for debate. We decided among ourselves that we would all go to the front podium and surround the speaker. We had taken a blood oath to not vote for any other bill until our set of bills came up. He said, "We'll do it tomorrow." Well, tomorrow came and went. We met as a women's caucus and we decided the only way to make progress was to talk to our sisters—our sisters who are the spouses of our colleagues. We started making phone calls. Well, the guys came back the next day and said, "Why'd you call my wife?!" We said, "We gave you fair warning." The bills were set.

When we went to the governor's mansion for the bill signing, then Governor Bush said, "You can't play tricks with me. You can't call my spouse." And I said, "We were never thinking about calling Laura. We're going to call your mother." He said, "I'll sign the bill." We know that we can be effective as women, but as women it's not just the network of women legislators. We have to look at our sisters and use that network effectively.

Connor: We've done something similar. One of our legislators has a daughter and some sensitive issues were being discussed. We kept saying to him, "This could be your daughter." The daughter was a page on our floor and we just called her over and said, "We really need your dad's vote. We need you to lobby your dad." It made a difference.

Gard: I encourage women legislators to use their own personal experiences. I'm a breast cancer survivor and the year after my experience I sponsored a bill dealing with reconstruction after mastectomy. I went to the insurance committee to present this bill; there was not a woman on the committee. There was a plastic surgeon who made a very professional, but graphic presentation. All of the men on the committee sat there staring at the table. They wouldn't look anybody in the eye. When the bill was presented on the floor, it passed unanimously. There was some problem in the House and getting the speaker to come on board. So all of the women in the women's caucus held a televised press conference. The speaker was furious because we used that tactic, but the speaker let the bill get on the calendar and the bill became law.

Jones: There are enough women in the House that when there is legislation that is not favorable to women or issues of concern to women, we can influence an outcome of a bill by walking off the floor if need be. As speaker pro tem, I try to talk to women, particularly the freshman, and ask how they're doing. I try to encourage them because sometimes they don't get that from anybody else. In Maryland, we have one of the largest women's caucuses in the country, which is also a great help in terms of support.

SL: What Is One Final Piece of Advice?

Gard: The advice that I would give is spend your first year or two learning the process, developing relationships and learning the rules.

Connor: My dearest friend advised me to remember to refill my cup. Don't keep emptying yourself every day. If you don't have a way to refill it, you're going to be of no help to anyone. So, I get a manicure every week. Remembering to refill your cup is important so you can get up and do battle the next day.

Van de Putte: Have a sense of humor, don't take yourself so seriously. Be professional, be prepared. Know that there are going to be pitfalls and that it is a long process. You don't have permanent coalitions. Work by the issue. Remember that not everything is partisan. I'm reminded that there's a saying "an unreliable ally is more dangerous than a clever opponent." Remember that we can reach across the aisle on issues and find common ground.

For More Advice . . .

Listen to a longer version of this dialogue on the new CD entitled, "Wise Women: Sage Advice from Seasoned Lawmakers," the latest in the NCSL's How To Be An Effective Legislator series.

The CD offers women legislators valuable tips from carrying legislation to providing constituent service, from building consensus to maximizing your strengths. More information is available at: www.ncsl.org/programs/wln/wisewomen.htm.

V

Governors and Executives

T erm limits may be a relatively new phenomenon for legislators, but they are business as usual for most governors. Delaware, for example, constitutionally limits a governor to two four-year terms. That constitution was adopted in 1787 and more than two hundred years later governors in the state are still limited to an eight-year stay in the governor's mansion.

Many more states place term limits on executive offices than on legislative offices. Whereas fifteen states term limit legislators, more than twice that number place term limits on governors. In most cases, these provisions extend to other elected executives as well: the lieutenant governor, secretary of state and attorney general generally share the same service limitations as the chief executive.[1]

The pressure term limits place on executives is summarized fairly easily: get something done, and get it done quickly. The chief executives of most states do not have the luxury of long time horizons, and little opportunity to gain on-the-job experience before tackling complex issues. The clock starts ticking pretty much as soon as the ballots are counted, and the pressure to deliver begins.

And governors are expected to deliver a lot. As we shall see in this section, they occupy the most visible positions in state government, and are expected to address an astonishing array of difficult and complex problems. These range from education to illegal immigration to economic development to dealing with natural disasters. It's not a job for the faint of heart, and it demands a skillful blend of leadership, sharp administrative skills and political savvy. In recent years governors have had those skills repeatedly tested by everything from tight budgets to hurricanes, abortion to kickbacks and corruption. Some succeed in this high-pressure environment and make a real impact, leaving a significant legacy for their states. Others do not.

THE ORIGINS AND DEVELOPMENT OF ELECTED EXECUTIVES

State and local governments differ from the federal government in the number of executive positions that are elected offices. With the exception of the president and vice president, all important executive offices at the federal level are appointed. Filling the top jobs in the executive branch through the appointive powers of the president gives the chief executive more control over government because the president has the power to hire and fire the heads of the key bureaucracies.

This is not the case at the state and local levels, where many executive offices are elected and thus have a measure of independence from the governor or local-level equivalent. Everyone from the insurance commissioner to the head of a state's education bureaucracy may be elected. Attorney generals, for example, are mostly independently elected officials; they owe their job to the voters, not to the governor. This can create friction between executives, whose loyalties understandably lie with the issues and groups that got them elected, not necessarily to whoever serves as the chief executive. In many states, the executive branch of government consists of a group of independent electoral fiefdoms, not a strictly hierarchical system in which the chief executive has the power to hire and fire as he or she sees fit.

Explaining how and why this system came to be requires a little history. Governors represent the oldest executive office in the United States, predating the founding of the country. Early colonial governors were agents of the monarchy rather than officials elected by the people. They nonetheless often wielded considerable power, including the ability to veto bills passed by colonial legislatures or even to dissolve these legislatures outright.

After winning its independence, the newly formed republic was understandably suspicious of concentrations of power in executive office. Accordingly, state governments typically were organized so that governors occupied a comparatively weak position. Some states had plural executives—essentially, the governor's job was done by committee—and in other states the governorship was little more than an honorary position.

Most governors had no veto power, had very short term limits (often only a year), little appointive power and no real budgetary power. Real power belonged to the legislature.[2]

Executive power became even more fragmented during the 1800s by the implementation of the "long ballot." The aptly named long ballot was a reform designed to give citizens the final say in who held a wide variety of public offices—not just governor and lieutenant governor, but treasurer, attorney general, and, at the local level, county executive, sheriff, and county treasurer. All of these offices, and many more, were put on the ballot, making the process of selecting executives at the state and local levels as much elective as appointive.

In time there was something of a countermovement against this executive fragmentation, mainly as a response to corruption in the legislature. In the late nineteenth and early twentieth centuries, a number of states pursued reforms designed to centralize more power in the hands of chief executives. Few states actually trimmed the long ballot—by shifting elective offices back to appointive offices—but many undertook reorganizations of the executive branch that included creating line-item veto powers, granting greater discretion in hiring and firing personnel, increasing the length of terms and providing increased budgetary authority.[3]

For much of the first half of the twentieth century, however, the executive branches of state government did little to change or modernize. Events such as the Great Depression, World War II, and the Cold War shifted citizen expectations and attention to the federal government. In addition, the malapportionment of state legislatures allowed state government to be dominated by rural interests, which were content to stick with the organizational status quo.

THE DEVELOPMENT OF THE MODERN EXECUTIVE

The most significant reforms in the executive branches of subnational government did not begin to gain momentum until the 1960s and 1970s. Malapportionment ended in the 1960s with the "one-man, one-vote" ruling of the U.S. Supreme Court. This radically reshaped the nation's legislatures, shifting them from institutions focused on rural interests to institutions more oriented toward urban interests. In urban areas there was strong demand for the public services that fell under the jurisdiction of the executive branch. Therefore one outcome of the shift in legislative emphasis was an increased willingness to reform the executive branch, to make the chief executive of government more like that of a corporation. These reforms included strengthening veto powers and creating new state agencies to meet the demands of urban populations. Unlike many existing state agencies, the new agencies were more likely to be led by gubernatorial appointees than elected leaders.[4]

Such executive branch reforms gained particular importance in the 1970s, 1980s, and 1990s. Increasing federal budget deficits and a popular movement to push power away from the national government and back to the states (New Federalism), put governors in the spotlight. Broadly speaking, governors not only gained real executive authority, they faced a string of complex problems that required them to use it. Governors today are expected to do everything—keep property taxes down, improve the economy, make sure the roads get paved. They don't just take care of business within their state borders either. They also play an important political role nationally. The National Governors Association (NGA), an organization of governors designed to promote collective action on policy issues important to states, is judged by many experts to be one of the most powerful and influential lobbying organizations in Washington, D.C.[5]

Some of the reforms of the last thirty years even gained executives what term limits are designed to take away: time. Currently all states but two have four-year terms. New Hampshire and Vermont are the only holdouts that still have two-year terms. But while a number of states have extended the length of terms, they have largely stuck with the limits on the number of consecutive number of terms that can be served. The average governor is elected to a four-year term, and can be reelected once before being term limited out.

The readings in this section examine what governors have to do, and be prepared to do, in the time they serve in office. They also examine the relative success or failure of different executives in living up to the demands of being governor. Rob Gurwitt's essay takes a look at the occupant of the last remaining one-term state. Virginia is the sole holdout in legally restricting governors to serving a single term. This means that the state's governors face more pressure than their counterparts in other states to get things done, and get them done quickly. Critics of the single-term limit argue that Virginia's governors could get more done if they were allowed a second term. Changing leaders too often—especially when they seem to be doing a good job and have broad popular support—undercuts effective governance. Supporters, however, argue that the strict term limit actually promotes effective government in ways that critics overlook.

The next essays consist of two chapters from *A Governor's Guide to Emergency Management.* In the aftermath of Hurricane Katrina, chief executives at local, state and federal levels came in for severe criticism for not doing enough to prepare for, and handle the aftermath of, the storm that ravaged a large chunk of the Gulf Coast. In retrospect it can seem obvious what should have been done. Yet, as these readings show, an executive needs to know a lot about a lot of things in state government in order to lead in such high-pressure situations.

Laura Coleman's essay summarizes the policy challenges emerging from recent gubernatorial state of the state messages. As the list makes clear, a governor has to be prepared for more than natural disasters. Education, health care, transportation infrastructure and a host of other issues clamor for the attention of state government in general and the governor in particular.

Notes

1. The Council of State Governments, *The Book of the States 2005,* Table 4.9 (p. 231), www.nga.org/Files/pdf/BOS4-9.pdf (accessed April 24, 2006).

2. Larry Sabato, *Goodbye to Good-Time Charlie: The American Governorship Transformed,* 2nd ed. (Washington, D.C.: CQ Press, 1983).

3. Nelson C. Dometrius, "Governors: Their Heritage and Future," in *American State and Local Politics,* ed. Ronald E. Weber and Paul Brace (New York: Chatham House, 1999), 38–70.

4. Ibid., 50–52.

5. National Governors Association, www.nga.org/nga/1,1169,C_FAQ^D_302,00.html (accessed May 3, 2005).

19

The Last One-Term Statehouse

Rob Gurwitt

If Virginia governors could serve two terms, they'd get a lot more done. But would the state be better off?

Mark Warner and Jim Gilmore do not have much in common politically, but Virginia's Democratic governor and his Republican predecessor share one strong conviction: that their commonwealth has been hamstrung by an archaic provision that weakens it in a competitive world. Virginia is the only state in the country that bars its governors from seeking reelection. Gilmore had to step down after one term in 2002; Warner, who is highly popular among the voters right now, will be leaving in January. Whoever wins the office next month—Democrat Tim Kaine or Republican Jerry Kilgore—will get four years to enact his agenda. Then he, too, will be gone.

Warner tried and failed to get the law changed during his term in office; Gilmore was with him on that issue. "We're the only state in America that does this, and it's really stupid," says Gilmore. "If a governor is trying to be a change agent, to change the culture of the state, that is a hard thing to do in four years." Warner's secretary of administration, Sandra Bowen, sums up her boss's views in similar fashion: "How would you like to run a *Fortune* 300 company and try to reengineer it and make it more competitive in the global marketplace, and it's guaranteed that all of top management will change every four years?"

It's an issue that students of Virginia government might want to ponder as they prepare to vote in a new regime next month, just as they have done quadrennially since the 1870s. Are Warner and Gilmore pointing to a serious flaw, one that condemns the state to the status of an unstable governmental backwater, too stuck in its ways to thrive in the 21st century? Or does Virginia's "archaic" system offer benefits that should not be overlooked?

From *Governing*, October 2005.

To hear some of the critics, you might imagine that the state simply changes leadership too often to practice sound and consistent management. But you would be wrong. Virginia ranks among the best-administered states in the nation. It is a national leader in electronic procurement systems and workforce management, in clear-eyed budgeting processes, strategic planning, performance measurement and IT practices. When the Government Performance Project, a state management assessment funded by the Pew Charitable Trusts and carried out by *Governing*, looked at all 50 states earlier this year, Virginia was one of only two (the other was Utah) to get top overall marks. "There is little that Virginia does not do well in government management," the authors of the report wrote in our February issue. "Virginia has an ethos of good management that has genuinely been institutionalized."

Those who like Virginia's single-term system, such as former governor and current U.S. Senator George Allen, don't argue that it has single-handedly turned the state into an administrative model, but they do point out that it doesn't seem to be hurting much—and that there are virtues on the political side. The one-term limit, they believe, promotes balance between the executive and the legislature and ensures that the top ranks of state government will be open to new blood every few years.

Others say that Virginia's reputation as a well-run state has mostly to do with other historical factors besides rotation in power. Most important, says University of Virginia political scientist Larry Sabato, "is the political culture in the state. Ever since the Civil War, we've had an emphasis on good management, elimination of debt and a kind of pay-as-you-go mentality." And that leads proponents of change to insist that if their state can function this smoothly with a four-year revolving door, it could function even better without it. "Virginia's doing pretty well," admits Bowen, the administration secretary. "But we could do it so much more efficiently and cost-effectively."

Still, while it might be overreaching to suggest that Virginia is well-governed because of the unique law, it's

> *"You have to use all the power of the governorship in order to effectuate your program, because otherwise the legislature can just wait you out."*
>
> Former Governor Jim Gilmore

worth wondering whether there is at least a link between the two—whether, that is, the discipline imposed by the one-term cap has forced state government to adapt institutionally in ways that help, rather than hurt, it. And while it's unlikely that any other state could or would want to move in Virginia's direction, there might be lessons in Virginia's experience that other states might want to heed.

REPEAL EFFORTS

Virginia's status as odd state out in gubernatorial tenure is, in fact, relatively new. Half a century ago, some 15 states prohibited their governors from succeeding themselves, including Pennsylvania, Indiana and the entire South except for Arkansas. That began to change in the 1960s, and by the 1980s, only three states were left: Mississippi, Kentucky and Virginia.

Mississippi repealed its one-term law in 1986 as part of a wide-ranging push by reformers to modify a Reconstruction-era constitution that had left governors almost powerless and made the speaker of the House the most powerful figure in the state. The switch in Kentucky came in 1992, after voters changed the constitution to allow succession in various offices. That decision, taken in conjunction with an effort to modernize and professionalize state government, passed only after the incumbent governor at the time, Brereton Jones, agreed not to use it to seek a second term himself.

Virginia has seen its own repeated efforts to repeal the law. For the past 14 years, a Republican legislator from Virginia Beach named Harry "Bob" Purkey has agitated for it, repeatedly filing legislation in the House of Delegates to change the constitution to allow second terms. "This is something he does as much as breathing, I suppose," remarks Delegate Bob Marshall, a Republican colleague of Purkey's who held hearings on the measure and wound up opposing any change. "I didn't necessarily find any inherent connection," Marshall explains, "between the benefits supposed to come from having the governor able to succeed himself and the two terms." (By law, Virginia governors are allowed to seek the office again after being out for four years, but hardly any of them try; it has been done successfully just once in the past century.)

For Purkey, the issue is clear-cut: It comes down to economic development and political accountability. "We have to create 55,000 new private-sector jobs every year to accommodate our population growth," he says. "But governors get right in the middle of an economic development issue and are involved in bringing jobs to Virginia, and by the time some of these deals come to fruition, they're out of there. Then it takes time for the new governor and staff to catch up." Moreover, he argues, a single term limits the degree to which a governor feels liable for his actions. "Being accountable to the public by virtue of the fact that you can be thrown out," he says, "is so overwhelmingly important."

Opponents counter that not many governors elsewhere are thrown out after one term anyway, and at least Virginia can guarantee a spirited campaign every four years for the most important office on the statewide ballot. "We have very little competition in Virginia politics today," says Paul Goldman, who was a top aide to former Democratic Governor L. Douglas Wilder and is now Wilder's right-hand aide in the Richmond mayor's office. "If you go to a two-term governor, you would eliminate the only area of competition we really have now, which is at the statewide level."

The one-term rule might seem to be a recipe for wild political swings and a certain inconstancy to state government life; in truth, however, it has produced just the opposite—a political system that places a premium on moderation. "People generally think of us as stick-in-the-mud, not very innovative or creative," says Sabato. "Generally that's true, but it also means we rarely engage in dangerous experimentation that ruins the state."

In fact, the single-term governorship has forced state government to learn how to keep itself on an even keel. To begin with, governors and their political appointees simply don't have time to conduct wholesale shakeups or lard the bureaucracy with their own hires. "Time is their enemy," says Sabato. "Governors have to jump right in and get their agenda adopted or they're going to have an empty term. They don't have the luxury of a lot of administrative turmoil."

As a result, over the course of its history, Virginia has developed a civil service that has become a stabilizing force in its own right. "We have a long tradition of qual-

ity civil servants who are apolitical and perform good public service," says former Democratic Governor Gerald Baliles, who served from 1986 to 1990. "They become indispensable: They possess the institutional knowledge that allows a governor to perform good service, and they constrain the opportunity for political mischief, where you have civil service positions filled by campaign operatives, which is a recipe for disaster."

For the most part, the nature of the budget cycle also hems in the governor. Virginia works on a two-year budget calendar, so a new governor's first budget is, in fact, crafted by his predecessor, and his only full chance to put his stamp on the budget comes halfway through his one term. "There are some disadvantages to that," says Baliles, "but it also tends to moderate enormous swings in budget priorities and governmental policies. If a new governor wants to make changes to the budget by the outgoing governor, it requires him to work together with the legislature."

As a result, the legislature—like the budget cycle and the civil service—has become a force for stability in state government. Legislators in Virginia are not term-limited, and over the years, the members of the various money committees have developed a reputation for careful stewardship of the state's finances. In 2002, with Warner's collaboration, the legislature also mandated a six-year budget forecast, which serves to constrain politically popular tax cuts or budget additions that carry a hefty price tag in the out-years. Moreover, the legislature has developed a nonpartisan research infrastructure—in particular the Joint Legislative Audit and Review Commission—that gives it a solid oversight footing.

None of this means that governors are doomed to irrelevance during their single terms. Doug Wilder, for instance, fixed a $2 billion revenue shortfall by cutting some services while seeking to protect social services for the poor; he also created the state's first "rainy day" fund so that his successors would have a freer hand in a sour economy. Allen focused on education standards, overhauling the state's juvenile justice system, and crafting welfare reform. "The four-year term limit," he wrote recently, "does not prevent an administration from taking action that can have a positive impact on the lives and opportunities of Virginians."

When a governor has especially broad ambitions, however, the single term can indeed bring him up short. It is no accident that the most adamant voices calling for constitutional change belong to Gilmore and Warner, who each in his own way set out to overhaul Virginia and found four years to be maddeningly short.

THE TICKING CLOCK

Gilmore, an ideological and partisan conservative, set out as governor to place his stamp on Virginia but found that his time in office constrained him. His signature issue was a massive reduction in the car tax, a politically popular move that eventually embroiled him in a standoff with the Republican-controlled state Senate when it became clear that the loss in revenues was setting the state on unsound financial footing. Gilmore contends that in a second term, he could have set things right. "If I'd had an opportunity to bring the state back out of recession," he says, "then people would have seen that running the state while cutting car taxes and not raising taxes was possible." He still resents the fact that not only was he denied that chance but also that he had to yield after four years to a governor determined to undo what he'd done. "It was absolutely unnecessary for [Mark Warner] to raise taxes," Gilmore says, "in order to fix some fictitious shortfall."

Warner, of course, doesn't see it that way. He points out that he took office facing an estimated $800 million shortfall that was quickly revised to $3 billion and eventually to $6 billion. The 2004 tax increase, part of a larger restructuring package that also cut some taxes, came out of Warner's belief that the state had no other way to get back on solid ground. "We had cut each agency by an average of 20 percent," says Finance Secretary John Bennett. "We had enacted reforms. We'd looked at a long-term financial projection that showed we would continue to have budget shortfalls unless we did something more aggressive. So it was born of long-term planning and cuts and reforms, because even after those things, it was clear we would not solve our problem."

Warner was able to enact the plan in concert with a Republican-controlled legislature in part because the state's fiscal circumstances demanded a response, and in part because his administration worked closely with the legislature's money committees, which have enormous power over fiscal affairs in Virginia. This, too, is a rigor imposed

> *"The four-year term limit does not prevent an administration from having a positive impact."*
>
> U.S. Senator George Allen

by the single term: Without the leverage of reelection, governors have little chance to use public sentiment to challenge the legislature. "Rather than having time to persuade people," says Gilmore, "and even take your case back to the people if you can't persuade members of the legislature, you have to use all the power of the governorship in order to effectuate your program, because otherwise the legislature can just wait you out."

Given the realities of the ticking four-year clock, most Virginia governors have focused on policy and barely tinkered with the structure of government—another source of stability when it comes to management. "When you have X days," says William Leighty, an executive-branch veteran who is Warner's chief of staff, "you'll spend them on the policy issues, not reading audit reports or driving process improvement. You'll say, 'I just want all those things over there to run well and not get in my way.'"

Warner has not played things that way. A technology entrepreneur in private life, he has spent an unusual amount of his limited time remaking the state government apparatus to instill greater efficiency, performance standards and a more business-like approach. This has included changing the budget process to include long-term financial planning, setting performance requirements for agency heads and reconfiguring the state's procurement processes and information technology structure.

Warner's accomplishments here have been substantial, but they have been affected at every point by the difficulty of trying to implement such massive managerial reforms in just one term. Paradoxically, this has helped make them stronger. Haunted by the worry that state employees might simply wait them out, administration officials have worked especially hard to institutionalize them.

They have done this by finding influential supporters outside the bureaucracy who can ensure that the changes last beyond a single term. Warner, as part of his effort to reform state purchasing and real estate management, built a coalition that included private contractors as well as public officials. In the case of purchasing, says Administration Secretary Sandra Bowen, "we invited in all the people who had been selling office products to agencies of

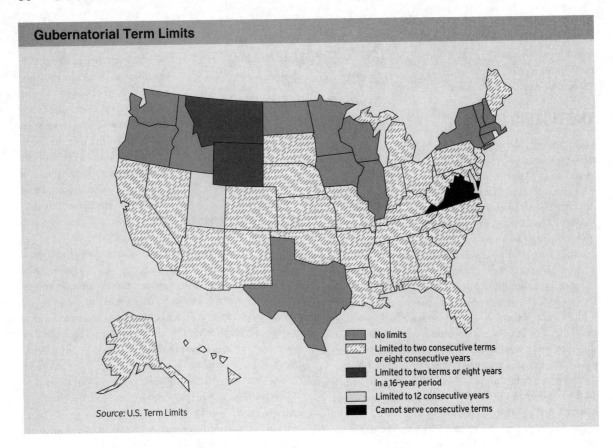

Gubernatorial Term Limits

- No limits
- Limited to two consecutive terms or eight consecutive years
- Limited to two terms or eight years in a 16-year period
- Limited to 12 consecutive years
- Cannot serve consecutive terms

Source: U.S. Term Limits

the commonwealth and filled up a room. What we were doing was a little threatening to them, because they'd been able to take advantage of our not doing our work smartly. I told them, 'We respect that you're in business to make a profit, but now take that hat off and put your taxpayer hat on.'" The result, Bowen believes, is that the new procedures now have private-sector advocates who will still be doing business with the state once she and Warner leave office—and will do it in a more rational way.

This determined marketing of change, pursued under the pressure of Warner's impending departure, "gives me confidence that the vast majority of our management changes will remain," says Leighty. But he still thinks that the one-term limit restricts how much can be accomplished. "Why do we have 90 separate financial accounting systems?" Leighty asks. "Why, as a governor, would anyone really want to invest a lot of time rebuilding the financial system when it'll take five or six years to get that done? Why even start? In a second term, we could have done something about this."

These are understandable frustrations, but even there, Virginia has created a partial answer. The legislature, at the urging of Warner and a group of business leaders, has set up and funded an agency called the Council on Virginia's Future. Its goal, says retired communications executive John Wynne, a leading player in the effort, is essentially to become an institutional force for sound state planning and good management.

In the end, it could be rendered moot. Bob Purkey is confident that if he can bring his two-term measure to a popular vote, it will pass. "The greatest fear opponents have is it will get on the ballot," he says, "because their fear is that it will pass overwhelmingly." If that should happen, Virginia would lose its unique status. But it would be left with some crucial ingredients of the old system: bureaucrats who know how to build political support for change; a legislature willing to take the lead on crucial issues; and a broad-based public council with a mandate to plan for the state's future. That might not be a bad legacy for an "archaic" law to leave behind.

20

A Governor's Guide to Emergency Management

Ann M. Beauchesne

What governors should know, and who they should know, before a natural disaster strikes.

WHAT A NEW GOVERNOR SHOULD KNOW

A new governor must be prepared should a disaster occur during the early days of his or her administration. The key first steps for a governor are to understand the existing emergency management system of the state and to establish informed policies and sound priorities to address critical needs. **A new governor should:**

- identify the key members of his or her emergency response team;
- compile essential emergency management information, including gaining an understanding of existing systems and processes for dealing with crisis events;
- assess the state's emergency management resources and capabilities; and
- review emergency powers and responsibilities authorized by state statutes.

Identify Key Members of the State Emergency Response Team

Although several agencies are involved in state emergency management, the governor relies heavily on two people—the state emergency management director and the chief of staff. The state emergency management director is responsible for coordinating emergency and disaster response and recovery, and the chief of staff serves as the principal contact in the governor's office and commu-

For more information on the Emergency Planning and Community Right-to-Know Act, go to the National Governors Association Web site at www.nga.org or the EPA Chemical Emergency Preparedness and Prevention Office Web site at www.epa.gov/swercepp.

From *National Governors Association,* February 2000.

nicates directly with the state emergency management office, state agencies, and local governments. The governor should meet with the chief of staff and the director of the state emergency management office to define their emergency management roles and responsibilities.

In addition, the governor should meet with all state agency officials involved in emergency management to ensure they understand how they should interact with the governor's office and state emergency management agency during an emergency.

A new governor should ensure that state department directors, particularly if they are also new to government, understand the importance of emergency management. Agency officials involved in emergency management should be experienced in these issues and should be given a direct line of communication to department directors. The governor should also tap into the resources of the entire state organization and ensure that an interagency perspective and approach are established.

Governors should be aware that all states have some form of a state emergency operations center where all departmental emergency management officials can gather during an emergency to execute the state plan.

The 1986 Emergency Planning and Community Right-to-Know Act, authorized under Title III of the Superfund Amendments and Reauthorization Act, requires each governor to establish a state emergency response commission (SERC) to oversee implementation of the federal act. In most states, the SERC is composed of state agency representatives and is the principal coordinating body for chemical-related emergencies.

Compiling Essential Emergency Management Information

A governor's staff should compile essential information that the governor will need when an emergency occurs.

Assessing the State's Emergency Management Resources and Capabilities

During the transition or the first week in office, a governor should have the office staff review the state's basic emergency management system. Within the first month of the governor's term, the staff should compile a hazard analysis and an assessment of the state's emergency management laws, capabilities, and resources from their state emergency management agency. The assessment should include answers to the following questions.

Essential Emergency Management Information

- A list of procedures to be followed by the governor.
- A description of the powers and responsibilities of the governor during a declared emergency.
- A description of the roles and authorities of the state emergency management office and other agencies.
- A sample executive order or proclamation* declaring a state emergency.
- A sample letter to the President requesting a federal disaster declaration.
- A description of the types of state and federal disaster aid available to victims.
- A review of emergencies that have occurred in the state in the last five years.
- A communications strategy.
- An assessment of the state's emergency management resources and capabilities.

*In some states, an executive order is not required to declare a state of emergency.

- Is the emergency management program comprehensive enough to meet the needs of the state?
- Are the goals, objectives, and mission of the state's emergency management system being achieved?
- Can the state redirect strategic resources and help communities and citizens avoid becoming disaster victims?

How to Declare a Disaster

Most emergencies or disasters do not reach the magnitude of a presidential declaration. These are the most difficult. The governor may be under intense pressure to request federal assistance, but if there is not sufficient damage it may be denied. Consequently a state must have the capability to provide assistance to victims without the benefit of federal disaster aid. Many programs exist in a state that can provide this type of assistance. In those cases when state and local resources are insufficient to respond to a disaster and thresholds for federal disaster assistance are met, a governor may request that the President declare a major disaster or emergency. Chapter 7 [of *A Governor's Guide to Emergency Management*] lays out, step-by-step, the processes for declaring a major disaster as well as for receiving federal assistance that is available without a presidential declaration. The authority and powers a governor has during a declared emergency are explained in Chapter 4 [of this text].

POWERS, ROLES, AND RESPONSIBILITIES OF A GOVERNOR AND STATE AGENCIES

State laws require the governor to carry out emergency preparedness, response, and recovery actions. Many states have recently included mitigation as an authority of the governor. During a declared emergency, a governor has extraordinary powers and responsibilities. In most states, the governor's emergency powers and the role of the state emergency management office are described in the same law, often titled the Emergency Management Act or Civil Defense Act.

The governor establishes policy and performance standards for the state's emergency management program. Just as national emergency management must have the interest, support, and confidence of the President, the state emergency management program should have the interest, support, and confidence of the governor. Further, governors may wish to see that the state's emergency management operation maintains a high degree of professionalism and that its director has direct access to the governor.

Governor's Powers and Responsibilities During a Declared Emergency

As the state's chief executive, the governor is responsible for public safety and welfare. The state constitution sets certain limits on the governor's powers, but the size and complexity of today's state government add many more responsibilities to the governor's office. These include preparedness and recovery activities that the governor typically delegates to the state emergency management office. State emergency management laws usually delineate how the governor may declare and terminate a state of emergency and what gubernatorial powers accompany a declaration. The governor's legal counsel should review the governor's emergency powers before a disaster occurs. A clear understanding of the governor's powers saves time during critical situations and enables the governor to proceed confidently.

Declaration of a State of Emergency

According to the state-specific statutes, the governor declares an emergency either by executive order or by proclamation. The order, or proclamation, typically describes the nature of the emergency, its location within the state, and the authority by which the governor makes the declaration.

Of course, response activities often begin before and without an emergency declaration. Governors generally use the order only when they need to have special emergency powers or request a presidential disaster declaration. Although state laws vary, the declaration of a state of emergency generally gives a governor several powers.

Activating the National Guard and enhancing liability protection and funding activities are three of the main reasons for a governor to declare a state of emergency. The National Guard can provide staff and equipment needed for response activities, including helicopters, trucks, four-wheel drive vehicles, and heavy equipment. A declaration may provide enhanced abilities for emergency procurement and protection of emergency workers. Any emergency or disaster can have a significant fiscal impact and, as such, governors may need to obligate vast sums of money in the early hours and days of an event.

Emergency powers can be a mixed blessing. Although they provide the governor with necessary authority, exercising that authority can lead to criticism. For example, a governor can face political problems if the public later perceives his or her actions as excessive. Further, if a governor orders the evacuation of an affected area, local officials may criticize this action as usurping their authority. Maintaining the needed balance and preventing

A Governor's Emergency Powers

- mobilize the National Guard and transfer and direct state agency personnel for emergency management purposes;
- require and direct the evacuation of all or part of the population within a disaster area;
- prescribe routes, transportation modes, and destinations in connection with evacuation and prohibit certain activities in the disaster area;
- commandeer or use private property;
- suspend state statutes, as necessary;
- authorize emergency funds; and
- enter into mutual aid arrangements with other states.

criticism during an event can be reduced through effective planning and understanding of authorities and responsibilities by all involved prior to an event. When circumstances allow, governors should consult with affected local officials before exercising gubernatorial emergency powers. In some states, gubernatorial emergency declarations may be a necessary step to making state funds available to local communities. This may provide rationale to declare an emergency even when actual state agency response activities are not needed. It can also guarantee political pressure to declare emergencies when declarations may not be warranted.

In the event of a disaster declaration, most state laws allow the governor to delegate special powers and authorities to the state's emergency management director or the appropriate cabinet secretary. Delegation promotes a coordinated response effort among the various state agencies that share emergency management responsibilities. The governor may authorize the public safety secretary, adjutant general, or emergency management agency director to use and allocate state resources to manage the emergency.

Roles and Responsibilities of the State Emergency Management Agency

The state emergency management agency (SEMA) coordinates the emergency management program and writes the state emergency operations and mitigation plans. Required by federal and state laws, the plan governs all emergency operations and defines the roles and responsibilities of state and local agencies. These plans provide for the coordination of linkages—vertically between local and federal government agencies and horizontally within state government. SEMAs must continually update the plan and ensure that other state agencies are fulfilling their emergency management responsibilities.

How State Directors Are Chosen

Most state emergency management directors occupy appointed political positions. Of the 50 state directors, half are appointed directly by the governor. Cabinet-level officials appoint the rest: 11 by the adjutant general, 8 by the secretary of public safety or local affairs, and 2 by the state police chief. Of these, three are appointed by the officials with the governor's consent. Finally, four state directorships are merit-based, civil service positions,

hired by the adjutant general in three states and the public safety secretary in one state.[1]

State Director Reporting

Ten state directors are cabinet-level officials themselves and answer directly to the governor, while the rest answer to another state official (usually the same person that appointed the director). Nineteen directors report directly to an adjutant general; nine report to a public safety or local affairs secretary; two report to a state police chief; and three report to an attorney general, a chief of administration, and another cabinet-level official, respectively. The remaining seven directors report directly to both the governor and another state official, depending on the situation: four report to the adjutant general, and three to the public safety secretary.

Regardless of the normal reporting chain, the state emergency-management director must be able to communicate directly with the governor when state emergencies occur.

Location within State Government

States have different emergency management organizational structures. In 10 states, emergency management agencies are cabinet-level agencies within the office of the governor. However, in the majority of states, emergency management agencies are located within other state agencies: within the state department of military affairs in 22 states; within public safety departments in 12 states; within joint public safety-military affairs agencies in 2 states; within departments of community affairs or local affairs in 2 states; and within the state police in 2 states.

Roles and Responsibilities of Other State Agencies in Emergency Management

Several agencies share responsibility for some state emergency management activities. The key to successful emergency management is teamwork. All state government departments' personnel and resources should be viewed as components of the state's overall emergency management

[1] *The Face of NEMA: A Look at State Emergency Management Agencies and Their Directors,* National Emergency Management Association, February 2000. (Note 5 in original text.)

Location of State Emergency Management Offices

Office of the Governor or Executive Agency
Alabama, Arkansas, California, Georgia, Illinois, Indiana, Mississippi, New Hampshire, Oklahoma, and Pennsylvania

Department of Military Affairs
Alaska, Arizona, Connecticut, Hawaii, Idaho, Iowa, Kansas, Kentucky, Louisiana, Maine, Maryland, Montana, Nebraska, New York, North Dakota, Rhode Island, South Carolina, South Dakota, Tennessee, Washington, Wisconsin, and Wyoming

Department of Public Safety
Delaware, Massachusetts, Minnesota, Nevada, New Jersey, New Mexico, North Carolina, Ohio, Texas, Utah, Vermont, and Virginia

Department of Military Affairs and Public Safety
Missouri and West Virginia

Department of Community Affairs or Local Affairs
Colorado and Florida

State Police
Michigan and Oregon

system. Some state agencies provide support for all types of emergencies, while others have lead responsibility for a particular type of disaster. A state's emergency operations plan describes agencies' specific roles and responsibilities; appendixes contain plans for various types of emergencies, such as chemical spills. All states have some type of emergency operations center—an emergency office where all departmental emergency management officials can gather during an emergency to execute the state plan.

- **Adjutant General's Office.** In 22 states, the adjutant general's office or the military department is the principal emergency management agency. The state emergency management office and the National Guard are located within the department. The adjutant general heads the department and usually has a military background. However, the adjutant general and other department staff are state employees.

- **Department of Public Safety.** In many states, the state emergency management office is located in the department of public safety. This department also contains two other important emergency management offices—the state police and state fire marshal. The office of the state police safeguards the lives and safety of all people while the office of the state fire marshal helps police and other authorities respond to fires and hazardous-material incidents. The state fire marshal and other fire officials within the state also have extensive backgrounds in risk reduction and prevention that can be beneficial in growth planning before and after disasters strike.

- **State Energy Office.** State energy agencies prepare state energy emergency plans, which include steps to alleviate the effects of shortages or disruptions of petroleum, natural gas, or electricity supplies. The underlying philosophy of most of these plans is to rely on the market and intervene only to protect public health, welfare, and safety. The more comprehensive plans establish programs for responding to shortages, ensure essential services are provided, and reduce inequities in fuel distribution.

- **State Environment Department.** The state environment department handles hazardous material emergencies and conducts hazard mitigation measures. Often it heads a state chemical emergency response team that responds to chemical spills or releases. The environmental management or natural resources agency handles flood management. These officials should be part of the governor's growth strategy team to ensure that the state's growth investments are protected from the impacts caused by disasters. The state environment department often plays a primary role in nuclear emergencies for those states with nuclear power plants.

- **Transportation Department.** The transportation department responds to emergencies that may impede transportation, such as hazardous material incidents and weather-related emergencies. It cleans up debris; handles evacuations; and repairs roads, bridges, airports, and transit systems.

- **Attorney General's Office.** The attorney general's office determines the party or parties responsible for a chemical emergency, terrorist incident, or other manmade disaster. In most cases, this determination is needed before contingency funds can be activated. The office also provides consumer protection assistance.

- **State Comptroller or Treasury Office.** In some states, this office disburses and accounts for funds for disaster relief, as well as for prevention and mitigation opportunities.
- **Health Agency and Welfare Agency.** The health agency provides sanitation and medical services and conducts exposure assessments following a toxic chemical release. The welfare agency issues food stamps and provides individual and family grants, often serving as a conduit for individual assistance provided by the federal government.

- **Labor Department.** This department provides disaster unemployment assistance benefits.
- **State Emergency Response Commission.** The 1986 Emergency Planning and Community Right-to-Know Act, authorized under Title III of the Superfund Amendments and Reauthorization Act, requires each governor to establish a state emergency response commission (SERC) to oversee implementation of the federal act. In most states, the SERC is composed of state agency representatives and is the principal coordinating body for chemical-related emergencies.

21

States of Progress

Laura Coleman

Governors outline plans for the future in state of the state messages.

In January 2005, the "Nation's Report Card" revealed no progress for high school students in 30 years. The United States is ninth in the world in high school graduation rates among 25- to 34-year-olds. The 1 million students who drop out of high school each year cost our nation more than $260 billion in lost wages, taxes and productivity in their lifetimes.

During the first two months of this year, governors across the country pledged to get to work and cooperate with their legislatures to improve conditions in their states. But their plans are not limited to improvements in K–12 education. Health care, public safety, and improving infrastructures also topped governors' agendas.

K–12 EDUCATION

According to a 2004 report from the American Federation of Teachers, for every new real dollar gained in the private sector, teachers only gain about 18 cents. In 2004, the average beginning teacher's salary was $31,704 and the average teacher's salary overall was $46,597.

Governors across the country, and in particular from states with below average teacher salaries, vowed to provide better compensation, thus ensuring that the best teachers remain in the classroom.

"We need to bring teacher pay in line with teacher responsibility," said Arizona Gov. Janet Napolitano. "Teaching shouldn't be the 'last resort' for students as they enter college and begin to think about future careers."

From *Statenews*, March 2006.

Napolitano called for legislation to increase the base salary in Arizona so that every teacher makes at least $30,000 a year. She also called for more professional development.

Kentucky Gov. Ernie Fletcher spoke about a similar plan. "I will propose an enhanced professional compensation plan that pays teachers more who receive professional development that is directly related to their classroom work and who take voluntary actions to teach subjects where there is a need or to teach at a low-performing school," he said.

Attracting K–12 teachers in low-performing schools was an issue inextricably linked to compensation.

Hawaii Gov. Linda Lingle laid out a plan to draw teachers to areas where there has been a shortage. Her plan is to allow retired teachers to be hired for up to 24 months without any loss of retirement benefits, start a Master Teacher Program with bonuses for any National Board Certified Teachers who agree to teach in an underperforming school for three years, create an emergency certified teacher program to allow any person with a bachelor's degree to teach, and use $500,000 to re-establish the Hawaii Educator Loan Program for loan forgiveness.

"Education must be one of our highest priorities, and is deserving of more support," said Lingle. "It is our hope for a better tomorrow, both for us as individuals and as a state. Over time, it can wash away the barriers of disadvantage."

Dr. Keon Chi, a senior fellow in CSG's national office in Lexington, Ky., agrees that education should be a top priority. "Hopefully, legislatures will support governors' initiatives, including more money for education programs and teachers' salaries," he said. "Legislators should do their best to raise compensation levels for K-12 teachers in order to improve student performance. Education is the best investment states can make for the benefit of their citizens."

HIGHER EDUCATION

"In 1970, half of the people in the world who held science and engineering doctorates were Americans," said U.S. Department of Education Secretary Margaret Spellings. She pointed out, however, that projections show that figure will drop to 15 percent by 2010.

Several governors proposed plans to increase enrollment in state colleges and universities and make higher education a reality for more residents.

Colorado Gov. Bill Owens addressed what he calls the "Colorado Paradox." Colorado ranks second in the nation in college degrees per capita, but lags behind in the percentage of Colorado students who pursue college education.

Among Owens' ideas to address this issue are limiting tuition increases and allocating more state funding for financial aid.

Illinois Gov. Rod Blagojevich proposed a $1,000 annual tax credit for every freshman and sophomore attending a state college or university. These credits would be awarded to students who keep a B average.

"For many families, this is a tax credit that can help make the dream of college affordable and the dream of college a reality," said Blagojevich. "Washington has its priorities all mixed up. On one hand, their policies encourage the outsourcing of jobs. On the other, they're trying to cut college scholarships. As a nation, we are falling behind."

Steps such as these are examples of how state governments hope to compensate for federal cuts to student loan subsidies.

TOUGHER PUNISHMENTS FOR SEX OFFENDERS

Governors across the nation made it clear that sex offenders should face tougher penalties to reduce recidivism.

South Dakota Gov. Mike Rounds announced that he will introduce a sex offender bill to increase penalties for repeat offenders, require a description of the offender's crime to be listed on the registry, specify procedures for registering incarcerated sex offenders, and create a new felony for harboring a sex offender. The bill would also create a process where certain offenders can be determined ineligible for parole.

According to Kansas Gov. Kathleen Sebelius, protecting children from these criminals is common sense. She asked Kansas' legislature again this year to double prison sentences for sex offenders who prey on children. Then she asked to add another penalty.

"When they've served their prison time, I want to require all repeat sex offenders to wear electronic tracking devices—for the rest of their lives," said Sebelius. "These tracking bracelets will allow law enforcement officers to monitor their locations at all times. I've put money for this in my budget because, again, it's just common sense."

HEALTH CARE

Nearly every governor mentioned health care during this year's State of the State addresses. Governors in several states mentioned increasing budget allocations for health care as a response to federal spending cuts.

California Gov. Arnold Schwarzenegger asked for the federal government to permit the import of prescription drugs into the United States.

"I ask myself, what's the quickest way we can help the greatest number of people with the spiraling health care costs? I believe in the free market. I believe in free trade," said Schwarzenegger. "I mean, we buy food from overseas. We buy cars from overseas. Why not prescription drugs?"

Oklahoma Gov. Brad Henry also called for the importation of prescription drugs from other industrialized countries. "Prescription drugs are one of the chief drivers of increased medical costs," he said. "When needy Oklahomans must choose between food and medicine while drug companies spend more than $4 billion on advertising, something has gone terribly wrong. The status quo is unacceptable."

Idaho Gov. Dirk Kempthorne announced that Medicaid reform is at the top of his agenda. "Medicaid is among the fastest growing parts of the state budget," said Kempthorne. "But to cure the systemic problems and reign in the escalating costs, we must do more to modernize the sys-

Nearly every governor mentioned health care during this year's State of the State addresses. Governors in several states mentioned increasing budget allocations for health care as a response to federal spending cuts.

Vermont in particular faces a demographic challenge with the prescription drug benefit: its population is the second-oldest in the country. "We need to work together to address the federal Medicare implementation challenges that are currently afflicting the entire nation."

—Gov. Jim Douglas, Vermont, CSG's 2006 president

tem. Unless we do something, we'll be forcing the care of our grandparents to be in direct conflict with the education of their grandchildren."

Kempthorne's reform strategy includes plans to redesign Medicaid into three distinct programs: one for low-income children, one for individuals with disabilities or special health needs, and one for the elderly. Each program would be specialized to meet the needs of its population.

Vermont Gov. Jim Douglas announced his directive to the Agency of Human Services to reinstate benefits to seniors who were previously enrolled in one of Vermont's prescription drug programs. "This means that no senior who relied on state government for medicine will be turned away from a pharmacy," said Douglas. "They will get the drugs they need and Vermont will guarantee their affordability."

Vermont in particular faces a demographic challenge with the prescription drug benefit: its population is the second-oldest in the country. "We need to work together to address the federal Medicare implementation challenges that are currently afflicting the entire nation," said Douglas, who is CSG's 2006 president. "We must ensure that Vermont seniors have access to the prescription drugs they need at the price they were promised."

West Virginia Gov. Joe Manchin unveiled a "Preventive Care Clinic-Based Plan" as one of his two public/private health initiatives to help provide West Virginians affordable health care. The plan sets up sites at primary care clinics or private doctors' offices and would allow subscribers access to primary care services—checkups, sick visits, X-rays or lab tests—at the participating clinic or doctors' office for a monthly fee. According to Manchin, the plan would provide basic preventive care for a low price.

Additionally, in Arizona and Kentucky, proposals are on the floor to offer tax breaks for health insurance costs to small businesses. In Arizona, 17 percent of residents are uninsured, and in Kentucky, 13.9 percent of residents lack coverage.

TRANSPORTATION AND STATE INFRASTRUCTURES

As a result of more fiscally stable states, allocations for repairing and updating infrastructures were in governors' budgets this year. Years during the economic downturn left roads and highways neglected, and this year governors pledged to make long-needed repairs.

Alaska Gov. Frank Murkowski introduced his "Bottleneck Busters" transportation initiative in October 2004. The proposal included $97 million in state funding for congestion relief projects. During his recent state of the state address, Murkowski asked legislators this session to jumpstart the program with $30 million of state funds. Murkowski's budget also includes allocations to reconstruct dangerous sections of Alaska's roads.

Virginia Gov. Tim Kaine's address included his ideas for improving the state's transportation system, especially in evacuation routes.

"The hurricanes that devastated the Gulf Coast last year taught us many things about the need for preparing for the worst," Kaine told legislators. "I will initiate a thorough review of evacuation and emergency plans. I will insist that state and local agencies be prepared to aid and evacuate residents in an emergency,

> *As a result of more fiscally stable states, allocations for repairing and updating infrastructures were in governors' budgets this year. Years during the economic downturn left roads and highways neglected, and this year governors pledged to make long-needed repairs.*

especially elderly and poor residents and those without their own transportation."

In addition, Kaine told legislators that Virginia's transportation woes are far-reaching and can be felt in both rural and urban areas.

"Because fiscal accountability shouldn't depend on a single election, Virginia needs a constitutional amendment to protect transportation dollars permanently," said Kaine.

Oklahoma Gov. Brad Henry asked legislators to allow voters to decide on a similar measure.

Several states have enacted legislation protecting transportation funds, which seek to prevent policymakers from dipping into money from hybrid funds to use for general allocations. Hybrid funds—like transportation funding—are often in better shape than general funds because of revenue from gas taxes.

OTHER PRIORITIES

Governors in Alaska, Idaho, Michigan, Missouri, New York and Washington specifically mentioned skyrocketing energy costs and announced plans to help their residents.

Gov. Kempthorne's budget includes more than $63 million in one-time energy assistance to help Idahoans with energy costs. Every Idaho resident who filed a 2004 tax return or the grocery tax credit will receive a check for $50 for each qualifying man, woman and child. Kempthorne asked lawmakers to approve the legislation immediately.

Proposals also have taken shape in New York, where Gov. George Pataki announced a $500 fuel tax credit for senior citizens, and in Missouri, Gov. Matt Blunt asked the state legislature to approve a $6.1 million budget allocation for the state's Utilicare program.

Several governors also mentioned using state funds to research alternative energy sources in order to reduce dependence on foreign fuel.

Increasing state technology made the agenda in Georgia and Rhode Island with the governors of those states introducing initiatives to support establishing broadband connectivity in their states. Gov. Donald Carcieri announced that Rhode Island is poised to become the first state in the country to be wireless border to border. He told legislators that investments in technology yield solid rewards.

"The opportunities for business, health care and education are limitless," said Carcieri. "It requires a public investment, but promises to pay off in the future with new jobs."

THE FISCAL STATE OF STATES

As a result of an economic upturn in the 2005 fiscal year—revenues exceeded expectations in 45 states and were on target in five—talk of tax cuts have entered governors' agendas.

Almost every state is looking at a cap on property taxes, and many states have enforced a limit. Another trend, says Sujit CanagaRetna, fiscal analyst for the Council of State Governments, is lowering property taxes and compensating with a hike in sales taxes.

However, experts warn that despite fiscal stability, states will be wary of increases in program spending in the next year.

"The revenue situation for states has improved radically," said CanagaRetna. "But when you look at it from the perspective of the depths we were plunged to, we still have a long way to go."

CanagaRetna said that states are expecting a series of looming expenditures, such as health care, retirement, and education including court-mandated education costs, so those areas will soak up a lot of revenue.

"So although revenue is improved," said CanagaRetna, "we are not out of the woods."

VI

Courts

Sooner or later, all the big issues of politics end up in court. In the past few years state courts have weighed in on such hot-button issues as gay marriage and abortion, and have made many more decisions that were important to no one outside the parties to a particular case. Regardless of who is involved in the conflict, or how high-profile the conflict is, the bottom line is that in the American political system all conflicts at some point end up in front of someone in a black robe whose job is to decide a winner and a loser.

That job description means judges can be pretty unpopular folks in some quarters. And, as we shall see from the readings that follow, some who have been on the losing side of judicial decisions are not just getting mad. They're getting even.

One of the most notable trends in state court systems in recent years is the increasingly overt politicization of the judicial branch. Evidence for this comes in the increasingly competitive world of judicial elections. Time was that judicial elections were backwater affairs that attracted little in the way of money and partisan firepower. No more. In 2004, candidates for state supreme court raised almost $47 million nationwide. In some states the money spent on these races rivaled the cash spent in races for the U.S. Senate.[1]

The money—and the hardball political campaigns it funds—reflects the growing awareness by special interest groups of the central role of state courts in the political system. If important issues sooner or later end up in front of judges, it makes sense for those involved in those issues to try and get a receptive hearing from the bench. What better way to do that than playing a direct role in choosing the person wielding the gavel?

This increasingly open political nature of state court systems is in stark contrast to the federal system. Once appointed, federal judges can serve for life. Voluntary retirement, impeachment and removal from office, or death are basically the only limits to the job security of a federal judge. Not so at the state level. Most state judges have to face the voters in some fashion. The idea behind electing judges was to make them accountable to the people, an idea that sounds good in practice. Recent trends, however, indicate that making judges stand by the ballot box has a downside. Attack ads, mudslinging, and the rest of the less savory components of open elections are an ever more common gauntlet that must be run by those seeking a seat on a state court bench. The readings in this section will explore some of those trends, and their implications for the important role that state courts play in the broader political system.

THE STRUCTURE OF STATE COURTS AND THE SELECTION OF JUDGES

The United States is unusual in that it has a dual judicial system. This is a product of federalism, which makes the federal government and state governments (at least in theory) coequal partners. Broadly speaking, the federal courts are set up to deal with issues of federal law and interpretation of the U.S. Constitution. State courts are set up to deal with state law and state constitutions. The U.S. Supreme Court sits at the top of both systems, mainly to ensure that state courts stay within the confines of the Constitution, which as the supreme law of the land sets the boundaries of state lawmaking.

State courts, however, are not subordinate to federal courts; they constitute an independent system with their own jurisdictions. State criminal justice systems are structured by state constitutions and state law, which includes most criminal law (cases that involve violations of the law) and much civil law (cases that involve disputes between private parties). State courts thus handle everything from traffic tickets to murder and gay marriage to divorce. The state courts' caseload is staggering, with about one hundred million cases filed every year; that's a court case for every three citizens.[2]

Most state court systems are organized into a basic three-level hierarchy. At the bottom of this hierarchy are the trial courts, or courts of first instance. A trial court is where a case is initially heard: the parties involved make arguments and present evidence to a judge and often a jury. It is the job of the judge and jury to decide what the facts are and which side the law favors. Trial courts are the most numerous type of state court, and they are the workhorses of the system. Roughly thirty thousand judges, magistrates, and similar court officers serve in the state trial courts. Each year there are roughly 1,600 cases filed for every state trial court judge.[3]

Above trial courts are courts of appeal. The basic job of an appeals court is to examine whether the law and proper procedures were followed by the trial court—not to provide the losing party in a trial court with a "do-over," or an opportunity to have the entire case reheard. A successful appeal must be based on a claim that the trial court made some legal error that damaged the loser's chances of winning the case.

At the top of most state court systems is a state-level supreme court. This constitutes the highest legal authority within the state—the only place to appeal a state supreme court decision is the U.S. Supreme Court. To do so requires making a federal case of a dispute through a credible argument that some element of the state court process or state law violates the U.S. Constitution. That's a tough argument to prove, and relatively few cases make it from a state supreme court to the U.S. Supreme Court.

Although this basic three-level system serves as a reasonably accurate description of state court systems, individual states have any number of variations. Some have courts specializing in criminal or civil cases. Some have such specialized courts as family courts or juvenile courts. Some have separate appellate courts for different parts of the state. A handful of states have only trial courts and a supreme court, with no intermediate appeals courts (these tend to be smaller and less populous states).

States also vary in how they select judges to staff their court systems. The process of selecting judges is important because it must reconcile two conflicting values. Most people are in favor of an independent judiciary; we want judges to make decisions based on an honest reading of the facts of a case and the applicable law, not on the basis of partisan or political interests. It is generally reckoned that judges are less likely to submit to political or partisan pressure if they are free to make rulings without worrying if their decisions will cost them the next election or prompt the legislature to remove them from the bench. Yet while most people see this as a good reason to support judicial independence, we also want judges to be accountable for their decisions. We don't want people who can legislate from the bench and never have to face the voters.

There is no objective way to decide whether independence or accountability should take precedence when it comes to selecting judges. At the federal level, independence is put above accountability. Once appointed, federal judges serve until they retire voluntarily, are impeached for flagrant misconduct, or die. In short, federal judges are insulated from the larger political process, the idea being that life terms will make them more likely to make the "right" decisions even when it is unpopular to do so.

At the state level, though, accountability is given more of a role. Some states elect rather than appoint judges. The argument for doing so is that judges who periodically have to face the voters are less likely to try to impose their own policy preferences from the bench. The downside, of course, is that elected judges may be tempted to do what is popular rather than what is legally proper, a fear some political scientists have argued is well founded.[4]

The extent to which judges are exposed to the ballot box varies from state to state, and sometimes even within a state. Roughly half the states use a form of popular election to select at least some judges. Many of these are non-partisan elections, but a few states still use partisan ballots for judges. Most of the other states use some form of appointment system. Only a handful of states use pure appointive systems in which the governor or legislature selects judicial nominees. More states, though, use a hybrid appointment system called "merit selection." Under merit selection a nominating committee, typically a nonpartisan committee that often includes representatives from the court system and the legal profession, is charged with drawing up a list of candidates highly qualified to serve as judges. The governor (usually) or the legislature (more rarely) picks judges from the list.[5]

Judges in appointive or merit selection systems still may have to face the voters. They often have to run in retention elections, in which they run uncontested; voters are simply asked to vote whether they want to retain a judge in office.

RECENT TRENDS

An increased attention to the electoral end of judicial selection is the most notable trend in court systems over the past few years. There are two lengthy readings in this section that explore this trend in-depth. The first is by Zach Pat-

ton, and it explores how elections increasingly mean that judges can no longer avoid partisan political campaigns.

The second is an academic study by Mathew Manweller that may shed some light on why judicial elections have increasingly attracted special interest attention, and the money and tough campaign tactics that accompany them. Manweller's study suggests that the tough, competitive electoral environment may be linked to ballot initiatives. Why? Because the groups who win these direct democracy campaigns are not happy when they are challenged in court, and even less happy when the courts overturn an initiative that won at the polls. Groups that win direct democracy campaigns know a thing or two about winning elections, and they seem to be willing to put that knowledge to good use by going after state judges when they are up for reelection.

The final article is by Luke Bierman, a board member of Justice at Stake, a nonpartisan group seeking to insure a nonpartisan judiciary (you can visit its Web site at: www.justiceatstake.org/). In this article Bierman lays out why courts are different from other branches of government, and why recent trends—including the increasingly partisan nature of judicial elections—threaten its historical role in the political system.

Notes

1. Peterson, Kavan, "Cost of Judicial Races Stirs Reformers," Stateline.org, www.stateline.org/live/ViewPage.action?siteNodeId=137&languageId=1&contentId=47067 (accessed April 25, 2006).

2. National Center for State Courts, *Examining the Work of State Courts 2004,* www.ncsconline.org/D_Research/csp/2004_Files/EW2004_Main_Page.html (accessed April 25, 2006).

3. Ibid.

4. Melinda Gann Hall, "State Judicial Politics: Rules, Structures, and the Political Game," in *American State and Local Politics,* ed. Ronald E. Weber and Paul Brace (New York: Chatham House Publishers, 1999), 114–138.

5. For an overview of the selection systems see David Rottman et al., "Courts and Judges," in *State Court Organization 1998* (Washington, D.C.: Bureau of Justice Statistics, Department of Justice, 2000), NCJ 178932, www.ojp.usdoj.gov/bjs/pub/pdf/sco9801.pdf (accessed June 3, 2004).

22

Robe Warriors

Zach Patton

If you think judges should be above petty politics, try not to watch them campaign this year.

Justice Martin Johnstone's first campaign for the Kentucky Supreme Court was a big deal. It was 1996, and state judicial elections had always been small-time affairs. Judicial candidates rarely advertised on television, and fundraising consisted mostly of asking for small contributions from friends and associates within the state. But Johnstone's election became a milestone. He and his opponent, an independently wealthy plaintiff's lawyer, set a new spending record: Theirs was the first million-dollar judicial contest in Kentucky history.

A decade later, the million-dollar mark is ancient history. The race to succeed Johnstone, who is retiring at the end of this year, will be a high-spending, high-stakes event, propelled by unprecedented levels of special-interest spending and politicking more akin to a U.S. Senate campaign than an election for a state court. And it won't just be costly: It will be, in all likelihood, shrill. In the 10 years that Johnstone has served on the Kentucky Supreme Court, judicial elections have become angrily politicized, with candidates offering their opinions on issues certain to come before them on the bench. "When I ran in 1996," says Johnstone, "we were forbidden from giving our views on God, gays, guns and all the other hot-button issues of the day. This year, we're going to deteriorate into the same gutter politics that partisan politicians have been wallowing in for so many years."

The fight for Johnstone's seat isn't unique. In fact, it's more the rule than the exception. In a staggeringly short time, state judicial elections across the country have become vastly more competitive. The influx of special-interest money and influence, coupled with court decisions and legislation that gives judicial candidates more

From *Governing*, March 2006.

latitude to campaign, has drastically changed the ground rules. Judicial candidates, once perceived to be above the fray of partisan campaign issues, are no longer insulated from them. There's no question that this grants them greater freedom of speech and allows for a judicial bench that reflects the opinions of a state's citizens. But there are also signs that it is threatening the independence and impartiality of the state judiciary in America.

> *"When I ran in 1996, we were forbidden from giving our views on God, gays, guns and all the other hot-button issues of the day."*
>
> —Justice Martin Johnstone

This election year will be a watershed for state courts. Nearly 80 Supreme Court seats will be on the ballot in 30 states, with hundreds of other judicial contests further down the ballot. The perennial battlefields of Ohio, Michigan and Alabama will attract a lot of attention. So may Tennessee and South Dakota, in which every sitting Supreme Court justice is facing a vote. But an even better state to watch may be Kentucky, where a recent constitutional change has dictated that all but two of the state's 274 judges—circuit, district, appellate and supreme—must face a vote this year. As one court watcher puts it, "Kentucky is going to be as close to a free-for-all as you can imagine."

MONEY EXPLOSION

The methods for choosing judges vary enormously from state to state, ranging from appointment, in which a judge never faces voters at all; to retention elections, in which appointed judges later face a yes-or-no vote on their performance; to full head-to-head campaigns, which are nonpartisan in some states and partisan in others. More than 87 percent of the country's 11,000 judges face some form of voter scrutiny, including Supreme Court justices in 38 of the 50 states. That ratio hasn't changed much in the past few decades; recent efforts to alter the judicial selection process in states such as Missouri and Indiana have been non-starters.

What has changed, however, is the amount of attention—and money—that judicial elections receive from special-interest groups. "In the past four to six years, there's been a real explosion in this arena," says Jesse

Rutledge of Justice at Stake, a public education group that tracks state judicial spending. "Interest groups are playing larger roles than ever in these campaigns. They are seeing state courts as a place to install 'their' judges."

From 1998 to 2000, in just one election cycle, spending in state judicial elections increased 61 percent. The average cost of winning a judicial election jumped 45 percent between 2002 and 2004, to more than $650,000. The 2004 campaign year also saw the single most expensive state judicial contest in United States history. Two Illinois Supreme Court candidates combined to raise more than $9.3 million, far exceeding the previous national record, set in Alabama in 2000, when spending reached $4.9 million.

The interested organizations involved in these campaigns generally fall into two broad categories. The first involves cultural and social issues—the "God, gays and guns" groups that Martin Johnstone says used to be absent from judicial politics. More groups are pressuring judicial candidates to commit themselves on issues such as abortion and capital punishment—and then contributing money accordingly. The other interest-group battle centers around tort liability. Plaintiffs' trial lawyers, who want a judiciary amenable to generous damage awards in civil cases, are opposed by chambers of commerce and other business alliances that seek to limit what they see as frivolous lawsuits against them. In terms of spending, this category far outstrips the social and cultural lobby. In the 2004 judicial elections, direct campaign contributions to judicial candidates from lawyers and business groups totaled nearly $47 million. That's almost eight times the amount those groups donated in 1990.

But it's only the tip of the special-interest iceberg. Business groups and trial lawyers spend millions more in independent advertising and promotional efforts. "The trend now is that these groups are going much more undercover, channeling their money to tax-free 527s or 501(c)(3) groups," says Rachel Weiss, a researcher for the Institute on Money in State Politics. The groups often have vague, innocuous names, such as Justice for All, a group of trial lawyers and labor leaders that spent heavily in the 2004 Illinois Supreme Court election. In West Virginia in 2004, coal company money was used to form a group called And for the Sake of the Kids, which was specifically created to unseat a state Supreme Court justice.

The real power player on the business side is the U.S. Chamber of Commerce, which has dedicated millions of dollars in recent elections to reshaping the state-level judiciary with business-friendly judges. The chamber, which represents the interests of more than 3 million businesses across the country, has reportedly spent $120 million in just the past four years, most of it through the Institute for Legal Reform, a tax-free affiliate. All that spending is paying off: In 2004, the chamber won every single contest in which it was involved. Those triumphs all but guaranteed that spending by groups on both sides of the tort overhaul debate would continue to rise. "We're going to see more of the same for 2006, if not worse," Weiss predicts.

One reason judicial campaigns are costing so much is that they're being waged more and more on the television screen. From 2000 to 2004, the number of states that saw judicial TV ads quadrupled to 16, meaning there were ads in four out of every five states in which candidates ran head to head. Spending on TV ads in 2004 totaled $24.4 million, obliterating the previous record of $10.6 million set in 2000.

Advertising consultants and focus groups are now as much a part of judicial campaigns as they are a part of legislative elections. And the advertising is showing up sooner. As recently as 2000, television ads for judicial campaigns were clustered in the few weeks preceding the general election. Now, they are appearing in primaries. The number of

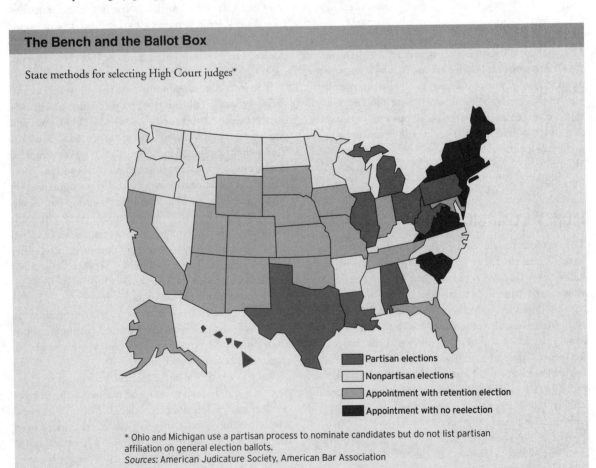

The Bench and the Ballot Box

State methods for selecting High Court judges*

- Partisan elections
- Nonpartisan elections
- Appointment with retention election
- Appointment with no reelection

* Ohio and Michigan use a partisan process to nominate candidates but do not list partisan affiliation on general election ballots.
Sources: American Judicature Society, American Bar Association

states with television commercials in judicial primary campaigns jumped from two in 2002 to nine in 2004.

Whenever in the campaign season they appear, the ads seem to make a difference. In 2004, 34 judicial elections featured some television advertising, and in 29 of them, the candidate with the most ad expenditures won.

A RACE TO THE BOTTOM

A trend that parallels the meteoric rise in campaign spending—and perhaps contributes to it—is the increased willingness of judicial candidates to voice their opinions on issues of law. Courts and legislatures have given these candidates greater freedom than ever to campaign, align themselves with a party, and personally solicit funds; in short, to behave in almost every way like a candidate for any other office. For decades, states that elect judges have imposed strict canons restricting them from discussing topics in their campaigns that may come before the bench later. But in 2002, the U.S. Supreme Court struck down restrictions of that sort in Minnesota, saying they violated the candidates' free speech rights. Subsequent lower courts have used that case to throw out similar canons in other states. Then, this January, the U.S. Supreme Court took another step in knocking down judicial campaign restrictions: It declined to review a lower court ruling (again in Minnesota) that had prohibited judicial candidates from identifying party affiliation or personally soliciting campaign funds.

The net effect of these changes is that voters will be able to find out more about the views of judicial candidates than they ever have before. That's an important—and positive—evolution, says James Bopp Jr., a First Amendment lawyer who successfully argued against restrictive canons in the 2002 Supreme Court case. "Citizens will be more informed about their judicial philosophy, and the judges will be held accountable by the people." Bopp, who also has argued successfully against the canons in other states, says the changes will help the candidates themselves. "They will now be able to fully participate in their elections," he argues. "Before, they had to stand there and be silent and hear special-interest groups talk about them. Candidates can be criticized fairly, and they can be criticized unfairly. They should be able to respond."

But critics say that lifting restrictions on judicial campaigning only leads to more special-interest money and more polarized judicial politics. Once candidates are allowed to voice their opinions, interest groups will do everything in their power to make sure they do. "Candidates are now being pressured by interest groups to take sides and engage in the kind of politicking you'd expect of a political race," says Jesse Rutledge of Justice at Stake. "There's this systemic pressure that just keeps growing and growing. It becomes a race to the bottom."

That's the fear some have in Kentucky. This past October, the state Supreme Court there relaxed its judicial campaign canons, in response to a lawsuit brought by the Family Foundation of Kentucky, represented by James Bopp. The result, says Justice Johnstone, is that the elections this year will be more caustic and more expensive. "Before," he says, "there wasn't very much special-interest participation because you couldn't get your money's worth. Judges couldn't say whether they supported your position or not. Now, we're going to see a great influx of special-interest participation."

Many of the groups that spend money on judicial contests continue to insist that there is no connection between the money they spend and the tendency for judicial candidates to announce their opinions on the stump. "There are those that suggest we want to get judicial candidates to make promises on issues," says Keith Ostrander, executive director of the Family Foundation, the group that successfully sued to strike down the canon in Kentucky. "That couldn't be farther from the truth. We simply want to establish a good dialogue between judicial candidates and the public. If you don't know the philosophy of a judge, you're just voting for a pig in a poke."

REFORM EXPERIMENT

In response to the spiraling costs and the increased electioneering in judicial elections, some states have taken steps to rein in the campaigns. High courts in Florida, Illinois, Kentucky, Ohio and elsewhere have established campaign conduct committees to oversee judicial races. These committees, typically made up of both public officials and private citizens, aren't empowered to censure candidates. But they can call attention to actions they consider unethical or improper. Other states have begun producing voter guides, profiling judicial candidates and outlining their stated positions. Still others have lowered campaign contribution limits, in an effort to attract small donors to balance the interest groups.

No state has done as much to limit the scope of judicial campaigns as North Carolina, which currently has the nation's only system of full public financing for judicial candidates. (It's also the only state that mails official voter guides to every resident.) Six years ago, the state saw its first million-dollar judicial campaign. As a result, lawmakers in 2002 went to a non-partisan election process and approved public financing for the campaigns. In 2004, the first year the new system was used, 14 of the state's 16 judicial candidates attempted to qualify for public funds; 12 ultimately did. One result was that private contributions to judicial campaigns in North Carolina fell by half.

The program produced benefits beyond the reduced expenditures, says Chris Heagarty, executive director of the North Carolina Center for Voter Education, which fought for the reforms. "There was an initial panic, especially from incumbents, but it worked to equalize everyone's fundraising. Even the candidates who ran with public financing and lost commented on the fairness of the system."

In order to qualify for public money, a judicial candidate in North Carolina must raise a threshold amount in small-dollar contributions before the primary. After the primary is over, those who accept public funding cannot take any donations from private sources. "That whole package of reforms is going to help judicial candidates stay above the political fray," says Heagarty.

Of course, there are those who believe judicial elections are better when they are more political, not less. Bopp and others argue that greater competition and more open campaigning from potential judges serve the public interest and the interest of democracy. Still, it is difficult to watch the developments of the past few years without picking up at least a hint that something unsavory might be going on. Some critics go further than that. "People now believe that if they contribute enough money, they can put judges on the bench who will be friendly to their issues," says Michael Greco, president of the American Bar Association. "It's corrosive and damaging to our justice system, and it's dangerous to the integrity and the independence of the judiciary."

Martin Johnstone is certainly worried. The outgoing Kentucky justice says the politicization of judicial elections "will seriously erode the confidence and the esteem in which people hold the judiciary." In January, even before the state's filing deadline, three candidates were already vying for Johnstone's seat. They were already out campaigning and raising money, largely unhindered by any restrictions on voicing their opinions. That, says Johnstone, is not a positive sign. "I really fear that this is going to be a new day," he says. "And not a good day for judicial politics."

23

The "Angriest Crocodile": Information Costs, Direct Democracy Activists, and the Politicization of State Judicial Elections

Mathew Manweller

Losers don't always just get mad at judges, sometimes they get even. Supporters of ballot initiatives overturned in court take their fight to judicial elections.

Between 1960 and 1998, the people of Oregon, Colorado, and California passed 127 citizen-sponsored state ballot measures. More than half of those ballot measures were challenged in court, and eventually half of those were partially or completely invalidated by state and federal courts. Understandably, those who draft and bear the costs of passing these measures become frustrated when they are invalidated by one or a handful of judges. Initiative drafters have little recourse against unelected federal judges. But state courts, to varying degrees, are subject to democratic elections and are therefore more likely to face political responses from disgruntled initiative activists. This article examines how the invalidation of initiatives by state courts affects the politicization of state judicial elections. Specifically, it is argued that initiative activists who have had their ballot measures overturned will increasingly bear the costs of challenging sitting state justices, primarily by assuming the "information costs" associated with electoral politics.

From *State and Local Government Review*, 2005.

Between 1960 and 1998, the people of Oregon, Colorado, and California passed 127 citizen-sponsored state ballot measures. More than half of those ballot measures were challenged in court (Miller 1999). In all, state and federal courts invalidated 33 of them (Miller 1999). Twelve initiatives were invalidated by federal courts, and the remainder, by state courts. Many of the ballot measures invalidated by the courts were both popular and highly salient to the public. A 2002 Oregon Supreme Court ruling in *Lehman v. Bradbury* (333 Ore. 231; 37 P.3d 989; 2002 Ore) invalidated a popular term-limit initiative. In *Amalgamated Transit*

Union Local 587 v. State (142 Wn.2d 183; 11 P.3d 762; 2000 Wash), the Washington Supreme Court invalidated a popular tax limitation measure. And in California, a federal district court, in *LULAC et al. v. Wilson, et al.* (908 F. Supp. 255 [C.D. Cal. 1995]), invalidated a popular but divisive immigration limitation provision. With increasing frequency, courts are being called upon to nullify direct democracy initiatives. Understandably, those who draft and bear the information costs of passing these measures become frustrated when they are invalidated by one or a handful of judges.

Initiative drafters have little recourse against unelected federal judges.[1] But state courts, to varying degrees, are subject to democratic elections and are therefore more likely to face political responses from disgruntled initiative activists. This article examines how the invalidation of initiatives by state courts affects the politicization of state judicial elections. Specifically, it is argued that initiative activists increasingly bear the costs of challenging sitting state justices, primarily by assuming the information costs associated with electoral politics. It can be argued that state justices are insulated from electoral reprisal because voters rarely have enough information about judicial candidates (incumbents and challengers) to hold them responsible for actions contrary to their own political preferences (Brody 2004). However, if initiative activists begin to bear the information costs in state judicial elections, there likely will be an increase in the politicization of state judicial races.

Recent political events have encouraged scholars to take an increasing interest in state judicial elections. For example, sitting members of Congress have become involved in state supreme court elections,[2] unpopular tort liability decisions have involved state supreme courts,[3] and more often, sitting justices have faced electoral competition.[4] As a result, campaign spending in judicial elections is increasing, as is the use of campaign advertisements. According to the Brennan Center on Justice, between 1998 and 2000, there was a 61 percent increase in the level of funds raised by state supreme court candidates (Goldberg and Holman 2002). Much of the money is spent on media advertisements. Even so, the U.S. Supreme Court, in *Republican Party of Minn. v. White* (536 U.S. 765; 122 S. Ct.), invalidated state measures limiting state judicial candidates from raising and spending campaign money.

All of these events have led social scientists to examine the conditions that lead to judicial electoral challenges (Bonneau and Hall 2003). The following variables have been identified: the type of institutional mechanism for electing and retaining judges (Brace and Hall 1995), the salience of issues to be ruled upon (Hall 1992), and the amount of money and interest group participation in the election (Dubois 1986). However, completely ignored in these empirical studies is the role of direct democracy activists who seek recourse against judges who have invalidated state ballot measures. The omission is glaring given that, *ipso facto,* any successful ballot measure has garnered the support of at least 50 percent of the voting public. Therefore, any judge or court that invalidates such a measure is, by definition, acting contrary to the majority will of the public. It seems logical that these types of rulings would attract the ire of not only voters but especially the activist(s) who spend considerable time and money to ensure the passage of the ballot measure. However, judges need only fear electoral reprisal if the voting public has enough information to connect the judge or court to the invalidation of the popular initiative, which typically is not the case (Lovrich and Sheldon 1984; Baum 1987). Yet, direct democracy activists increasingly provide such information to the voters.

RATES OF JUDICIAL REVIEW OF STATE BALLOT MEASURES

Fifty percent of all successful state ballot measures are challenged in court, and of those, 54 percent are eventually invalidated (see Tables 1 and 2). These rates of

Table 1 Rates of Initiative Challenge

Decade	Initiatives Challenged in Court	Percent Challenged
1960s	3 of 6	50
1970s	10 of 20	50
1980s	21 of 41	51
1990s	35 of 60	58
Totals	69 of 127	54

Notes: Data are only for California, Oregon, and Colorado. However, these states historically use the initiative process more than any others.
Source: Miller (1999).

Table 2 Rates of Initiative Invalidation

Decade	Initiatives Challenged	Invalidated in Part	Invalidated in Full	Percent Invalidated
1960s	3	0	3	100
1970s	10	5	0	50
1980s	21	6	4	48
1990s	35	8	7	58
Totals	69	19	14	54

Notes: At the time these data were published, nine cases were still pending.
Source: Miller (1999).

judicial nullification are significantly higher for state ballot measures than for either federal or state legislative acts.[5] Comparatively, state ballot measures are 54 times more likely to be invalidated by the courts. The high rate of judicial nullification necessarily draws judges and courts into highly salient political disputes threatening the political insulation so vital to the court's independence. Former California Supreme Court Justice Joseph Grodin observed, "It is one thing for a court to tell a legislature that a statute it has adopted is unconstitutional; to tell that to the people of a state who have indicated their direct support for the measure through the ballot is another" (quoted in Uelman 1972, 1147). When one judge is required to overrule the wishes of two million voters, it is unlikely that the public will respond by applauding the integrity of the checks and balances system. The rejection is felt and reacted to personally.

It is unclear whether the high rates of judicial invalidation represent a story of institutional success or failure. From one perspective, the fact that initiatives are nullified so often is a sign that America's Madisonian system is working exactly as it was designed. From another perspective, high rates of nullification raise the specter of Platonic judges acting as a supralegislature, wielding an indiscriminate scythe against the majority's will. As with most dilemmas in American politics, the answer probably lies somewhere in between the two extremes. The high rate of ballot measure nullification entails a defense of minority rights so critical to Madison's vision of what a republican form of government should entail (Read 1995). At the same time, when judges are drawn into political debates and are called upon to mediate chal-

lenges to popularly elected initiatives, there is a risk of politicizing the courts. Unlike the public in general, many initiative drafters have access to well-financed political organizations that can mobilize fundraising and voter outreach.[6] Uelmen (1972, 1147) notes that the initiative "crocodile" can be labeled the "angriest" because "the promoters of the initiative measures tend to take personal pride in their handiwork, and take personal offense when a court messes with it." Feeling personal offenses often translates into political and institutional action.

THEORIES OF INSTITUTIONAL COMPETITION

The positive theory of institutions posits that institutions react to other institutions' actions. More accurately, individuals within institutions, working in the context of some aggregation rule (voting, for example), act to prevent the encroachments of other individuals within an institutional setting. Some political analysts refer to this dynamic as political systems or separation of powers models (Clayton and Gillman 1999; Freejohn 1995). The general argument is relatively Madisonian in nature: institutions strategically react to one another in order to maximize institutional autonomy. When one institution encroaches upon the powers of another, theory predicts that the first institution will countermand such an encroachment. The literature suggests that institutions, or individuals acting within institutions, adopt strategies based on current institutional relationships. When those relationships change, the strategies also change. For example, if the Supreme Court continuously strikes down congressional enactments, the positive theory of institutions predicts an increase in congressional action to either restrict the court's power or adjust the way in which it drafts legislation.

Given the theoretical tenets of the positive theory of institutions, coupled with consistently high rates of ballot measure nullification, the behavior of initiative activists should be predictable. Initiative activists should react to judicial review by maximizing their own autonomy and limiting the autonomy of the courts (or any other institution that seeks to limit the ability of initiative activists to pursue their political goals). Specifically, in the context of direct democracy and public law, initiative activists are expected to take steps to reduce initiative invalidation rates.

THE INSECURITY OF STATE COURTS

Although initiatives may be invalidated by both federal and state courts, federal courts are insulated from backlash by the nature of the appointment process and lifetime tenure of judges. In contrast, most states employ democratic forms of election and retention of judges. Consequently, state courts are more vulnerable to recourse by political elites.

Research has shown that state supreme courts are indeed more susceptible to political pressures than are federal courts (Hall 1987; 1992; 2001; Hall and Brace 1988). State courts are more influenced by politics because sitting judges must face the voters from time to time (Richardson and Vines 1970; Jaros and Canon 1971; Hall 1987; Brace and Hall 1995). More specifically, the literature indicates that state judges are more likely to be influenced when dealing with popular initiatives and highly salient issues such as the death penalty and abortion law (Brace and Langer 2002).

Uelmen (1972) and Eule (1994) argue that initiatives present an especially difficult problem for state judges. There have been anecdotal cases in which judges have invalidated popular initiatives and were subsequently defeated at the next election.[7] Judges therefore may decide not to reject unconstitutional measures for fear of losing their seats.

Hall (1992) notes that 38 states exercise some form of popular control of judges, but not all state judicial electoral systems are the same. States use three types of judicial elections: partisan elections, nonpartisan elections, or retention elections. A few states use a combination of the three methods. Eule (1994) notes that most states that permit popular initiatives also hold judges accountable through some form of democratic election.[8]

Despite evidence suggesting that judges should be wary of nullifying popular initiatives, they do so quite often. Over half of all challenged initiatives are rejected by the courts, including highly popular term limit, campaign finance, and anticrime statutes. Yet, even in competitive judicial elections, the incumbent almost always wins. According to Hall (2001), incumbent justices receive a lion's share of the vote regardless of electoral system. In retention elections, incumbents average about 71 percent of the vote. In partisan elections, they garner 72 percent; in nonpartisan elections, 80 percent. Between 1980 and 1994, only 1.7 percent of incumbents in retention elections lost. In nonpartisan elections, the number jumped to 8.6 percent, and to 18.8 percent in partisan elections. Given these data, initiative elites might be expected to be most active in states that have partisan elections, moderately active in nonpartisan states, and minimally active in states that hold retention elections.[9] The most likely reason state judges rarely experience electoral defeat is that voters have very little information when it comes to judicial elections (Brody 2004). Given the empirical evidence, it is an informed voting public that makes a difference: It is only when judges vote contrary to the ideology of the public and the public is aware of those votes that judges face electoral defeat. As long as voters forget that a particular judge has nullified a popular initiative, the courts will remain politically insulated. Such a situation is likely, given that most judges face retention elections only once every 10 years. This research suggests that initiative activists are becoming increasingly willing to inform voters about judges and their records and thereby politicize state courts.

METHODOLOGY

The data for this study were generated by 45 confidential in-depth interviews of "initiative elites,"[10] examination of internal e-mail documents and listservs, and in some cases participant-observation opportunities.

Miller's (1999) data set identifies every initiative that passed in California, Colorado, and Oregon from 1960 to 1998 (see Tables 1 and 2). From his data set, state records were used to identify the chief petitioner(s) for each ballot measure, from whom an interview was sought and categorized accordingly. In most cases, the chief petitioner was the person or persons most responsible for the initiative's content. However, in a few cases, the chief petitioner was an honorary or symbolic figure. In those cases, the chief petitioner was interviewed to determine who was actually responsible for the content of the measure.

Miller's (1999) regional focus is expanded to include activists in Idaho, Washington, and Montana who also had been influential in passing at least one statewide initiative. Whereas Miller's data stop in 1998, this data set includes elites who were actively involved in the initiative process up to 2000. However, interviews were limited to individuals who were actively involved in the initiative process no earlier than 1990. In some cases, elites who actively participated in the 1990s also had drafted measures in the 1980s, and a few had done so in the 1970s. These interviewees were not disqualified from the research population. The time frame was limited for a variety of reasons. Individuals who participated in the system prior to 1990 were very difficult to locate. Some were deceased; those who were interviewed often were unable to remember events.

Miller (1999) identifies 60 initiative campaigns between 1990 and 1998. The chief petitioner(s) from each campaign were contacted, and the data were supplemented by including initiative elites who were active between 1998 and 2000. In total, 71 subjects were identified in the research population. From this population, 45 in-depth interviews were conducted.

The sampling procedure was not randomized. Once individuals for the research population were selected, the sample was no longer a randomized sample but rather a "purposive sample," or what Warwick and Lininger (1975) call a parallel sample. Warwick and Lininger explain that a parallel sample is needed when a specific individual must be included in the sample or when the research population is so small that randomization is irrelevant. In an effort to find subjects, interviewees were asked to help locate other initiative elites. This approach may raise the concern that the data set reflects a "circle of friends" or a "snowball" sample. However, the research population was determined before asking respondents for contact information. In addition, potential respondents were not selected from suggestions by other respondents. Each of the 71 members in the research population was contacted to schedule interviews. Several individuals were selected

based on the inordinate amount of influence they wielded. For instance, a credible sample of initiative elites in Oregon, Washington, and Montana included individuals such as Bill Sizemore, Tim Eyman, and Rob Natelson. Because it was essential to include specific individuals in the sample, more effort was made to contact and schedule interviews with certain subjects.

Using semistructured interview questions as suggested by Merton (1954; see also Merton, Fiske, and Kendall 1990), in-depth interviews provided most of the data for this research project. In some cases, data collected during interviews were supplemented: access to internal and/or personal e-mail correspondence and legal documents was offered; internal meetings were observed; or access to internal listservs of initiative groups was permitted. Access to the listservs allowed additional observations to be made of how members of an initiative coalition make decisions.

CHALLENGING THE AUTONOMY OF STATE COURTS AND JUDGES

Only in rare cases, in which the media plays a significant role in "educating" voters about a particular judge or a particular ruling, do judges face credible electoral consequences. In other words, voters are unwilling to bear the information costs associated with judicial elections. Therefore, one relatively simple and cost-effective way for initiative activists to challenge judges and courts is to bear those information costs on behalf of the voters. If voters are made aware of judicial decisions that are contrary to their political preferences, they likely will have enough information to vote their preferences in judicial elections.

Initiative activists have found four ways to bear information costs in judicial elections. First, activists can gather information about a particular judge, his or her controversial decisions, and any popular initiatives that were invalidated and release that information to the media or through grassroots newsletters. They also may release information to campaigners who challenge judges.

Second, disgruntled activists can find and support qualified candidates to run against sitting judges when their term is up. Typically, most coalitions that are formed to draft ballot measures include at least one lawyer, usually more. Because they may have been intimately involved in the ballot measure campaign, lawyers may feel an intense bitterness when their measure is overturned, and they may be convinced to run against judges who invalidated their measure. Unlike other members of the coalition, lawyers are qualified to serve as judges. These factors, together with a well-financed initiative coalition to support the candidacy, make it appealing for them to run.

Third, changing the way in which judges are elected can lessen the need for information costs in judicial elections. Some direct democracy activists are attempting to make it easier for voters to remove judges or to select judges who share voters' ideology. For example, candidates who are appointed and elected from a specific area will likely represent the political values of that geographical region. Voters are thus provided with informational cues about a judge's ideology. Voters may assume that judges from rural areas will have "rural values" and that those from urban areas of the state will have "urban values." Other activists have pursued the inclusion of a "none of the above" option in judicial elections. With this option, voters who have no information about specific candidates can still "retaliate" against sitting justices.

Fourth, symbolic measures raise awareness of issues, especially issues that reflect poorly on the courts. Many direct democracy activists assume that judges are not held accountable for unpopular decisions because the public at large has little information about how judges arrive at those decisions. Therefore, they engage in symbolic protests that attract media attention or force electoral action. For example, an Oregon activist proposed an initiative to change the state judicial oath. He accepted the fact that the measure likely would not pass, and if it did the courts would invalidate it. However, the press coverage that the measure would attract was a sufficient reason to advance the initiative.

Table 3 identifies the number of initiative elites who adopt various strategies to inform the public. Engaging in electoral campaigns is the most common approach, followed by promoting media campaigns or symbolic measures. Seeking institutional reform is the least common approach. The data are divided into three subsets. Thirteen of 45 activists (29 percent) engaged in some type of retaliation against judges or courts.[11] This percentage, though small, does indicate that not all of the proposals posed by the 45 respondents were nullified by judges. Some initiative elites successfully enacted legislation (one or more ballot measures) without ever having a court invalidate any of their proposed measure(s). These activists are not expected to expend any resources in responding to the courts.

Among activists whose proposals were nullified at least once, 12 of 38 activists (32 percent) engaged in some type of retaliation against judges or courts. The numbers show a slight but not significant increase in the percentage of elites challenging judicial autonomy. However, as noted earlier, not all ballot measures are invalidated by state courts. Ten of the 38 activists' proposals

Table 3 Types and Rates of Challenges to Judicial Autonomy

Challenge	All Respondents[a]		Respondents Whose Proposals Were Nullified by Federal or State Court[b]		Respondents Whose Proposals Were Nullified Only by State Court[c]	
	N	Percent	N	Percent	N	Percent
Media Campaigns	3	7	3	8	3	11
Electoral Campaigns	5	11	5	13	5	18
Institutional Changes	2	4	1	3	1	4
Symbolic Measures	3	7	3	8	3	11

[a]Number of total respondents = 45. Number of activists who assumed information costs on behalf of voters = 13, or 29 percent of total N.
[b]Number of respondents whose proposals were nullified by either federal or state = 38. Number of activists who assumed information costs on behalf of voters = 12, or 32 percent of respondents whose proposals were nullified.
[c]Number of respondents whose proposals were nullified only by a state court = 28. Number of activists who assumed information costs on behalf of voters = 12, or 43 percent of respondents whose proposals were nullified by a state court.
Note: The ballot measures proposed by one activist who challenged judicial autonomy were not invalidated by any court.

were nullified by federal judges or courts. Because elites are relatively powerless to respond to federal court nullifications, these activists rarely expend resources responding to the courts.

Twelve of 28 activists (43 percent) whose proposals were nullified by state courts engaged in some type of retaliation against state judges or courts. There is a substantial 14 percent increase in the likelihood of retaliation among elites whose proposals were invalidated in state court. These data suggest that these elites are quite likely to expend resources responding to state courts.

THE MOTIVATIONS OF INITIATIVE ELITES

What political pundits may call "politicizing," initiative activists call "democratizing" the courts. Most of the cases presented in this article illustrate ways in which initiative activists are trying to make the courts more democratic. They are finding new judicial candidates, they are trying to alter the ways in which judges are elected, and they are engaging in judicial campaigns in the same way they would legislative campaigns.

The culture of initiative activists attracts people who are attracted to direct democracy. Initiative fights take place in a social narrative that pits the will of the people against established and isolated political elites. It should be no surprise, then, that direct democracy advocates react most viscerally to judicial review, the most autocratic of institutions. As democratic activists, initiative activists adopt the old Populist mantra, "the cure for the ills of democracy is more democracy." From this perspective, initiative activists are simply trying to fix a "broken" system by bringing more democracy to the courts.

Unhappiness with insulated courts is not a new phenomenon in American politics. Early Supreme Court justices were impeached by the Jefferson administration. President Roosevelt tried to pack the Supreme Court with friendly judges after much of his New Deal legislation was invalidated. Congressman Gerald Ford spent much of his time in the House trying to impeach Supreme Court Justice Douglas. However, in each of these cases, Congress refrained from politicizing the courts. Jefferson's Congress refused to remove Justice Chase on purely political motives. The New Deal Congress balked at Roosevelt's power move. And Ford's work never got out of committee. In the past, the courts' independence was maintained.

The current threat to state courts is that voters will not provide those courts with the same protection that Congress traditionally has provided for federal courts. Frustrated initiative activists may turn an unpopular decision overruling a ballot measure into a referendum on the institutional design of the entire state court system. Voters, perceiving that a state court acted inappropriately in one particular case, may offer knee-jerk support for an initiative "democratizing" the court system. As of yet, it is unclear how far voters will support the attempts of initiative activists to make judicial elections more competitive or alter state court systems, but initiative activists are already trying to do so.

ASSUMING INFORMATION COSTS THROUGH MEDIA CAMPAIGNS

As an example of how information costs are borne out in media campaigns, one proponent of a controversial property rights measure (Measure 7) in Oregon said, "If they strike down Measure 7, it's war. We're going to go after the judge with everything we've got. We found out he let a child molester go on a technicality. We're going to use that against him [in the next election]" (confidential interview, April 3, 2002). Measure 7 passed in Oregon with 51 percent of the vote, but the decision was overturned by a lower court judge and eventually found unconstitutional by the Oregon Supreme Court.[12] Several ballot measures proposed by the initiative activist quoted here were invalidated, Measure 7 being the most recent. Although many of the initiatives he worked on were upheld, the courts invalidated two initiatives about which he cared passionately. In addition, he lost many lower court decisions regarding title hearings and signature-gathering lawsuits, for example. His response was to compile "opposition research" on sitting judges. At the time of the interview, this activist was in the process of identifying a select number of judges who were responsible for invalidating prominent initiatives. His goal was to create a dossier for each judge, highlighting decisions that the public might find controversial. He intended to disseminate the information in television commercials and press releases. This initiative proponent did not emphasize specific cases in which ballot measures had been overturned; rather, he focused on any decision that might reflect badly on the judge.

This strategy clearly was designed to increase the political costs to judges for nullifying ballot measures. The activist was aware that judges typically are reelected because voters have very little information about candidates, and they will not bear the costs of finding that information. To remedy the situation, the drafter acquired and processed information on behalf of the voter for his own purposes. His ultimate goal was to strip the courts of the traditional insulation that judges have in political disputes: "I don't want an independent judiciary, I want an accountable judiciary" (confidential interview, April 3, 2002).

Similarly, disgruntled direct democracy activists are able to bear information costs directly by running media commercials for judicial candidates. In 1999, the Oregon Supreme Court invalidated Measure 40, which altered many aspects of criminal proceedings. In response to this decision, attorney Greg Byrne ran for a position on the Oregon Supreme Court. To assist the campaign, Crime Victims United, a prominent backer of Measure 40, paid for campaign commercials for candidate Byrne (confidential interview, October 28, 2003). Crime Victims United assumed some of the information costs associated with judicial elections by broadcasting advertisements providing positive information about a favored candidate rather than disseminating negative information about a disfavored candidate.

In 2000, Idaho Supreme Court justice Cathy Silak became the first justice to be voted off the bench in Idaho in more than 50 years. She was the victim of two unpopular decisions: one on water rights and the other invalidating a "gold star" term limit initiative. (An Idaho term limits group had secured passage of an initiative that would have put a gold star on the ballot next to the names of candidates who had voted in favor of term limits.) Citing U.S. Supreme Court precedent in *Cook v. Gralike* (2001), Silak authored a four to one majority opinion invalidating the measure. That same year, Dan Eismann, with the help of $53,000 in independent expenditure advertisements from the Term Limits Campaign, unseated Justice Silak (Dicaire and Watson 2002). In 2002, Justice Eismann heard an appeal concerning the constitutionality of a term limit initiative. Despite calls for him to recuse himself, he upheld the measure's constitutionality.

The preceding examples illustrate that direct democracy activists inherently understand what could be termed the "law of judicial elections." That is, judges need only fear countermajoritarian rulings if the public is aware of the ruling and can associate the ruling with a particular judge or court.

ASSUMING INFORMATION COSTS THROUGH ELECTORAL CAMPAIGNS

For some activists, simply becoming involved in judicial elections at the periphery is not enough. Some activists decide to run for judicial openings themselves. Attorneys are involved in most political coalitions that draft ballot measures. They are needed to navigate the complex procedural regulations for passing initiatives and to warn drafters about unconstitutional provisions in the measure. Consequently, an existing population of opposition candidates is ready to challenge sitting judges once a highly popular ballot measure is nullified. Attorneys who are involved with drafting ballot measures often take personal offense when courts invalidate their measures, and unlike the average voter or other activists in a ballot measure coalition, they have the political qualifications to run for judicial positions. The strategy of supporting candidates to unseat judges who have invalidated popular initiatives is gaining popularity among initiative activists.

For example, in response to Judge Lipscomb's reversal of Oregon Measure 7, David Hunnicutt, the principal attorney involved in drafting the measure, ran for a judicial position in the next election. In his campaign message, he promised Oregon voters that he would be a "judge who followed the law, not wrote the law" (*Official 2002 General Election Voters' Pamphlet* 2002). Hunnicutt lost the election, with 41 percent of the vote. However, Charles Beggs noted, "The court race was high-spending by usual standards. His incumbent opponent, Judge David Schuman, raised more than $200,000, mostly from lawyers, and a family farm group with ties to OIA garnered $165,000 to help Hunnicutt" (Beggs 2002). Furthermore, the Money in Politics Research Project (2002, 1) noted that independent contributions, a rarity in judicial elections, were a relevant factor in the judicial race, noting, "The Oregon Family Farm Association PAC spent $128,000 on independently produced radio ads attacking Schuman and supporting David Hunnicutt through May 12th. During the same period, the Oregon League of Conservation Voters spent $36,500 for mailings opposing Hunnicutt. Adding the campaign contributions plus independent expenditures reveals [that] $138,000 [was] raised to support Hunnicutt and $225,500 raised by Schuman's allies."

The case of Montana's Constitutional Initiative 75 (CI-75) provides another example. The Montana Supreme Court, in *Marshall v. Conney* (293 Mont. 274; 975 P.2d 325), invalidated CI-75, a constitutional amendment that would have required public approval of all tax increases. The chief sponsor, Robert Natelson, was particularly upset with the court. In response to the court's decision, Natelson launched a statewide campaign to change the makeup of Montana's highest court. He focused his particular attention on Justice Leaphart, who was up for reelection just three years after the *Marshall* case. Natelson characterized the court as "what we call an outlier. Their direction is dramatically different than a traditional court. I've never seen anything like it in my 30 years in the law business, except maybe the California Supreme Court in the 1970s" ("Law professor challenges the court" 2002, A1).[13] The chairman of Natelson's anti-tax organization was more critical, referring to the justices as "seven black-robed terrorists" who had "overturned the wishes of 176,000 voters" (Montana Human Rights Network 1999).

Natelson's sentiments were echoed by the many state legislators who had supported CI-75. Rep. Scott Orr commented, "The court is out of control. It's time for a revolt at the ballot box." Calling for a new constitutional convention, another representative noted, "The Montana Supreme Court is a bunch of ultra-liberal supreme dictators" (Sienger 1999).

Sensing a change in the political environment, Natelson embarked on a statewide campaign to encourage lawyers to run for positions on the state supreme court. In particular, Natelson drafted a former teaching assistant, Bob Eddleman, to run for the seat held by Justice Leaphart.[14] In addition to drafting candidates, Natelson put forth a five-point judicial reform plan, which called for partisan elections in all judicial races. Jeff Renz, who was a critic and colleague of Natelson and director of the ACLU in Billings, called the plan "politicizing [the courts] to the hilt" and claimed that it would result in a loss of judicial independence (Sienger 1999).

However, many initiative proponents do not want an independent court. Having succeeded in the very populous arena of direct democracy, they are often angered by what they see as elitist courts subverting the "will of the people." Initiative drafters are starting to realize that despite the rarity of truly competitive judicial campaigns, justices do indeed have to survive in a democratic system. From the perspective of the initiative proponent, the problem stems from the fact that judges usually run unopposed. The natural strategic response is to find qualified candidates to run against judges who have invalidated their measures.[15]

Running for a judicial position, or finding others to run as proxies, challenges the autonomy and independence of the court in a more direct manner than simply broadcasting advertisements or collecting "opposition research." However, the overall approach is the same. In both instances, direct democracy activists see the dissemination of information to the general public as the key to making the courts more accountable to majority political preferences.

ELIMINATING THE NEED FOR INFORMATION COSTS THROUGH INSTITUTIONAL CHANGE

The two preceding cases offer examples of initiative activists concentrating their efforts on the electoral aspects of state courts. Either by assuming information costs or promoting opposition candidates, their goal was to increase the political costs to judges for invalidating state ballot measures. In the following cases, the initiative activists have adopted a different strategy. Rather than participating in judicial elections, they have sought to alter the judicial institution by changing the "rules of the game."[16]

Don McIntire, a successful initiative proponent in Oregon, was the chief sponsor of Measure 5, a tax reform measure that acted as a catalyst for other tax rollback measures. He was a strong advocate of the initiative system in general and felt that the courts had become too activist in nullifying initiatives. In response, he drafted and qualified Measure 21 for the 2002 Oregon ballot. The measure required, "[i]n all elections for the position of judge, 'none of the above' shall be listed on the ballot as an official candidate in addition to all other candidates.... [W]hen more votes are cast for the 'none of the above' candidate than for any other, special elections will be held in May and November, until the position is filled" (www.sos.state.or.us/elections/nov52002/guide/measures/m21fav.htm).

In the *Official 2002 General Election Voters' Pamphlet,* McIntire explained the rationale for his initiative in these terms: "We don't really vote for judges, we simply rubber stamp lone candidates. In most elections for judge, voters know that virtually every seat will list but one candidate. That's why people don't pay attention to the judges. Judges have a tremendous impact on our society, and to many Oregonians, not always for the better. Now, the voters will have a significant, democratic method of getting the attention of those who wear the black robes."

Gregg Clapper, the co-chief petitioner, made clear that Measure 21 was a direct response to the way judges had invalidated numerous initiatives. In the *Official 2002 General Election Voters' Pamphlet,* he noted, "If you get angry when some judge invents a reason to throw out a voter approved amendment like Ballot Measure 7, or when another judge reaches into the Constitution and yanks out the Term Limits amendment, approved overwhelmingly by Oregon voters ten years earlier, Ballot [M]easure 21 will provide you with a powerful way to effect a return of common sense to our sometimes autocratic and elitist judges."

Also in the voters' guide, one of the proponents of Measure 7 made a similar argument: "Maybe your issues about some judges [*sic*] decisions aren't the same as mine. Perhaps you don't care that some of our judges have gone overboard to frustrate the death penalty, or thrown out Measure 7 or Term Limits, or that they let the murdering Dayton Rodges off the hook on a technicality.... [U]se the ballot box as a means of making believers out of some of our 'untouchable' judges."

Clearly, McIntire and his supporters understood that information costs and the lack of challengers affect judicial elections. However, their response to judges who invalidate ballot measures was different from that of those who seek an electoral response. Initiative activists who become involved in judicial elections must find and finance qualified candidates on a continuous basis, or they must continuously gather information about judicial candidates and then disseminate that information to the voters. In contrast, the "solution" provided in Measure 21 was a one-step answer. Measure 21 sought to alter the system of electing judges and therefore create a permanent response; specifically, reducing the need for voters to have specific information about judicial candidates.

Based on the arguments made in the Oregon voter pamphlet, the proponents of Measure 21 felt that individuals should be mobilized when judges invalidate measures, but the power of incumbency is too strong to overcome. Therefore, people continue to reelect the same judges. By offering a "none of the above" option, voters can vote against a judge they dislike without having to vote for a judge about whom they have no information. The written arguments in the voters' pamphlet suggest that the indirect goal of the measure's proponents is to make judges conscious of the "none of the above" option and therefore aware that they will not necessarily retain their positions in a noncompetitive election. As one proponent said, "It also challenges the [judicial] candidate to earn the vote of his/her constituents" (*Official 2002 General Election Voters' Pamphlet,* 32).

Measure 21 would have contributed to the politicization of the courts. It would have required sitting justices to raise money, actively campaign for office, and consider the effects of their rulings in context with the voting public's policy preferences. The goal of initiative activists was not to accomplish the first two effects, but clearly they did want judges to consider the political effects of their rulings.

On the same Oregon ballot was a second measure, strongly supported by initiative activists,[17] that altered the way in which judges would be elected. Measure 22 would have required that Supreme Court justices be elected from regional districts rather than appointed at large by the governor (Oregon Secretary of State 2002).[18] The declared purpose of the measure was to ensure that judges represented all regions of the state. The more subtle purpose was to reduce the need for voters to bear information costs because geography can be a significant information cue. It is often assumed that congressional and state representatives represent the values of the voters from their geographic region and that the more specific a region, the more conservative the representative will be. For example, a representative from Yakima, Washington, likely would be more conservative than a representative from Seattle, Washington. From a voter's perspective, there is little need to study the voting record of each representative. The geographic region the representative hails from is enough of an information cue for the voter to make a decision.

The activists behind Measure 22 hoped to create the same type of information cue for judicial elections.

More conservative voters in Eastern Oregon could select judicial candidates from their region, creating a more conservative court, but they would not need to amass information about a judge's voting record.

ASSUMING INFORMATION COSTS THROUGH SYMBOLIC MEASURES

Some initiative activists respond to judicial activism with purely symbolic measures. These measures are designed to catalyze public opinion rather than directly affect the court system. The examples of Oregon's Lon Mabon and Washington's Monte Benham illustrate this approach. In both cases, the activists have sought to highlight their assertion that judges have ignored state constitutions when invalidating initiatives.

Most initiative proponents who had their proposals nullified argue that courts have misapplied constitutional principles or created entirely new constitutional principles. Mabon and Benham's response was to make the voting public aware of the courts' perceived activist nature. Their intention has been to educate the public about the "proper" role of judges and their state constitution. Both men have drafted and have sought to qualify measures that would have little effect on judicial behavior in the short run but would stimulate public debate about the interpretive power of justices.

Mabon was pursuing a judicial oath initiative as of this writing. The measure would alter the oath that Oregon judges swear when assuming office. The new oath would read,

Notwithstanding any other provision of this constitution every judge of Oregon law, before entering upon the duties of his office, shall publicly take and subscribe, and transmit to the Secretary of State, the following oath:

I, _____, do solemnly swear or affirm that I will support and defend the national constitution of United States of America (1789), and the constitution of the Union State of Oregon (1859). And when discharging the duties of this office I will give allegiance to no other like jurisdiction, whether foreign or domestic. I will faithfully and impartially, in a manner free of all bias, discharge the duties of the judge of said state, according to the best of my ability. I further swear or affirm that I will honor and maintain the separation of powers doctrine *and I will not use my official duties to create law from the bench; as an interpreter of the law I will not substitute my opinion or preference, or that of any social faction, for the will of the people* [my emphasis], but shall adhere strictly to the intent of the framers, both of the law and of the constitution. Where such intent cannot be discerned, I will defer to the legislative branch to provide it. I will not accept any other office, except judicial offices, during the term for which I have been elected or appointed.

The italicized words indicate the drafter's desire for a court that would defer to the will of the people, which could readily be interpreted as the will of the people as articulated in the initiatives they pass. Mabon felt that the courts had abused their discretion when ruling on challenged initiatives, acting more like a supralegislature than interpreters of the law. The initiative limits the discretion of the Oregon judges with a new oath of office that emphasizes a philosophy of judicial restraint.[19]

However, Mabon was pragmatic when discussing the likelihood that his initiative would be enforced or have any immediate effect on judicial behavior. Although he understood that the oath could not be enforced other than by the judges themselves, he believed that the initiative would promote a dialogue about the behavior of judges and force judges to become aware that voters were focusing their attention on them. He noted, "I know there is no way our courts will enforce this. But I also know that a lot of people will ask, 'Why is this initiative even on the ballot?' Once they start asking that question, they [the voters] are not going to like what they find out" (personal interview, May 15, 2002).

Similarly, Monte Benham of Washington has a similar and, most likely, ineffective strategy to challenge the autonomy of Washington state judges. Benham is convinced that Washington judges invalidate state ballot measures for political rather than legal reasons because voters are unaware that such actions are unconstitutional. He felt that judges in his state could write new constitutional law because the voters would be unaware of anything new or "contrary" to the existing constitution and that judges would have less leeway if citizens understood their own constitution better.

In response, Benham pursued Initiative 285, titled "Teach the Children." The intended purpose of the measure was to require that public high schools teach the state constitution and thereby apprise Washington residents of "the constitutional powers of the initiative drafters." If residents knew about their own constitution, they would not let judges "get away with what they do to our initiatives." Indirectly, Benham pursued the same strategy as those activists who want to bear the information costs for voters in judicial contests. The earlier examples focused on how activists want to disseminate information about the behavior of judges. In this case, the drafter wanted to provide information to voters about the limits of judicial powers in the hope that it would be used against "renegade" judges.

CONCLUSION

All of the case studies presented in this article highlight one principle: Initiative elites who become frustrated with courts or judges who invalidate their ballot measures seek to use the electoral process to restrict the power and discretion of judges. Although each case illustrates a unique way of pursuing that goal, bearing the costs of information on behalf of voters is common to all. If voters have more information about judicial candidates, the courts may become more responsive to the preferences of the public, but at the same time, state courts will become more politicized.

Initiative drafters compel the courts to consider the ramifications of their own behavior. For example, if measures implementing a "none of the above" option or requiring a new judicial oath ever were to pass, these measures likely would be challenged in court. Thus, the courts would be in a position to rule on the legitimacy of measures restricting their own autonomy and could therefore simply invalidate the threatening measure.

Nevertheless, initiative elites pursue these types of measures to attract media attention and make judges rethink their decision to invalidate measures. Even a symbolic measure that is electorally defeated or judicially invalidated can affect future campaigns. A defeated symbolic measure, such as a "none of the above" measure, may have the effect of influencing a judge the next time he or she challenges a measure on the docket.

Initiative elites who become involved in judicial elections, either by directly soliciting candidates or indirectly conducting "opposition research" and subsequently promoting media campaigns to unseat incumbent judges may greatly affect the courts. Competitive elections will force sitting judges to raise money, campaign, and engage in other political activities to stay in office. Given that the U.S. Supreme Court recently ruled that judges cannot be barred from raising money and cam-

paigning in judicial elections, the institutional setting is ripe for more contested judicial elections. The result may be a more political court and less confidence in the impartiality of the courts.[20]

Two institutional changes may serve to limit the number of judicial invalidations and, in turn, the level of frustration felt by initiative activists. First, courts could introduce the process of preelection judicial review of ballot measures. Second, constitutions could be amended to require legislatures' legal counsel to "fix" measures before they are placed on the ballot.

In rare cases, the courts have ruled on an initiative before it comes to the ballot. In *Senate v. Jones* (21 Cal. 4th 1142/988 P.2d 1089; 90 Cal), California's Supreme Court removed Proposition 24 from the ballot before election day. In general, however, most courts prefer not to rule on initiatives before they have become law. Courts tend to view these types of actions as "advisory" and outside the role of the courts. Despite resistance, the use of preelection judicial review would prevent clearly unconstitutional initiatives from ever making the ballot and thus gaining salience with the public or wasting the resources of initiative activists. If measures are rejected before elites spend thousands of dollars gathering signatures, waging a political campaign, and feeling the elation of election-day victory, the resentment may be far less than when their initiatives are nullified.

The state of Colorado requires that every ballot measure be submitted to the legislative council, a group of trained lawyers who examine it for constitutional and legal defects. However, Colorado along with Idaho, Massachusetts, Montana, Oregon, and Washington are the only states that require such review. If all states required such a procedure, legal mistakes could be rectified prior to the commitment of significant resources by initiative elites.

Indirectly, one way to limit the number of invalidations is to limit the number of challenges. The reason why initiatives are challenged so often is that the courts are the only minority veto in the process. In the legislative process, passionately interested groups have an opportunity to amend or block legislation before it becomes law. The initiative process offers no such opportunity. Therefore, angry initiative opponents often use the courts as a way of fighting initiative-implemented policy because they have no other vehicle. If direct democracy was altered to allow for minority vetoes, the process would produce less polarizing initiatives. Less polarizing initiatives would be challenged less often.

However, there is a fine line between "fixing" the initiative process and creating a parallel legislative process. Each time the initiative process is changed to make it more like the legislative process, direct democracy loses its *raison d'etre* because minority interests in the form of small but influential interest groups are permitted to pigeonhole popular legislation. Nevertheless, polls suggest that public support for direct democracy, as a general principle, remains very high.[21] Therefore, a state-sponsored rollback of the initiative system is very unlikely. Initiative drafters will continue to place measures on the ballot. Voters will continue to pass a large percentage of these measures. And if courts are continuously required to invalidate over half of all challenged initiatives, initiative elites will protect their autonomy by attacking institutions, primarily the courts. The essential component of reforming direct democracy is therefore to create a system of judicial review that does not engender the animosity of initiative elites and at the same time preserves the essence of the institution.

Notes

1. An exception is the case of Craig Holman, an activist involved in the passage of California's Proposition 208. Immediately after the passage of this campaign finance reform initiative, a federal district court enjoined its implementation for four years. In the ensuing time, a legislative initiative was passed that completely invalidated Proposition 208. In response, Holman wrote a law review article critical of the federal court's behavior. He notes, "I wrote the article out of my own frustration with the courts intervening in an initiative that I was promoting (Proposition 208, a strict campaign finance reform measure in California). A federal district judge stalled implementation of the measure for four years, until most people in California believed the measure ceased to exist and voted in an alternative measure" (personal interview, May 25, 2004).

2. The 2002 Illinois Supreme Court election pitted Republican Rita Garman against Democrat Sue Myerscough. Most of Garman's funding came from the Speaker of the House Dennis Hastert's (R-IL) political action committee. Most of Myerscough's funding came from Senator Richard Durbin's (D-IL) political action committee (see *Eyes on Justice* 2002).

3. After the Ohio Supreme Court invalidated the state's tort reform law, interest groups representing doctors, insurance companies, and business interests started raising record amounts of money for Supreme Court election races (see *Eyes on Justice* 2002).

4. According to Hall (2001), in 1980, 54.8 percent of incumbent judges faced challengers. By 1994, that number had increased to 66.7 percent. However, there was variation across types of judicial elections. In states with nonpartisan elections, the percentage fell from 56.5 percent in 1980 to 16.7 percent in 1986 but then increased to 56.3 percent by 1994. In states with partisan elections, there has been a steady rise in judicial challengers between 1980 and 1994, from 52.6 percent to 81.8 percent. In the same study, Hall also measured how often judges face "close" elections (i.e., winning with 55 percent or less of the vote). She notes that between 1980 and 1995 only 2.6 percent of retention elections were considered close. Nonpartisan and partisan races had close elections, 25.4 percent and 35.6 percent, respectively.

5. The Supreme Court nullifies, on average, only one congressional statute per two-year term. In all, the court rejected only 97 statutes between 1789 and 1972. The highest judicial veto rate came in 1963–72, when 25 statutes were rejected (see Landes [and Posner] 1975). Similarly, Emmert (1989) has studied how state courts use the power of judicial review. He has found that on average, state supreme courts hear 13 challenges to the constitutionality of a state statute per year. Subsequently, about two laws per state per year are invalidated by state supreme courts (see Emmert 1989).

6. For example, Bill Sizemore runs an organization called Oregon Taxpayers United, and Tim Eyman runs an organization called Permanent Offense. In addition, Ward Connerly has an organization called America's Civil Rights Institute, Lewis Uhler runs the National Tax Limitation Committee, and Ted Costa directs The People's Advocate.

7. For example, in 1996 Justice David Lanphier (NE) was removed from office one year after invalidating Nebraska's popular term limit initiative (see Uelmen 1972, 1148).

8. All of the states from which data were drawn have a democratic process for electing or retaining judges.

9. It is difficult to thoroughly measure the impact of institutional design upon initiative elite activism in judicial elections. Only 3 of the 10 states that employ some form of partisan election for judges have any form of direct democracy (New Mexico, Mississippi, and Arkansas). Two of those states (New Mexico and Mississippi) have never passed an initiative and therefore have no experience with judicial nullification. Arkansas has only passed nine initiatives since 1980. As mentioned in the methodology section, Arkansas, Mississippi, and New Mexico are not included in the data set. Of the states included in the data set, three use nonpartisan elections (Idaho, Oregon, and Washington), two use retention elections (California and Colorado), and one uses a combination of nonpartisan and retention (Montana).

10. "Initiative elites" includes initiative writers, high-level advocates, and organizational leaders. "High-level advocates" refers to individuals who are able to add or remove clauses to the final draft of an initiative. For example, many initiative elites do not draft their initiatives but instead hire lawyers or other activists to perform this function. However, they still have significant influence over the initiative's content and what kinds of pre- and postelection campaigns strategies are pursued.

11. Of the 13 instances, 2 occurred in Idaho, 1 in Montana, 1 in Washington, 3 in California, and 6 in Oregon.

12. The judicial politics of this case did not end with the Supreme Court's decision. The lead Oregon state attorney defending Measure 7, David Schuman, was appointed to the Oregon Court of Appeals soon after his failure to successfully defend the measure. A day after his appointment, Robert Swift, a supporter of Measure 7, filed a complaint with the Oregon State Bar, arguing that Schuman deliberately lost the case as a *quid pro quo* with Governor Kitzhaber for the appeals seat (see Merritt 2002).

13. This California court was also the subject of much controversy, and three of its members were eventually recalled by the voters.

14. Leaphart retained his seat with 60 percent of the vote. See sos.state.mt.us/Assets/elections/2002Gen/2002GenState.pdf.

15. In 2003, using a slightly different approach, angry Nevada activists initiated a recall effort against six of the seven Nevada Supreme Court justices after the court invalidated Measure 11. In 1993, the Nevada legislature failed to pass an amendment that required a two-thirds vote on all tax increases. The following year, the proposal was adopted by the voters of Nevada using the initiative process. Per Nevada law, the constitutional amendment had to be ratified by the voters a second time, which it was in 1996. However, in 2003, following a budget impasse in the legislature, the Supreme Court ruled that the legislature did not have to follow the rules enacted by Measure 11. In the ensuing months, George Harris, a member of the Nevada Republican Liberty Caucus, announced a recall effort aimed at the six judges who signed the majority opinion (*Guinn v. Nevada State Legislature* [71 P.3d 1269; 2003 Nev]). However, the effort was abandoned when Harris and his supporters realized they could not obtain enough signatures in the required amount of time.

16. For example, in 2002 the Florida legislature altered in a state referendum the jurisdiction of the Florida Supreme Court. The action was taken in direct response to an earlier Florida Supreme Court decision that overturned a ballot measure incorporating the death penalty into the Florida Constitution. In 1998, Florida voters, with over 70 percent of the vote, added a death penalty statute to the constitution. The Florida court argued that the language describing the ballot measure was misleading, and it therefore invalidated the measure. A highly critical Florida legislature reintroduced the measure in 2002 with added provisions that stripped the Florida court of much of its discretion in death penalty cases. The measure again passed with 70 percent of the vote. This example is exceptional in that the elites pursuing the initiative were Florida legislators, not a private citizen. However, it illustrates that altering the institutional "rules of the game" (in this case, jurisdictional change) is seen as a legitimate tool to rein in activist courts.

17. Dan Meeks (Oregon Measure 9) and Larry George (Oregon Measure 7) both drafted arguments in favor of Measure 22 in the *Official 2002 General Election Voters' Pamphlet.*

18. Measure 22 lost by only 14,000 votes out of 1.1 million cast.

19. The drafters of California's Proposition 115 (1990) attempted to achieve a similar goal. Section 3 of Proposition 115 required that the California State Supreme Court grant criminal defendants only the rights recognized by the federal Supreme Court. According to the primary drafter of the proposition, the goal was to "put a lid on judicial activism" (confidential interview, January 22, 2001). The California Supreme Court invalidated Section 3, claiming it was a revision rather than an amendment to the constitution. See *Raven v. Deukmejian,* 52 Cal. 3d 553 (1991). The drafting of Section 3 is not included in the data set because the drafting was not done in response to the invalidation of an initiative but rather to convey a general dislike of activist courts.

20. See "Politics, money erode US trust in judiciary" (2002). An American Bar Association poll suggests that 75 percent of citizens express concern about the impartiality of judges who raise money for political campaigns.

21. The 2000 Portrait of America poll reported that respondents in all 50 states registered greater than 50 percent support for the initiative process. In most cases, support levels were greater than 60 percent (see Waters 2003, 477–80).

References

Baum, Lawrence. 1987. Explaining the vote in judicial elections: The 1984 Ohio Supreme Court elections. *Western Political Quarterly* 40:361–71.

Beggs, Charles. 2002. Schuman keeps Appeals Court job. www.kgw.com/news-local/stories/kgw_0521_news_eln_appealscourt.a40e62c.html. May 22.

Bonneau, Chris, and Melinda Gann Hall. 2003. Predicting challengers in state supreme court elections: Context and the politics of institutional design. *Political Research Quarterly* 56:337–49.

Brace, Paul, and Melinda Gann Hall. 1995. Studying courts comparatively: The view from the American states. *Political Research Quarterly* 48:5–29.

Brace, Paul, and Laura Langer. 2002. The preemptive power of s[t]ate supreme courts: Enactment of abortion and death penalty laws in the American states. Working paper. Rice University.

Brody, David. 2004. The relationship between judicial performance evaluations and judicial elections. *Judicature* 87, no. 4:168–77.

Clayton, Cornell, and Howard Gillman. 1999. *Supreme court decision-making: New institutionalist approaches.* Chicago: University of Chicago Press.

Dicaire, Lori, and Tom Watson. 2002. Tipping the scales: How money threatens the independence of Idaho's courts. www.idahoansforfairelections.org/TIPPING%20THE%20SCALES%20report.pdf.

Dubois, Philip. 1986. Penny for your thoughts? Campaign spending in California trial court elections 1976–1982. *Western Political Quarterly* 39:265–84.

Emmert, Craig. 1989. Judicial review in state supreme courts, 1981–1985. PhD diss., Florida State University.

Eule, Julian. 1994. Crocodiles in the bathtub: State courts, voter initiatives and the threat of electoral reprisal. *University of Colorado Law Review* 65:733–41.

Eyes on Justice. 2002. faircourts.org/files/EyesonJusticeforOct24.pdf.

Freejohn, John. 1995. Law, legislation, and positive political theory. In *Modern political economy: Old topics, new directions,* edited by J. Banks and E. Hanushek. Cambridge, MA: Cambridge University Press.

Goldberg, Deborah, and Craig Holman[.] 2002. *The new politics of judicial elections.* New York: Brennan Center on Justice. www.justiceatstake.org/files/JASMoneyReport.pdf.

Hall, Melinda Gann. 1987. Constituent influences in state supreme courts: Conceptual notes and a case study. *Journal of Politics* 49:1117–24.

———. 1992. Electoral politics and strategic voting in state supreme courts. *Journal of Politics* 54:427–46.

———. 2001. State supreme courts in American democracy: Probing the myths of judicial reform. *American Political Science Review* 95, no. 2:315–29.

Hall, Melinda Gann, and Paul Brace. 1988. Order in the courts. *Western Political Quarterly* 73:391–405.

Jaros, Dean, and Bradley Canon. 1971. Dissent on state supreme courts: The differential significance of characteristics of judges. *Midwest Journal of Political Science* 15:322–46.

Landes, William, and Ronald Posner. 1975. The independent judiciary in an interest group perspective. *Journal of Law and Economics* 18, no. 3:875–901.

Law professor challenges the court. 2002. *The Spokesman-Review* (April 2): A1.

Lovrich, Nicholas, and Charles Sheldon. 1984. Voters in judicial elections: An attentive public or an uninformed electorate. *Judicial System Journal* 9:923–39.

Merritt, Bill. 2002. Measuring up to the bar. *Willamette Week Online* (April 29). www.orcities.org/currentissues/M7/m7ns166.pdf.

Merton, Robert. 1954. 1990. *The focused interview: A manual of problems and procedures.* New York: The Free Press.

Merton, Robert, Majorie Fiske, and Patricia Kendall. 1990. *The focused interview: A manual of problems and procedures.* 2nd ed. New York: Free Press.

Miller, Ken. 1999. The role of courts in the initiative process: A search for standards. Paper presented at the annual meeting of the American Political Science Association, Atlanta, September 2–5.

Money in Politics Research Project. 2002. Independent expenditures: Who's paying for them and why? Press release. Portland, OR. May 17.

Montana Human Rights Network. 1999. Montanans for a Better Government sets political agenda. Press release. Helena, MT. April 2.

Official 2002 General Election Voters' Pamphlet. 2002. www.sos.state.or.us/elections/may212002/guide/np/hunnd.htm.

Oregon Secretary of State. 2002. Official results. May 5. www.sos.state.or.us/elections/nov52002/abstract/m22.pdf.

Politics, money erode US trust in judiciary. 2002. *New York Times* (August 12): A1.

Read, James. 1995. Our complicated system: James Madison on power and liberty. *Political Theory* 23:452–75.

Richardson, Richard, and Kenneth Vines. 1970. *The politics of federal courts: Lower courts in the United States.* Boston: Little, Brown and Co.

Sienger, Cathy. 1999. Has the high court gone too far? *Queen City New Service* (Jan[uary] 22): A3.

Uelmen, Gerald. 1972. Crocodiles in the bathtub: The independence of state supreme courts in an era of judicial politicalization. *Notre Dame Law Review* 72:1135–53.

Warwick, Donald, and Charles Lininger[.] 1975. *The sample survey: Theory and practice.* New York: McGraw-Hill.

Waters, M. Dane. 2003. *Initiative and referendum almanac.* Durham, NC: Carolina Academic Press.

24

Courts Are Different

Luke Bierman

Courts are different from the legislative and executive branches. Here's why they should stay that way.

Courts are different. The role of the judicial branch in the American republic is intended to complement, not duplicate, the roles of the legislative and executive branches. Separate institutions, with unique functions and responsibilities that are executed in distinct ways, lie at the core of American governance, which is rooted in the constitutional design. For well over 200 years, America has progressed with these fundamental distinctions intact. Recent trends give cause for concern about the continuing efficacy of these guiding principles, about whether courts will continue to remain different.

Separation of powers is a principle not mentioned explicitly in the federal Constitution but is so inherent in the constitutional design that its fundamental nature is not subject to serious question. Indeed, James Madison characterized the doctrine of separation of powers as "a first principle of free government" and Thomas Jefferson recognized the distribution of political powers into separate branches as "the first principle of a good government." The distribution of governmental powers—legislative, executive and judicial—into separate institutions was essential to the republican form of government contemplated by the Constitution and, in fact, guaranteed to the states.

This principle of separation is so basic to the governmental structure that it is not possible to imagine an American government—state or federal—organized without three separate branches of government executing distinct powers. We may allow variations in the organization of those branches, such as the unicameral legislature in Nebraska or the varied hierarchical structures of state court systems, but we would not tolerate a government that did not provide

From *League of Women Voters* (Web site accessed April 25, 2006).

127

for a separate branch to execute any one of the three functions of government. Separate institutions, exercising the legislative, executive and judicial functions, simply are not negotiable in the constitutional republic contemplated by and guaranteed to the states by the Constitution.

The judicial branch then is, by design, an essential element in this system. It exists with a distinct function and presence in the political and governance system. Its role is as much to check the other branches as it is to resolve disputes in a manner consistent with a civilized society. The debates focusing on the legitimacy of judicial review, settled over the course of more than 200 years of experience, seem to have been resolved. To encroach on this function diminishes the constitutional design and the guarantee of republican principles promoting self government.

For much of the country's history, this system has worked pretty well. The judiciary, although facing periodic crises, has executed its mission as the bulwark of the Republic, as characterized by Alexander Hamilton. In the last century, in particular, a variety of tools were devised to protect the judicial function. For example, a code of judicial ethics was formalized early in the 20th century and provided judges with insulation against speaking about issues likely to come before them. This code preserved important judicial attributes of independence, impartiality and accountability. Eliminating judicial elections in favor of appointive systems, known generally as merit selection, was also viewed as a mechanism to protect the judicial function from political encroachments that would diminish its capacity to serve as a check and, hence, its effectiveness.

Moreover, the judiciary operates in ways that distinguish it from the legislature and executive, supporting its unique role in the constitutional design. Judges employ a judicial process rather than a legislative or executive regulatory process. In stark contrast to other methodologies for resolving issues, the judicial process contemplates an adversary system focused on a particular legal dispute resolved with deliberation before decision making. Judges listen to competing presentations offered in accordance with strict rules of procedure, with very precise limits on how information is communicated. There is neither lobbying in the legislative or executive use of the practice nor discussions outside the presence of an adversary. Decision making is based on the facts and law

of particular cases, derived from prior decisions in the process known as *stare decisis* as applied against the background of legislative, social and personal circumstances. It is not intended to resolve broad policy disputes, although we recognize that judicial decisions sometimes have that effect. Unlike most other public venues where disputes are resolved and decisions are made, written decisions in judicial proceedings are the norm. Often such decisions are deduced through a collegial process of give and take, whether with colleagues in courts sitting in panels or with clerks in courts sitting solo. Errors can be corrected through the appellate process or a number of other available procedures. The ethical behavior of judges is maintained through adherence to the codes of judicial conduct that specify the bounds of proper judicial activity.

These distinctive characteristics of the judicial process are conducive to the role contemplated for the courts. As a check on the branches with more broad policy making responsibility and more immediate and direct representation of the polity, the judiciary is distinguished by insulation and isolation, by impartiality and independence. Rather than reflect the preferences of the electorate at a particular time, the factions that can coalesce in the legislature and executive as warned against by Madison in *Federalist No. 10,* the judiciary relies on principled decision making for its legitimacy and authority. It is the least dangerous branch. Impartiality, long horizons and deliberation are its hallmark, if it is to remain true to the intent and design of the constitutional contemplation. For the greater part, judges are able to do just that, resolving literally millions of cases each year, most without serious controversy over the propriety of the outcome. The brilliant Supreme Court Justice Benjamin Cardozo once observed that nine out of ten cases can come out only one way.

More recently, however, the judiciary has suffered from changes that can adversely affect its capacity to fulfill its constitutional role. For example, campaign fundraising in judicial elections has escalated dramatically in the past two decades. The spending in judicial campaigns now regularly hits million dollar figures, amounts unheard of just a few years ago. The participation of special interest groups also has become routine in judicial elections; something also not seen until recently. More nefarious, contributions and participants are coming from groups organized with names that mask the true identity and intent of its founders. Likewise, the

2002 Supreme Court decision in *Minnesota Republican Party v. White* and its progeny that eliminated some restrictions on judicial campaign speech have contributed to a judicial campaign environment that mirrors the worst examples of legislative and executive elections. Judicial candidates are called upon to describe their views on controversial issues without regard to the facts or law of particular cases. They are empowered to characterize others in shameless ways in pursuit of electoral success and encouraged to employ the worst campaign tactics in order to win. While these developments allow more information into the free exchange of ideas, they do so at the cost of undermining the differences that have contributed to the judiciary's success as an independent branch of government.

Also infringing on the capacity of the judiciary to fulfill its mission in the separation of powers is the incidence and use of court stripping legislation. The use of laws diminishing a court's jurisdiction is nothing new. Indeed, the famous 1803 case of *Marbury v. Madison* that established the judiciary's ability to declare acts of Congress unconstitutional was in part about court stripping. Still, the scope and aggressiveness with which we see this conduct appears to be on the upswing, especially with respect to state courts. For example, Congress regularly has had bills introduced to remove certain kinds of cases from the federal courts' jurisdiction. However, in the last 15 years a number of these bills, aimed at controversial issues involving prison, religion and death penalty litigation, have passed. Likewise, in many states there are significant bills intended to remove abortion, criminal justice and other controversial issues from the courts' jurisdiction. Apart from the impact of these laws on allowing individuals access to the courts, traditionally offered broadly in America to ensure protection of

rights and liberties, these approaches can intimidate courts and minimize their effectiveness as a check in the separation of powers.

Other avenues of change for the judiciary are now apparent. Some groups are petitioning to alter, in significant ways, the relationships among the branches of government. For example, in South Dakota a ballot proposal would impose limits and even penalties for judges who decide cases in ways that are at odds with certain standards established by those in power. This is precisely the opposite of what the judiciary is supposed to do in our republican democracy. Indeed, it may be that these kinds of adjustments in the role of the judiciary are precisely the kinds of changes that would so alter the relationships among the branches as to affect the fundamental nature of the separation of powers. Calls to remove judges through impeachment and other means or to discipline them for the results of their decision making can not only intimidate the judiciary but also run counter to the American tradition of judicial independence in decision making. Judicial budget cuts and other reductions in the resources allocated to the courts are other means used to coerce the judiciary into reaching preferred outcomes.

In these respects, then, perhaps the current trends for the judiciary are not so different from what is happening in the other branches of government. No longer are judicial elections quiet affairs run on shoestring budgets with little controversy and limits on judicial sloganeering. No longer are the courts left to decide cases in ways that comport with the judicial process and mission of the judiciary within the contemplation of separation of powers. These are unfortunate developments if we take seriously that the design of the American Republic intends for the judiciary to be different. Viva la difference.

VII

Bureaucracy

Bureaucracy is possibly the least loved branch of government. Its image is almost entirely negative, and it is generally equated with red tape and inefficiency. Yet here's the paradox: as much as we claim to hate it, we seem to be incapable of getting along without it.

For the part of government that is most disliked, there certainly seems to be a lot of it about. Collectively, state and local public agencies employ roughly eighteen million people. And despite its popular image, most professional students of the bureaucracy agree that most of the time it does a pretty good job.[1] Actually, most citizens think so too. Ask them if they like government bureaucracy and the answer is likely to be a firm negative. Ask them about teachers in the local schools, the local librarian, the cop on the beat, or the crew down at the firehouse and you're likely to get a much more positive evaluation.

The funny thing is that public agencies such as schools, libraries and police and fire departments *are* bureaucracies. Those who work for them, technically speaking, are bureaucrats. Governments rely on public agencies—what generically are called "the bureaucracy"—to get things done. It's not legislators or executives who enforce the law or actually implement and manage the programs they pass. The job of translating the intent expressed in budgets, bills, and executive mandates into action is turned over to the bureaucracy. A reading program might be required by a state legislature, for example, but somewhere along the line it's a teacher who actually has to make that program a reality. We seem to like teachers and what they're doing, even if we do not like the idea of bureaucracy.

This paradox of not liking the notion of bureaucracy, but actually being pretty positive about the reality of it helps explain the most notable trend in bureaucracy: reform. This is not a recent trend, but more of a permanent part of the American political system. For as long as the public sector has had an extensive, professional civil service arm—and that's been more than a century—people have been criticizing it for being too big, too slow and too inefficient.[2] In other words, people have been convinced there must be a better way to run the administrative side of government basically since there has been an administrative side of government. We like the things bureaucracy does for us, we just want those things done better. The past few years have been no different.

The readings in this section highlight the role of the bureaucracy in doing what might be termed the "dirty work" of government, the detail-oriented labor that makes the expressed wishes of representative institutions reality. They also highlight the current popular responses to reforming the bureaucracy: reorganize, leverage technology and privatize.

WHAT BUREAUCRACY IS, AND WHAT BUREAUCRACY DOES

Broadly speaking, bureaucracy can be thought of as all public agencies and the programs and services they implement and manage. Most of these agencies are housed in the executive branches of state and local governments and run the gamut from police departments to schools, state health and welfare departments to public universities.

These agencies exist to implement and manage public programs and policies. In effect, bureaucracy is the "doer" of government. When a legislature passes a law to, say, set maximum speed limits on state highways, it expresses the will of the state. The law, however, will not catch speeders zipping down the highway. To translate the will of the state into concrete action requires some mechanism to enforce that will, such as the state highway patrol in the case of speeders on state highways. Virtually every purposive course of action that state and local governments decide to pursue requires a similar enforcement or management mechanism. Collectively, these are public agencies and the people who work for them—the police, fire, and parks departments; schools; welfare agencies; libraries; and road crews. In short, the bureaucracy.

The bureaucracy is not just an agent of policy. In many cases bureaucracies and bureaucrats make policy. Public universities, for example, have broad leeway to set the required courses for their degree programs. Such policies affect the day-to-day lives of millions of college students, determining where they will be on certain days of the week and what they will be doing.

Public agencies do not just shape the lives of college undergraduates—they have an effect on everyone who lives within the jurisdiction of state and local governments. Consider, for example, the role of state regulatory agencies, which, among other things, are responsible for licensing a broad variety of professional occupations. If you intend to be a doctor or a lawyer, or a barber or a bartender, you may require a state license. To get that license means that at some point—and probably on an ongoing basis—you have to take the steps required and monitored by the relevant agency as a prerequisite to licensure.

Bureaucracies are thus heavily involved in rules and regulations; it's just the nature of what they do. And this goes a long way to explaining why bureaucracy has such a negative reputation. Few people relish filling out forms at the Department of Motor Vehicles, dealing with building inspectors, or getting a speeding ticket. Yet bureaucracies do not have much choice. Laws and public programs require rules, and the job of bureaucracy is to make sure these rules are enforced. This does not always make the bureaucracy popular, and there is a constant search to find a better way for it to do its job.

This section's readings provide a variety of perspectives on bureaucracy. The essay by Christopher Swope is a classic example of the sort of thing that gets bureaucracy a bad name: building codes, which are often Byzantine, and differ from municipality to municipality. There is an ongoing debate about how to bring more state- and national-level order to these important sets of rules and regulations that vary from detailed and complex to nonexistent. And make no mistake, such rules are important. Building codes are not just a matter of rules and paper shuffling; in an earthquake or hurricane zone they may literally be a matter of life and death.

Ellen Perlman's essay tells a story of bureaucratic reform in Iowa. In this state, bureaucracies are being pushed to be more entrepreneurial by being offered the option to become charter agencies. Ironically, the idea here is make bureaucracies, well, less bureaucratic. The basic deal Iowa agencies are being offered is this: less money, but more autonomy. The goal is that greater autonomy will lead to better decision making, and better decision making will result in a more efficient agency.

A second essay by Perlman examines enterprise resource planning, or ERP. This is another take on making bureaucracy more effective and efficient, this time by leveraging technology rather than organizational change. The idea here is to set up a centralized computer system to streamline such areas as budgeting and personnel across different agencies in the same level of government. While the efficiencies this can bring to government sound good in practice, the reality often brings a number of pitfalls, which can be as much political as technological.

The final essay by Laura Coleman takes a look at one example of a common approach to making bureaucracy more efficient, getting rid of it altogether and handing over its job to the private sector. Making this example noteworthy is what is being privatized: toll roads. Rather than having toll roads under a public agency, the City of Chicago leased eight miles of the Skyway Bridge and toll road to a multinational corporation for $1.82 billion.

Notes

1. Kenneth J. Meier, *Politics and the Bureaucracy: Policymaking in the Fourth Branch of Government*, 3rd ed. (Pacific Grove, Calif: Brooks/Cole 1993).
2. Charles T. Goodsell, *The Case for Bureaucracy* (Chatham, N.J.: Chatham House, 1994).

25

The Code War

Christopher Swope

As governments move toward uniform building codes, they are being lobbied by two rival groups that offer competing sets of standards.

Public meetings on building codes are typically subdued. Which is why Glenn Corbett, a fire-safety expert at the John Jay College of Criminal Justice in New York City, found it both satisfying and amusing when a code hearing last winter in Manhattan drew a raucous, standing-room only crowd.

"This is a code person's dream city council hearing," recalls Corbett, who has been working with governments on code issues for 20 years. "The place is packed. There's code officials there wearing suits, and union guys in denim jeans with tattoos. It's wild. People are screaming and swearing. The chair is slamming her gavel, threatening to take people out of the auditorium. It's unheard of, for a code hearing."

Building codes may be the DNA of all construction, but they are also the sorts of arcane regulations that most people hardly ever think about. What made this riotous council hearing especially strange is that everybody in the room agreed on the basic issue at hand: New York City's voluminous building code desperately needed streamlining. Where the fighting broke out was on a secondary question: Which of the two "model codes" in the United States should the Big Apple use as a blueprint?

It is a question that has boiled over, with a curious ferocity, in quite a few places lately. For years, the business community has been pushing governments to standardize building codes from state to state and city to city. The goal is to create enough uniformity nationwide to lower building construction and management costs—while still addressing unique local safety issues, such as hurricanes, earthquakes or, in New York's case, high-rise buildings. If that sounds fairly straightforward, the reality is anything but. Governments

From *Governing*, January 2006.

face an intensely lobbied choice between two rival sets of codes, each of which has its own fanatical base of supporters.

On one side is the International Code Council, a group dominated by government building officers and code enforcement officials. ICC's strongest supporters include architects and people who own or manage buildings in numerous states. On the other side is the National Fire Protection Association. NFPA draws its primary support from fire chiefs and unions representing certain building tradesmen. Not only do the two code-writing groups compete fiercely against each other for state and local business, they're also suing one another, each claiming that the other has ripped off chunks of their model codes.

The feud is something of a sideshow to an important and serious task. Model codes aren't just a boon to the building industry. They're also integral to public safety. Both code-writing groups revise their codes every three years—in fact, both have just released new versions for 2006. When states and cities adopt the codes, they are getting the latest thinking on how to handle new building materials and construction techniques. Contrast that to New York City's code—which was last comprehensively updated in 1968—or to Louisiana, which had no statewide code for single-family houses before Hurricane Katrina hit. "My experience with state and local officials," Corbett says, "is that codes tend to be a very ho-hum kind of thing. But it's also one of those fundamental regulations that, when a building burns down and a bunch of people are killed, it's propelled to the top of the heap."

BATTLE LINES

The code standardization movement is actually about a century old. As you might expect, the push for uniformity arose out of tragedies. Corbett points to Baltimore's great fire of 1904 as an early rallying point. Others look to New York's Triangle Shirtwaist Factory fire in 1911. To varying degrees, cities across the country had responded to their own local disasters with homegrown codes intended to prevent similar tragedies in the future.

What evolved during the 20th century was a regionalized approach. States and cities in the Northeast and around the Great Lakes collaborated on one set of building codes. Southern states developed a separate set. And Western and Midwestern states did their own thing. Other groups, meanwhile, developed ancillary codes that were widely used around the country. NFPA, formed in 1896, wrote model fire and electrical codes. Another organization, known as IAPMO, developed model plumbing and mechanical codes.

Pressure built on the code groups to consolidate as building and construction became more of a national business. That's when the current battle lines were drawn. The three regional groups merged to form the ICC, and published one integrated compendium of codes for the first time in 2000. When talks to bring NFPA into the fold broke down, it developed a brand-new building code of its own. It also formed an alliance with IAPMO in order to offer governments another full package of codes to compete with ICC's. This was horrible news, as far as many people in government and industry were concerned. What they had wanted all along was one code for states and cities to adopt as a baseline. What they got instead was two.

The result? Governments must choose between ICC and NFPA. If that sounds mundane, consider how intense the lobbying became in Phoenix. When city councilors presented the two codes side by side in 2004, they couldn't believe the volume of e-mail messages that poured in. NFPA supporters besieged residents with automated phone calls, claiming that the NFPA codes were safer. ICC, meanwhile, ran a full-page ad in the *Arizona Republic*. As in New York, council hearings were jam-packed with partisans on both sides. After leaning initially toward NFPA's codes, Phoenix ultimately picked ICC. "I've been in the code business 38 years," says Larry Litchfield, of the Phoenix development services department. "There was more attention to this code adoption process in Phoenix than anything I've ever seen."

A similar story unfolded in California, where a rewrite of the statewide building code is now underway. In 2003, the California Building Standards Commission selected NFPA's model code as its baseline. Given the state's size, California's decision sent shockwaves through the building industry. Other than a few small localities in Texas, Maine and Illinois, the Golden State was the first jurisdiction to adopt NFPA's new building code. At the time, the Building Standards Commission consisted mostly of Democratic Governor Gray Davis' appointees. They were largely seen as sympathetic to labor unions, who generally favored the NFPA codes.

NFPA's big victory was short lived, however. Within months, voters recalled Davis in favor of Republican Arnold Schwarzenegger, whose appointees changed the commission's outlook. After several tense hearings last winter, the commission reversed course in March. It dropped the NFPA codes in favor of ICC's. NFPA called the change "a purely political move." Not surprisingly, ICC called it a step forward for public safety.

MIX AND MATCH

To understand the battle between NFPA and ICC, it is useful to avoid thinking of the two groups as associations of code geeks. Rather, think of them as two publishing houses engaged in a war for book sales. Codebooks are a big business in the United States and abroad. When a city or a state adopts one model code or the other, it means that thousands of code officials, architects, engineers and others must purchase new copies to keep on their desks. In 2004, NFPA pulled in $58 million from publication sales, while ICC earned $25 million. (Both are nonprofits.)

Both organizations can make big claims when it comes to their influence. That's because jurisdictions commonly mix and match certain codes from each group. NFPA's electrical code is the single most widely used model code in the world. As far as building codes go, however, ICC is way out in front, with its code in use in 45 states. The building industry views ICC's building code the way most consumers view Microsoft's Windows: It's seen as eccentric and risky to test the alternatives. ICC is also helped by the star power of its CEO, James Lee Witt, the former FEMA director who took the job in 2003.

While partisans will claim one code to be better than the other, neutral observers generally agree that both are sound. "Building codes are based on physics," says Phoenix's Larry Litchfield. "That doesn't change from one book to the other." The major difference between them is a procedural matter relating to the way they update their codebooks. This, too, is a fine point. But considering that each group writes codes that are used across the country, it is an increasingly important process that receives very little outside scrutiny.

Both ICC and NFPA update their codebooks at conventions of their members. In each case, anybody—members or not—can propose a code change. What's different is how the two groups vote. At ICC, only building officials from government are allowed to vote. ICC believes this prevents special interests, such as trade unions or manufacturers of building materials, from advancing hidden agendas through the building code. By contrast, NFPA opens up voting to all of its members—although checks and balances theoretically prevent any one special interest from commandeering the code.

The difference in voting procedure explains why the fire services and trade unions generally support NFPA over ICC. "At NFPA, professional firefighters have a place at the table," says Peter Gorman, President of the New York City Uniformed Fire Officers Association. "The NFPA code addresses building safety from a firefighter's perspective." This also explains another curious wrinkle in the fight between NFPA and ICC—an oddly heated debate over plastic pipe that rears its head in one state after another.

ICC codes generally allow plastic pipe to be used in a building's plumbing system; NFPA codes generally do not. NFPA's stance reflects worries firefighters have about the fumes plastic pipe gives off when it burns. It also reflects some job-related concerns of plumbers. Plastic pipe, it seems, is easier for do-it-yourselfers to work with. More plastic pipe means less work for professional plumbers. That's why plumbers turned out in force at that heated New York code hearing. "The national plumbers union is extremely political," says Patricia Lancaster, the head of New York's buildings department, who is spearheading New York's code re-write. "The plumbers' storming of the first hearing was noted by a number of city council members."

> *"The plumbers storming of the first hearing was noted by a number of city council members."*
>
> —Patricia Lancaster
> Head of New York's Buildings Department

WINDOW FOR REFORM

The plastic pipe question is only one of hundreds that New York has to sort out. Over the years, the city's building code metastasized to the point that it spawned a cottage industry of consultants and "expediters" to help businesses decipher it. Tragically, the collapse of the World Trade Center towers opened a window for reform. Mayor Michael R. Bloomberg ordered an overhaul in 2002, riding an outpouring of goodwill that has, with a few exceptions, quelled political squabbling.

New Yorkers usually take pride in being different from the rest of the United States. But in the case of its building code, New York City officials have come to believe they might be better off looking a lot more like other states and municipalities. Bloomberg appointed a commission to weigh the ICC building code versus the NFPA code. It settled on ICC, largely because it's what most other governments are using.

What has been going on ever since is a painstaking line-by-line vetting of the old code and the ICC code. New York wants to keep some of the tougher provisions from its existing code, particularly those pertaining to high-rise buildings. To sort through it all, some 400 executives and technical experts from all parts of the building and construction industries have volunteered their time. They've divided into 13 committees and 72 subcommittees, and keep track of each other's work using a special Web site set up by the Buildings Department.

There are hundreds of examples of absurd local legacies that will disappear from the building code. Lancaster's favorite one is the initials used to designate "office occupancy" and "residential occupancy." "In the 1968 code,"

she says with disbelief, "office is called 'E' and residential is called 'J'." The new code, following ICC conventions and common sense, will call office "O" and residential "R." Lancaster says that New York may amend the code in ways that make it different from the rest of the country, "but for the most part we'll all be talking about the same thing."

As the committees were quietly working through arcane details, however, NFPA and its allies were lobbying the city council. The push was strong enough to persuade the council to revisit the city's original choice of the ICC codes. That's when the unruly code hearing happened. One plumber after another stood up to testify to the superiority of NFPA's code-writing process. As Karen Headley, a member of the major plumbers' union put it, "Don't you think that someone like me, with years of experience working in construction, would have some valuable input when it comes to safety codes? ICC doesn't really care what I think."

In the end, the plumbers' concerns were resolved. The code was amended to limit the use of plastic pipes to certain circumstances. The council went on to unanimously approve the first part of the code re-write in November, by a vote of 48 to 0. Lancaster hopes that the rest will be finished by next year.

At last, it seems, New York's bitter debate over model codes is winding down. Just about everyone involved is relieved. "If it were NFPA, it'd be perfectly fine," says Professor Corbett, who serves on one of the technical code committees. "The fact is that years ago, we picked ICC, and that's the horse we're riding.

"To tell you the truth," he adds, "I wish we didn't have two building codes."

26

A State Shapes Up

Ellen Perlman

With a bureaucracy grown rigid and rule-bound, Iowa is pushing its agencies to act like entrepreneurs.

From *Governing,*
November 2005.

I t was a harrowing highway moment. An official from Iowa's Department of Corrections was driving an agency van when he had a high-speed encounter with a deer. While the official was unhurt, neither the deer nor the van survived. That accident could have resulted in a secondary trauma: a delay of up to eight months to replace the van. Under Iowa's traditional procurement rules, all agencies had to use the state contract to buy vehicles—a process that often added months to the transaction.

Rigid rules such as these can be a major drag on agencies and their ability to do their jobs efficiently. But they can also be something else. In Iowa, they've become the impetus for a movement to shape up state government through entrepreneurship.

MAGNA CHARTER

One of Iowa's main—and most successful—thrusts is in chartering its agencies. Under this system, which got underway in 2003, agencies were offered a trade-off: If they volunteered for the program, their annual appropriation would be cut, but in return, they would get more flexibility in how they operate. Here was a chance not only to cut red tape but also to break away from a learned helplessness that a government can impart.

Participating agencies are exempt from any mandated across-the-board budget cuts, but they have to commit to producing measurable benefits and to helping close the state's budget gap—either by saving money or earning revenues. To achieve those goals, they are given incentives to act entrepreneurially. They can, for instance, retain proceeds from asset sales as well as 80 percent of new revenues

138

they generate and half their year-end general fund balance. Those are privileges few agencies in any state can lay claim to.

Five Iowa agencies volunteered for the charter movement—corrections, human services, natural resources, revenue, and alcoholic beverages—as well as the state's veterans home. All totaled, the volunteers represent nearly 30 percent of appropriated state funds and 50 percent of executive-branch employees.

For the corrections department, becoming a charter agency meant taking a $2.5 million cut in funding over five years. But the payback was nearly immediate. A few weeks after the department signed on to become a charter agency, the governor ordered across-the-board cuts in all agencies except those exempted through their charter status. If it weren't a charter agency, corrections would have lost $6 million from its budget right then and there.

Then, when the deer incident happened, the agency enjoyed another benefit. It didn't have to wait months for a state purchaser to get the van deal. DOC buyers marched right down to an auto dealership and made arrangements for quick delivery and at the same price the state had negotiated on the contract.

The charter privileges have jolted participating agencies into thinking differently. For example, the Department of Human Services had no impetus to sell residential facilities that were sitting idle and were likely to stay that way. As department officials saw it, the only thing they had to gain from a sale was a potentially large political headache. But as a charter agency, DHS had the chance to keep some of the money from the sale. That put the agency into a deal-making mindset.

Similar activities are going on in the other charter agencies. The director of the Department of Natural Resources is heartened by the exemption from legislatively set staff limits. Under normal budget appropriations, the department would be given a ceiling for the number of full-time-equivalent employees it can hire. Even if the department got additional funding through federal grants, once it hit its staffing limit that was that. Not so anymore. "The beauty of it is we now hire based on the ability to deliver a product, whereas before it was artificially limited," says Jeff Vonk, DNR's director.

The agencies now are looking at results rather than rules. "It's got them thinking about what they can do, not what they can't do," Jim Chrisinger, a team leader at the Department of Management.

COMPETITION'S EDGE

Two years ago, as part of its experiment in entrepreneurial government, Iowa combined four agencies that provide services to other agencies and changed the rules about who has to buy services from those providers. State agencies still have to purchase "utility services," such as heat, rental space and custodial services from the state provider, but they can buy other "marketplace services"—such as conference planning, surplus property, motor pool and repair services—either from the state or elsewhere.

What this means is that service divisions that used to automatically get business from other government agencies have to prove they are worth using. Their survival depends on it: Those agencies no longer receive legislative appropriations to provide their services. In trying to woo customers, the agencies will have to improve the quality and prices of what they offer—or go out of business.

That pressure has radically altered the business practices of the state print shop, which had been losing money on an annual basis. In order to be more competitive, the shop halved the number of employees and sold an underperforming offset printing operation to the state's prison industries. The print shop appears to be headed for a bottom line in the black this year—and it is attracting customers.

THE REPLICATION ROUTE

Iowa is borrowing a page from Washington State's budgeting playbook and purchasing results rather than funding departments. Administration officials look at the entire budget, set priorities and apportion spending by starting at the top of the list. When money runs out, funding is cut off and whatever was at the lower end of the list is out of luck. The idea is to get away from the "we're funding because it's always been funded" attitude.

To assess quality and progress, Iowa holds quarterly meetings during which departments meet with the governor and lieutenant governor. Discussions revolve around specifics: how things are going and what the department can do better. That's an idea borrowed from Baltimore, where the mayor holds regular meetings with agency heads to grill them on the progress of specific performance measures.

The state hasn't only turned to other governments for ideas. In its use of something called "kaizen," it is emulating business practices. The Japanese word means "continuous improvement," and the practice started in the manufacturing world as a way to boost productivity. In Iowa, it has meant putting agency people in a room and having them examine how they conduct their business. The point is to find ways to cut waste so money can be redirected to areas that are causing public dissatisfaction or frustrating agency personnel.

It's not as touchy-feely as it sounds. Before the DNR scrutinized how it was operating, staff took an average of 63 days to turn around a basic air-emissions permit, something businesses need before they get a new construction permit. The department mapped out its process, identifying areas of wasted time and areas of efficiency. "We eliminated dead time in the process," says Vonk. Within a week, the department had a streamlined process, and it now takes less than two weeks to issue a new permit. Similarly, over at Human Resources, officials went into a kaizen huddle and were able to shrink the time it took to renew a social worker license from 21 days to two.

Not all of the administration's flexibility experiments have worked out well. An effort to improve state-local relations, by offering municipal governments more leeway to raise taxes and fees in exchange for cuts in state aid, failed when the legislature reduced aid to localities but granted them almost no new revenue-raising authority.

Meanwhile, some chartered agencies have found that not every rule is meant to be broken. In some cases, the rules that everyone wanted to buck proved to have a useful purpose. That was the case when the DHS wanted to hire top people and pay salaries above the norm for the state. "Salary is a known entity in the public sector," says Mollie Anderson, director of the Department of Administrative Services. If one person is paid a lot more, others can become disgruntled. "There are some reasons why we have the rules we have," she adds.

For the most part, though, the state will be looking at charter agencies to see how the experiment has worked. "If it's good enough for them," Anderson says, "maybe we should think about it for the rest of our customers."

27

The ERPWORKS

Ellen Perlman

Recoding the guts of an enterprise can bring a city or state to the brink of failure, fatigue and notoriety.

"It's not for the fainthearted." David Otto, an information systems manager for the city of Tacoma, Washington, is talking about his city's experience installing a complex centralized computer system—an enterprise resource planning project or ERP, for short. In the nearly two years it's taken to replace 102 legacy computer processes with the new system for billing, financials and other administrative tasks, he and other city officials have been battered by battles with unhappy employees, the press and the city council, which was not happy when told there would be additional expenses for the $50 million system.

At least Otto can commiserate with several other large cities and states. From Arkansas to Iowa to San Antonio and beyond, ERP implementations have been tripped up and nearly deep-sixed by problems ranging from poor project management to under-trained employees to nasty political infighting.

That hasn't stopped states and localities from taking off down that rocky road. Faced with ailing computer systems, many large governments want to gain the efficiencies and advanced capabilities that can come with centralizing human resources and budgeting data and other technology software. When it is done correctly, employee productivity improves and information is better organized and more accessible to departments and policy makers. "You almost can't imagine running without this kind of software," says Joshua Greenbaum, of Enterprise Applications Consulting, a software analysis and consulting firm.

Governments may be buying a better mousetrap, but as they install it, they have to deal with users' fingers getting snapped and springs popping off here and there. For both human and technical reasons,

From *Governing,*
May 2005.

rolling out an ERP system is an arduous and long-running task—in both the public and private sectors. "These projects are the most complex human endeavors we undertake this side of building a bridge, a canal or the space shuttle," Greenbaum says, adding that large business organizations get it wrong "all day long." Unfortunately for governments, their missteps are scrutinized more closely and publicly. Even so, Greenbaum says, an ERP system "works much more often than it fails."

That said, failure or even its close approximation is messy. Arkansas' ERP experience, which began in 2000, is a case in point. There were technical hiccups: When the payroll piece of the system was rolled out, more than 500 state employees failed to get their paychecks; several vendors were not paid on time. There are legal tangles: Two employees sued the state, claiming the system was not accessible to the blind. Arkansas turned around and sued SAP, the vendor. But the state didn't limit its suit to accessibility. It also claimed that SAP had failed to provide a performance-based budgeting module as contracted and that the regular budgeting module it did provide didn't function up to expectations. SAP disputes the state's contentions. A trial date has not yet been set.

And there's been intra-governmental finger-pointing and fault-finding. Even as the project began, the top legislative leaders in the House and Senate, both Democrats, questioned whether Republican Governor Mike Huckabee gave authority for the project to too many people. Randall Bradford was hired as chief information officer in October 2001 to help fix the already troubled system. After he gave two weeks' notice in June 2002, he was fired, wrongly, he contends, for declaring he was going to publicly reveal problems with the ERP system.

Now that there is a lawsuit involved, most officials in the administration decline to speak about the ERP project on the record. One who will is Arkansas Attorney General Mike Beebe, who is running for governor this year. He questions the integrity of the project, cites lack of performance on the contract and criticizes the implementation as "slow, complicated and labor intensive."

Then there's the secretary of state. More than two years after the $60 million system was put in place, Charlie Daniels is using his own accounting software, which he finds superior to the state's new system.

THE LEARNING CURVE

Most ERP implementations are not as troubled as Arkansas'. But almost all face significant problems and major stumbling blocks. The slip-ups can begin very early in the process. Sometimes specs for the project are written incorrectly, the government isn't really clear about what it wants, or the vendor tries to oversell the product. Or once the project gets underway, officials start suggesting additional tasks for the system, leading to "scope creep," which means additions, changes and more expense. "The software," says Greenbaum, "is almost never at fault."

Projects also falter if there isn't visible leadership, consensus among those who have a stake in the project and good communication and marketing. And even when such pieces are in place, a city or state may not be prepared for change-management issues. "Most leaders do not adequately anticipate the amount of frustration and the change required," says Mollie Anderson, director of the Department of Administrative Services in Iowa, which is putting an ERP project in place.

Inadequate training is the subtext to many failures. Tacoma knew that and thought it had training under control. It had set up a four-month training program that was almost university-like in its approach. Some 1,700 "students" attended courses that were available all day, every day and some nights and weekends. And attendance at key courses was not exactly voluntary: Users could not get access to the system until they went through the training.

And yet, as the city started to implement several functions at once—a finance system and a billing system, followed quickly by business warehouse and management modules—an employee backlash flared up. City employees complained that they couldn't figure out how to do their jobs under the new system. The local press got wind of the workers' frustrations, investigated the ERP project and found, according to one reporter's story, that the city had designed a project that was too large to succeed, had refused outside oversight and had failed to give employees adequate training.

Otto takes issue with the findings but sees that the training program was not ideal. People were being taught to use the new system even as that system was still being configured.

Some ERP glitches come from a government being too ambitious, a phenomenon that is akin to trying to boil the ocean. And just as productive. "Doing too much is a recipe for disaster in enterprise software," says Joshua Greenbaum of Enterprise Applications Consulting. Tacoma, Washington, he says, fell into that trap. As he sees it, the city tried to do way too much and all at once by putting into play four applications within a two-month period.

Tacoma officials see it differently. They looked at the choices at hand. They could either go with a big-bang implementation or phase in various ERP applications over time. They went for the cost savings of a comprehensive startup. A phased implementation might have been less risky, says David Otto, the director of Business Information Systems for the city, but it costs money to build and unbuild technology bridges to legacy systems if each piece of the project is done separately.

Another trap is trying to customize the software too much. The less tailoring a city or state does for a particular function or agency, the more likely it is to achieve a positive return on its investment. Tacoma knew this going in but couldn't avoid fine-tuning software for the billing process for five different utilities. But customizing means that software has to be tested separately and that is time-consuming and costly. And then, when the vendor updates its product, modifications have to be made all over again.

Some customizing can't be avoided. But if you do too much of it, says Bev Wheeler, industry principal with SAP, "you end up with a brand-new legacy system." In some cases, governments that do too much tailoring of software might never be able to upgrade the system, either because it becomes too expensive or new software releases come with architectural changes that preclude updates and improvements to customized applications.

Iowa, too, ran into employee-based problems. During the first few months on the system, productivity faltered by as much as 40 percent. Vendors who had received payment within 15 days under the old system, for example, were now waiting 45 days. The chief financial officer for the Workforce Development Office complained that his agency's trust and confidence had been "shattered."

Anderson says things have improved since then but that the state learned that it had to go beyond just training employees. It needed to involve users in testing the design of the system to make sure it made sense for how they do their jobs. With the average state worker 44 years old, most people using the old system had settled into a comfortable familiarity with what they did. The new system, however, required employees to do a lot more data entry than they were used to doing. Previously, for instance, a central office took care of accounting. Now individual departments are responsible for it. That's a workload change tied to a new way of doing business, and employees have to be prepared for the change.

TAKING CHARGE

While the need for training cannot be underestimated, neither can the importance of project management. Iowa admits it didn't get that right either at first, and only realized it when things started to unravel—the project slipped in terms of being on time and on budget. Moreover, agencies—the system's customers—started complaining about various functions. Administration department officials couldn't get straight answers when they made inquiries. The number of change orders—requests to do something different than originally planned—was increasing.

Enough clues emerged for Iowa to realize the project needed an overall manager. There were people managing the technology and others overseeing different modules that were being put in place. But no one was watching out for the entire project—dealing with change orders, making sure things were completed on their due dates and taking action if things started to slip. "You need someone who manages from start to finish," Anderson says.

Denver also began its ERP project without a strong ERP manager or chief information officer. Without such key players in place, the city was not equipped to manage the complexities of the upgrade of its payroll system. Inaccurate balances in accounts and other problems surfaced. "We never missed a payroll," says Mike Locatis, the CIO who came on board after the project was underway. "But confidence in the system went way down."

STICKER SHOCK

Ballooning price tags have bedeviled many an ERP project. In San Antonio, the mayor and the council complained that project staff were not updating them on progress or the lack of it. According to an investigation by the local paper, the project director said the project was keeping to its budget, while costs were being tucked into other areas so the overruns didn't look so dramatic.

> With a project that already costs $50 million or more, city councils don't like to be blindsided by overruns.

Tacoma also had a price-tag issue. Early on, Otto explained that there would be additional and ongoing operations and maintenance costs but concedes he presented that aspect of the project to policy makers only once or twice, while the original estimate of $50 million was discussed at every meeting.

Later, the council was unpleasantly surprised when it learned there would be a higher operating budget for the new system than there had been for the old one. Project managers could have kept council members better informed about present and future costs. "It was sticker shock," Otto says. "We didn't do a good job at really hammering home that there were going to be ongoing costs."

Iowa didn't do well anticipating how much staff time would be needed in the construction phase. There is a substantial cost for staff as they work with a contractor. There may be an unconscious don't-want-to-know aspect to the calculations. "The fear is that if you fully articulated all those costs, no one would appropriate the money," says Anderson, adding that no one was purposely deceitful and that it's a lot like calculating the cost of having a family. "When you get into it, it costs more than you thought."

Despite all the ERP tribulations, there's no point for a government to cower in a corner and avoid an overhaul. Change brings angst, but most ERP projects eventually work. Besides, there is a price to pay for waiting until a system falls to pieces and for the inefficiencies that can be the hallmark of clunky old systems. The important mindset for revamping systems with ERP, Denver's Locatis says, is to approach it with "eyes wide open."

28

Toll Roads Tip
to Privatization

Laura Coleman

Indiana's 'major moves' may
signal a trend for maintaining
some state highways.

Chicago's decision in 2004 to lease the Skyway Bridge for 99 years
to a private corporation introduced the notion of toll road privatization in the United States. It was the first example of privatization
of an existing United States toll road.

It also raised questions for state officials to consider. Is the private
sector emerging as a viable alternative to state operation of toll
roads? Will leasing toll roads benefit motorists? What will be the
fiscal impact on states? In return for $1.82 billion in upfront cash,
the city turned the eight-mile Skyway Bridge and toll road over to
the Spanish-Australian consortium of Cintra-Macquarie beginning
in January 2005. Cintra operates and maintains the bridge and has
the flexibility to raise tolls.

THE EVOLUTION OF HIGHWAY FUNDING

While the discussion about privatizing highways has recently hit the
political forefront, toll roads have existed in the United States since
the late 18th century.

By the mid-1950s, most limited-access highways in the eastern
United States were toll roads. At the same time, the U.S. Interstate
Highway System was established. The program financed the construction of new limited-access highways with 90 percent federal
dollars and 10 percent state funds, which limited states' motivation
to expand their toll systems.

The main source of federal highway funding was the Highway
Trust Fund and most of that money came from fuel taxes specifically directed toward highways. There was a tight linkage between
the source of funds and projects, including highway construction

From *Statenews,*
April 2006.

and maintenance. That linkage, however, has broken down over the years, according to Sujit CanagaRetna, senior fiscal analyst with CSG's southern region, the Southern Legislative Conference.

"There has been a diversion of funds toward general projects—mass transit, and so-called 'pork' projects—instead of purely highway projects," said CanagaRetna. "And with fuel taxes becoming inadequate to deal with the rising need for additional roads and highways, you had a bit of a lopsided equation where demands for roads were increasing steadily. On the flip side, the source of funds was dwindling."

States had problems raising additional revenue, and Congress consistently refused to raise gas taxes—the last time those taxes were raised was in 1993. Those factors, said CanagaRetna, have spurred the notion of toll roads as a potential source of additional revenues.

STATE PRIVATIZATION PLANS

Indiana Gov. Mitch Daniels is possibly the person most responsible for the emergence of the privatization issue in state capitols. Daniels' plan, Major Moves, would use revenue for the lease of the Indiana Toll Road to fund the Indiana Department of Transportation's 10-year road plan, which includes developing new infrastructure across the state.

Cintra-Macquarie, doing business as Statewide Mobility Partners, won the bid for the 75-year lease for $3.85 billion upfront and $4.4 billion in improvements along the 157-mile Indiana Toll Road. The contract recently has passed Indiana's legislature.

Under Major Moves, Indiana would spend $150 million over the next three years to help local communities pay for road maintenance and repair. Daniels has also pledged to oppose any attempt to divert Major Moves revenues to other areas of the state budget. Without privatization, the state would make an estimated $7.5 billion in the next 75 years, but would also remain responsible for highway maintenance and upgrades.

Indiana has an estimated $2.8 billion in road projects pending, and the state says it can afford only about half those projects. Daniels expects privatization to make those projects possible and alleviate the need for increased gas taxes. However, the proposal allows an increase in the cross-state passenger car toll from $4.65 to $8, with future increases pegged to inflation.

SURVEY SAYS...

Although the public has been slow to come around to the idea, many transportation experts agree privatization is sound policy. However, Bob Poole, director of Transportation Studies for the Reason Foundation, warns that windfall amounts of revenue provided by public-private partnerships can be a double-edged sword.

"Large sums of money can lead to spending on ill-advised projects. But privatization leads to more professional, business-like management. It's useful for people to step back and take a different look at this phenomenon," said Poole. "Think about how we accept privately-owned utilities—gas, water, telecommunications. In a fundamental way, limited access highways that lend themselves to charges would be similar to these infrastructures. It is not really different in terms of the kinds of expertise required to build, manage, market and finance. They are all long-lived infrastructures that serve a vital public need."

Experts also project better customer service as a result of privatization. Peter Samuel, a journalist and researcher specializing in toll roads, wrote a report that contends privatization allows for the management of toll roads "to be free to take initiatives to market the toll road, hire and fire staff, and adjust services provided according to what customers are prepared to pay for."

State toll authorities tend to leave toll rates frozen for many years, said Samuel, and then suddenly drastically increase those rates. This so-called "price earthquake" leads to unnecessary disruption, he said.

"Traffic, particularly trucks, tends to divert onto local roads, at least for some months or a year or two after the big toll rate hike," he said. "There is great local annoyance, there are more accidents, and transport efficiency is reduced with trucks traveling on much slower roads."

Private companies monitor and adjust prices more regularly and in smaller and less disruptive increments, according to Samuel. Most companies adjust rates in line with inflation.

Poole agreed the key difference between privatization and keeping toll roads in state hands is that the private sector is more diligent about keeping tolls in sync with inflation. "Toll roads went from being in a position to generate surplus revenue to failing because of not raising tolls," he said. "Placing the roads in the hands of a private company depoliticizes business management decisions. This is difficult to do in the public sector."

Privatization in Other States:

- **Virginia:** The 14-mile Dulles Greenway is owned by TRIP-II, a company owned by local investors. In the past five years, traffic has increased to such an extent that the Greenway is being widened.
- **California:** SR 125-South, a 9.3-mile toll road along the eastern fringe of the San Diego metro area, is owned by the Australia-based Macquarie Infrastructure Group. It will connect area freeways and provide an alternative for international traffic. It is expected to cost about $650 million.
- **Texas:** A CINTRA-led group has been chosen by the Texas DOT to build 316 miles of new toll road, The Trans Texas Corridor-35. Construction is likely to begin in the next two years.

—Peter Samuel, "Should States Sell Their Toll Roads?" Available in PDF at www.reason.org/ps334.pdf

PRIVATIZATION CRITICS

Some critics of leasing toll roads consider the practice symbolic of America being sold, piece by piece. Others are concerned that if the private company goes belly up, the state will be left to repay bonds. Still others wonder about the future of state highway employees.

In general, the idea of imposing tolls often is unpopular because the public believes it already funds roads with gas taxes and vehicle registration.

Furthermore, Carl Ohrn of the Metropolitan Council in Minnesota indicates that each plan's goal is a key factor in determining how beneficial privatization can be. "Many metro areas want to manage traffic, so they charge a toll based on demand. Money is not as much an issue as providing a congestion-free alternative." According to Ohrn, these are conflicting goals or different goals, depending on the area of the country.

Some people believe it is bad policy to divest public assets, said CSG's CanagaRetna. However, most opponents of toll road privatization see a more immediate drawback: privatizing will increase tolls. "Tolls can become cost-prohibitive to some" regardless of who maintains the roads, he said.

As far as the job security of state highway employees whose jurisdiction faces privatization, the details—terms of the lease—make the difference.

Debra Minnott, director of Indiana State Personnel, said the state's plan will offer other positions in state government at the same pay and benefits to those employees who choose not to work for the private company. Employees who are vested by the time they leave state employment will still receive state benefits. "In addition," said Minnott, "there are several pieces of legislation currently pending which could assist employees by purchasing additional service credit for those who are near vesting or near normal or early retirement age."

Poole suggested those opposed to privatization peruse lease terms. He commended Indiana for making the documents so accessible to the public—they are available on the state's Web site. "These decisions were based on 30–40 years of other countries' experience," said Poole. "We're not dealing with something behind closed doors where terms are hidden. It's all out there in the open. Everything is publicly documented."

Poole also suspects if American companies were the main players in the lease agreement, the issue would not be as controversial. "But we live in a global economy," said Poole. "We have foreign investment in banking, real estate and everything else."

Major Moves Lease Agreement Summary

- Statewide Mobility Partners (SMP) may not sell or reassign lease, or hire third-party operator of the Indiana Toll Road without the approval of the State of Indiana.
- SMP is responsible for all costs and expenses, including operation, maintenance, restoration, resurfacing, reconstruction and tax liabilities.
- Example of Operating Standards Agreement: snow/ice—bare pavement within 4 hours and shoulders clear 8 hours after storm ends.
- SMP is mandated to interview all existing employees interested in employment. Those not hired will be provided opportunities elsewhere in state government.
- SMP shall give a hiring preference to qualified Indiana workers.
- SMP must adhere to "Buy Indiana" 90 percent guidelines for maintenance and construction contracts.

THE NEW WAVE IN TOLL ROADS?

So is privatization a trend? According to most experts, it is too early to say. But they agree that priced highway facilities, regardless of who operates them, will become more prevalent.

The push toward alternate forms of energy could also play a role in the future of toll roads, according to Canaga Retna. "Unless officials change the formula so that alternate energy is taxed also, there will be dwindling revenue from fuel taxes," he said. "That will put even more pressure on state and local governments to meet expenditures on highways. It will make the necessity for tolls even greater."

And while Poole won't call privatization a trend just yet, he sees more of it on the horizon. "There are four bona fide bids for the Dulles Toll Road in Virginia and three linked in Houston. There are discussions in Delaware and New Jersey," said Poole. "By our reckoning we have totaled active proposals at $20 billion in discussion stages, not including existing toll roads. This is just the tip of the iceberg for what is to come in the next 10 years."

VIII

Local Government

W hat do New York City, with its population of more than 8 million, and Plains, Texas, (population 1405) have in common? The obvious answer seems to be, well, not much. New York City is one of the largest and most cosmopolitan cities, not just in the country, but on the planet. Plains is a small county seat deep within the sparsely populated South Plains of Texas. Yet if nothing else they are both incorporated municipalities; in other words, they are both formally established local governments. What makes them different—including size, demographics, economics and density—makes a general point about what they have in common. It's often easier to figure out how local governments are different than how they are similar.

The simple reason for this is that there are a lot of local governments—close to ninety thousand according to the U.S. Census Bureau.[1] These governments provide many of the basic services that society has come to take for granted: law enforcement, public schools, fire protection and libraries, as well as such basic infrastructure operations as water, sewer and local road systems. It is possible to see rough similarities across governments at similar levels; big and small school districts, after all, have the same basic responsibilities, as do most cities. Mayor Michael Bloomberg of New York City and Mayor Shane McKinzie of Plains, Texas, face a lot of similar issues (for example, budgets, taxes, infrastructure, fire protection and law enforcement issues). It's the scale and complexity that's different.

Yet there are so many forms of local government, and so many different programs and services that they provide, that it is difficult to make general statements about local government with any degree of accuracy. Consider that under the umbrella of "local government" are not just New York City and Plains, Texas, but also the Port Authority of New York and New Jersey, the Plains Independent School District, and Zone 7 of the Texas Boll Weevil Eradication Foundation. Commonalities across these governments are hard to find. Filling potholes, regulating water ferries, teaching math, and killing bugs cover a pretty broad spectrum of government activity. Add in the bewildering variety of other local governments, everything from mosquito control districts to airport authorities, and it's easy to see why local government seems to be more defined by its differences than by its similarities.

Thus if the readings in this chapter seem to cover very different subjects (everything from illegal immigration to eminent domain), it is not without good reason. To provide a representative sample of all the things local governments do, and all the forms local governments take, would require something on the order of an encyclopedia. A single chapter's worth of readings cannot cover all of that ground, but it can convey a basic notion of the huge breadth and scope of what local governments are, and what they do.

WHAT LOCAL GOVERNMENTS ARE

Local governments come in three basic forms: counties, municipalities, and special districts. For governing purposes, states historically subdivided themselves into smaller political jurisdictions called counties, and turned over to these such basic local functions as road maintenance and law enforcement. Counties originated as, and to a considerable extent still are, local outposts of state government.

Municipalities are public corporations created to provide basic governance to defined geographic jurisdictions. They include familiar political entities, such as towns, villages and cities. They differ from counties in that they tend to be more compact geographically, are more urban and legally exist as independent corporations rather than as the local office of state government.

Special districts are something of a miscellaneous category that includes everything else, and when it comes to local government there is a lot of everything else. The most obvious difference between counties, municipalities, and special districts is that the former two are general governance units. They provide a broad range of programs and services. Special districts, on the other hand, are created to provide a specific program or service. School districts are the most common form of special district—they exist solely to provide public education. Other examples include water treatment and sewage management districts.

That said, it should be kept in mind that these definitions are fairly loose. For example, what constitutes a town or a village or a city is governed by state law, and the powers and policy responsibilities of these different categories of municipality may vary considerably. Counties, municipalities, and special districts are not even clearly separated by geography, but rather are piled on top of each other, which can be confusing to citizens and create coordination and control problems for public officials. A county may be almost completely covered by a municipality, or a series of municipalities. There may be several school districts crossing over county and city boundaries. Fitted across these jurisdictions may be other special districts. Local governments fit together like a sort of three-dimensional jigsaw puzzle with some pieces missing. Given this, it should not be surprising to hear that local governments sometimes get into arguments about who should be doing what.

Although local governments can seem to be something of a confusing jumble from a big picture perspective, there is a fairly clear difference between the vast majority of local governments and state government. Generally speaking, state governments are sovereign governments and local governments are not. What this means is that state governments get their powers and legal authority directly from citizens—this power and authority is codified in the state constitution.

Most local governments, however, get their power from state government, not directly from citizens. Their powers and legal authority are mostly set by state law, which is to say the state legislature. And what the legislature gives, it can take away. So, unlike the relationship between the federal and state governments, which at least in theory is a relationship of equals, the relationship between state governments and local governments is legally a superior-subordinate relationship. Some states grant local governments broad powers; others reserve much of these powers to themselves and delegate comparatively little. Even in the states that grant local government considerable independence, however, the state technically is still the sovereign government.

This hierarchy is codified in Dillon's Rule, which is the legal principle that local governments can only exercise the powers granted to them by state government. The independence and power of local governments thus varies enormously not just from state to state, but from locality to locality within states. Some municipalities are virtually city-states, powerful political jurisdictions with a high degree of self-rule. Others are little more than local extensions of state governments.

Regardless of their formal allocation of power, local government is the level of government that is typically the most visible to the average citizen, and the most relevant to daily life. Local governments maintain roads, run schools and have primary responsibility for health and welfare functions, such as law enforcement, fire protection, and ambulance service. These responsibilities alone present a considerable challenge, as a couple of the essays in this section show. Rob Gurwitt's essay details former Virginia governor L. Douglas Wilder's decision to reenter politics by getting elected mayor of Richmond. Although some might consider a move from the governor's mansion to the mayor's office a step down the political ladder, Wilder recognizes that it is at this level that some of the more pressing needs of a community can be best addressed.

John Buntin's essay shows just how important local government is, and how local politics can, quite literally, be a matter of life and death. Police and fire departments have historically been independent from each other, and relations between the two are often tense. That's now a central issue for disaster preparedness. No matter whether it's a hurricane or a terrorist strike, the first responders to any disaster are likely to be local law enforcement agencies and fire departments. Their ability to work with each other is of central concern to local governments trying to prepare for the worst.

Two other essays examine how some local governments are at the center of national issues. Alan Greenblatt's essay examines the impact of a controversial U.S. Supreme Court decision giving cities the right to force homeowners to sell to private developers under their powers of eminent domain. Jonathan Walters takes a look at how illegal immigration is creating conflict and challenges for local governments across the United States.

Notes

1. U.S. Census Bureau, "Census Bureau Reports Number of Local Governments Nears 88,000," 2003, www.census.gov/Press-Release/www/2003/cb03-10.html (accessed May 5, 2005).

29

Wilder's Last Crusade

Rob Gurwitt

Virginia's ex-governor has made a career out of accomplishing the unexpected. He is betting he can do it one more time as mayor of a proud but messed-up city.

For a short time after L. Douglas Wilder took office in January as mayor of Richmond, those who wanted to speak to him faced a dilemma: Should they call him "Mayor" or "Governor"? On the street, at meetings, even in city hall, people vacillated, unsure whether the respect due a former governor of Virginia somehow overshadowed his new political station.

It didn't take long to sort out. "Mayor Wilder" is what the city's new chief executive wants to be called, in part because he doesn't wish to leave any doubts about his position at the apex of Richmond life. "There's a guy who likes to call himself 'mayor' of one of the streets down here," Wilder says, gesturing out his office window. "I said, 'That's all over! I'm going to be the mayor of every alley, every street, every avenue, you name it.' I cede no part of the city to anyone!"

This is not hyperbole. Capping a lifetime of firsts—the first black state senator in Virginia since Reconstruction; the first black lieutenant governor; the first African-American elected governor anywhere in the United States, Wilder this year became the first directly elected, constitutionally powerful mayor of Richmond since the 1940s. At the age of 74, when most politicians would be pondering where to store the gilt-edged photographs of their past glories, Wilder has plunged into one last great act.

He has embraced it with the self-assurance of a man in the habit of playing the lead role. Another newly minted mayor, faced with weaning his city from diffuse governance by a city council and city manager, might move gingerly to avoid antagonizing interest groups accustomed to getting their way. Wilder has chosen the opposite tack. He has seized Richmond by the scruff of the

From *Governing,*
June 2005.

neck and thrown it and himself headlong into an unusual urban revitalization project: crafting a standard of strong leadership in a city that had forgotten what that looks like.

Wilder is convinced this is what Richmond wants. The 2003 referendum that created the new mayoralty produced a four-fifths majority in favor of the move, and Wilder himself got a similar margin when he ran for the post last November. "When you're 74 years old," he says, "and the people have reposed the confidence in you to say, 'Look here, old man, we believe you are the guy who can do what you say you'll do,' well, you can't rise any higher in terms of people's expectations."

You can, however, test the limits of what they expected. Now that he's getting down to brass tacks, Wilder is forcing the city to confront what it chose for itself. Business leaders who supported the change and helped fund the campaign for it have found their pet causes held up to new scrutiny in city hall. Nonprofit and community groups that relied on a steady stream of city funds have seen themselves zeroed out of the budget. Every week brings news of some high-level departure from a city agency, and sometimes rumors that an entire agency might disappear. In the few months it has taken Richmonders to get used to saying "Mayor Wilder," he has transformed the political landscape around them.

"It's not just the magnitude of the change," says John Moeser, a professor of urban studies at Virginia Commonwealth University in Richmond, "but the swiftness of the change. In many respects, it's unprecedented. But throughout his career, Wilder has been full of surprises, and this is going to be mainstay Wilder. He's going to call the shots as he sees them."

SENSE OF NEGLECT

That Wilder was presented with this opportunity is thanks in large part to, well, Doug Wilder. In 2002, he joined with Tom Bliley, a former Richmond mayor and longtime Republican congressman from the area, to form a commission exploring the possibility of abandoning Richmond's council-manager form of government, in which one of the city council members, chosen by colleagues, was given the title of mayor. Very little management authority went along with the title. It was a widespread feeling that the system lacked accountability that jump-started the city's makeover.

At the time, Wilder seemed pretty much to have given up on politics. A longtime Democrat, he had explored the idea of running for president in 1992 and ran a brief campaign for the U.S. Senate as an independent after finishing his term as governor in 1994. The Senate run in particular—a challenge to Democratic incumbent Chuck Robb—wound up alienating some longtime allies. Then, in 1997, Wilder was blamed by many Democrats for the party's gubernatorial defeat because he failed to support the Democratic nominee. Gradually, he slipped into what seemed to be a comfortable semi-retirement, teaching at Virginia Commonwealth University and occasionally commenting on state policy.

Richmond, however, was entering a particularly bleak stage in its history. Between 1997 and 2004, the city saw a mayoral aide plead guilty to cocaine distribution and racketeering; the mayor he served resign from the council and plead guilty to federal charges of mail fraud and obstruction of justice; a city councilman and his wife convicted on federal tax-evasion charges; the vice-chairman of the city's Industrial Development Authority convicted in a bribery scandal; and a former aide to the city manager plead guilty to charges in a city hall billing scam.

Quite apart from the ethical taint that all of this was giving Richmond, there was a pervasive feeling in the city that it was adrift—and that, especially in its African-American community, the lack of direction from city hall was proving disastrous. Decay downtown, neighborhoods that felt neglected, a high crime rate, widespread poverty, illiteracy and sexually transmitted disease—all of these fed the dissatisfaction. "You name the category—public health, education, employment, the economy—we were hurting and the leadership had not addressed it," says Marty Jewell, a longtime community activist who was elected to the city council last November. "No one was accountable. The mayor was saying, 'Well, under the statute I preside over meetings and cut ribbons'; the manager was not required to respond to any citizen or citizen issue; and the council was in a situation where you couldn't get three council members to agree on what was for lunch, let alone set benchmarks and hold the manager to those benchmarks."

For Wilder, who grew up in Richmond and built his political career there, the last straw was a meeting of a group called Richmond Renaissance, a biracial collection of heavy hitters from the political and business worlds.

The former governor had become increasingly vocal about Richmond's ills, going so far as to call the city "a cesspool of corruption and inefficiency." Asked to speak to the group about his concerns, Wilder was stung by the response: Rather than being challenged on his argument, he was castigated for criticizing the city. "That told me that the group's leadership was weak," Wilder says. "If this was what was supposedly the combination of forces directing the affairs of the city, then we were in bigger trouble than I had thought."

The problem was that, even if there was public sentiment for change, the obstacles were daunting. Virginia functions according to "Dillon's Rule," the hoary legal structure that makes cities and counties creatures of the state—any change to the way a community operates has to be approved by the state legislature. And the city council wasn't about to request that it be required to hand over power to a strong mayor. The ad hoc commission—for which Wilder recruited Bliley, a white conservative with strong ties to Richmond's business and social elite—was essentially designed to produce a proposal that, if adopted by the voters, would make an end run around the powers-that-be.

In Richmond, with its history of segregation and resistance to change, race is still a potent subtext in any political discussion, and this was true in the mayoral reform debate. The city is 58 percent African American, and while the move to a strong mayor elected citywide was supported by white business leaders, the black establishment—most of Richmond's state legislators, its African-American newspapers, and its organization of clergymen—opposed the idea, worried that citywide election would reduce the influence of black neighborhoods and allow a heavy turnout among white citizens to swamp lighter turnout among the African-American majority.

In answer—and to secure Justice Department approval under the federal Voting Rights Act—the commission proposed a twist: The mayoral winner not only had to win a majority of the citywide vote, but carry at least five of the nine councilmanic districts,

Richmond by the Numbers	
Population:	195,300
Ethnicity (2002):	
Black	57.2%
White	38.3%
Other	4.5%
Unemployment rate:	6.4%
Budget:	$536 million
Number of employees:	8,421

Source: City of Richmond

ensuring that he or she could not win without the support of African-American voters. After a frantic two-month effort to collect signatures—led by Paul Goldman, Wilder's longtime political and policy adviser, the commission's proposal went on the November 2003 ballot.

Wilder campaigned for it full-bore, countering his opponents' arguments by pointing out, as he puts it now, that "after 27 years of black-majority rule, we saw very little changing. Crime was up, we were losing jobs, health was deteriorating, economic development was down, school populations were decreasing. And we were not producing the quality of leadership that in my judgment was needed to correct those things." The electorate obviously agreed, not only giving the initiative 80 percent of the vote but approving it in all but six precincts. It went on to passage at the state capitol. "It was monumental that it took only a year and a half to accomplish," says Tom Shields, a political scientist at the University of Richmond. "If it had been anyone else behind it besides Doug Wilder, it wouldn't have happened."

> *In Church Hill, the neighborhood where Wilder grew up, residents wonder what's in Richmond's new power structure that will benefit them.*

NO DEBTS TO PAY

Given all this, it must have seemed inevitable to some that

Wilder would move in as the city's first strong mayor in 60 years. He insists, though, that he initially had no intention of running for the post. "I told people, 'I like my life, I go on my boat when I choose, my grandchildren come down to visit. This isn't anything I need.'" While there were various other possibilities—Bliley says that for a time he hoped the candidate might be Robert Bobb, a longtime Richmond city manager who had gone on to be administrator in Oakland, California, and is now in Washington, D.C.—none panned out. Meanwhile, some of the very people Wilder held responsible for Richmond's troubles were eyeing the mayoralty. "We didn't fight this hard to see a recapitulation of what we had," Wilder says. Once he got in, the race was essentially over.

Watching a man of his political skills, it's hard to believe Wilder could have done anything else. In person, he can be charming, warm and very persuasive. He has a way, as he works a crowd, of listening gravely to whoever is speaking to him at the moment, and people who meet him nearly always leave with the feeling that he has heard them. Underneath, however, Wilder is always pursuing his own agenda. "Rule No. 1," a local columnist reminded readers a few months ago in a "primer" for dealing with the new mayor: "Doug Wilder owes only Doug Wilder. Rule No. 2: Doug Wilder will not do anything unless it benefits him or his cause (in the current case, the city of Richmond). Rule No. 3: See Rules Nos. 1 and 2. Rule No. 4: No, really."

This reputation for holding no fast allegiances did not serve Wilder particularly well when he was governor, but it works in his favor now. Wilder and all around him are intensely aware that he is creating the template for what any strong mayor in Richmond will be expected to do, and his independence has allowed him to convince a lot of people that his only interest lies in seeing Richmond thrive. "The good thing about him," says a long-time nonprofit executive in town, "is that he isn't loyal to anyone. At his age, he can do pretty much what he wants, because he's not going to be running for some other office."

People who meet him nearly always leave with the feeling that he has heard them. Underneath, however, Wilder is always pursuing his own agenda.

The result is that Wilder gets the benefit of the doubt when he insists that the city needs wholesale change. In truth, the sense of urgency may not be quite as obvious as it would have been a few years ago. Even before Wilder became mayor, there were heartening signs: a solid bond rating; reduced crime rates; a new convention center downtown; a growing population and booming residential market in several neighborhoods on the edge of downtown; the re-engagement of a once indifferent corporate community in city life. "People sense that Richmond is back, that this region's time has come," says the Chamber of Commerce president, Jim Dunn. Bill Pantele, a city councilman allied with Wilder, tells a story about being summoned about a year ago to meet with constituents in a hard-pressed neighborhood. They wanted to complain about their tax assessments going up. "That was a conversation no one thought we would have five years ago," Pantele says. "We have homeowners concerned about normal homeowner issues now: getting sidewalks fixed, street trees, getting an alley resurfaced. Five or six years ago, no city council person would have had conversations like that."

Wilder and Goldman—who is now his chief city hall adviser and agitator for change within the government—tend on the other hand to see how empty the glass remains. They point to the city's 25 percent poverty rate, the loss of 3,500 jobs over three years, a decrepit public health system, plenty of downtown buildings that remain boarded up, schools with high truancy rates, neighborhood infrastructure that has gone ignored for years. Nor was the city apparatus they found when they moved into city hall anything to write home about. A commission appointed by Wilder to study its effectiveness found a litany of problems, from departments performing duplicate tasks, to services that cost several times what they do in cities of comparable size, to lax hiring, procurement and contracting processes.

"You look at the workforce in your utilities department, so much of that work is outsourced to the tune of millions of dollars," Wilder says. "You look at the housing authority, they're spending a million dollars in outsourced legal work when they could do that through the city attorney's office, yet they're coming to us for money? We've reached our debt capacity, we've got holes in our retirement account. So you start asking yourself the question, Who has been in charge? And bottom line, you come to the conclusion that there hasn't been anybody in charge."

NO TIME TO LOSE

Wilder has made it clear that someone is in charge now. To begin with, he went to the legislature and had it fill in the blanks left when it approved the city's move to a mayor elected at-large. These changes have given him veto power over council actions, authority over the city budget, even a measure of control over the school board. He jettisoned the previous city manager and police chief right away, and in the months since taking office has overseen the departure of a series of administrators from the old regime. He called in city employees and asked them not only what they did but what they actually accomplished—"It's amazing what you see when you ask someone what would not happen if they were not there," he says, laughing. With Wilder, one gets the sense that exercising mayoral power is not simply a means of furthering a policy agenda; exercising power as mayor is his agenda.

"I had a couple guys in the legislature say, 'Why don't you go slower, just take a year or so and see what happens,'" he says. "But I know what's needed now. I go back to that old axiom: If a thing is right, the time is always right. It's not a question of arrogating nor rushing. It's a question of clothing the office with what it should have. No more but no less."

This has been clearest in Wilder's dealings with Richmond's business community. In recent years, encouraged by business leaders, the council and manager cut a variety of economic development deals that looked promising but have left the city on the hook for millions of dollars. Particularly galling to Wilder and Goldman is an arrangement by which the city picks up the tab for shortfalls in running the convention center—a regional entity—while suburban counties are projected to receive rebates from the project. "These businessmen go on about how great the convention center is," Goldman fumes. "It's running in the red millions of dollars, yet only one locality has to bail it out? Who cut that deal?"

Wilder has turned a skeptical eye on a variety of other projects that have had strong business backing. He is openly questioning whether the city should live up to its pledge of $27 million for a performing arts center if the center's board is unable to come up with the private funding it has said it could raise. He is in an open spat with the Richmond Braves minor-league baseball team, which wants a new stadium in the historic Shockoe Bottom neighborhood. And much to the chagrin of many of the prominent businessmen who funded his strong mayor referendum, he has pulled city funding for Richmond Renaissance and for the Greater Richmond Partnership, a regional development organization that has, so far, been more successful at bringing businesses to outlying counties than to Richmond itself. "With every negotiation that takes place … for the remainder of my term," he said in April, "we are not going to have these types of open-ended, loose-ended commitments for the city with nothing coming back."

This is not to say that Wilder's goal is to put distance between himself and business leaders—just that he wants the city to be a lot more careful. Indeed, just before he said that, he announced a deal with tobacco giant Philip Morris for a $300 million research and development facility downtown that will involve a donation of city land and a 10-year rollback on taxes.

On balance, Wilder still enjoys the support of the city's corporate elite. While opposing cuts in the regional economic partnership, the Chamber's Jim Dunn sympathizes with Wilder's overall goal. "The mayor absolutely has to look at every nickel the city is spending," he says. "It takes resources to change the things that need to be changed."

That is, in fact, the whole point of Wilder's first budget, a 2-inch-thick document that landed with a decided "thud" the first week in April. It not only slights favorites within the business community, it cuts nonprofits that have long depended on the city for support. Instead, it gives funding priority to police, schools, street repairs and parks—basics of city government that Wilder argues went neglected for too long.

While conflict is inevitable as Wilder forges ahead, he is sanguine about the future—in particular, the future after he leaves office. Even though he has the better part of four years to go in his first term—and hasn't hinted one way or another whether he intends to seek a second—many are nervous about what will happen to the strong mayoralty when someone else is filling it. Wilder tells them that by then, city hall will be more responsive, more efficient and more accountable, and a less commanding figure will still be able to run things. "I tell people not to worry about what happens when I leave," he says. "Because if we're successful in creating the machinery that we want, the public won't allow it to become anything else. They'll say, 'Wait a minute, we know you can do this!' They'll know that government can be what they thought it ought to be."

30

Battle of the Badges

John Buntin

Tense relations between police and fire departments, long a fact of life in many cities, are now emerging as a serious domestic-preparedness problem.

"An airplane is falling on the company!"

"A what?"

"An airplane! An airplane!"

"An airplane hit your building?"

"Yeah, yeah, it hit the building. I need an ambulance, because one guy is hurt."

That was one of the stomach-churning calls made to emergency dispatchers in suburban New Jersey on a cold February morning earlier this year. A corporate jet had failed to take off from the Teterboro Airport and skidded across a busy highway in the middle of the morning rush hour before crashing into a warehouse.

Because of its proximity to New York City—Teterboro is just 12 miles west of midtown Manhattan—and its fleet of private jets, the airport is precisely the kind of facility that has worried counter-terrorism experts since the 9/11 attacks. Yet the initial response to this aviation disaster was chaotic. The smallest municipality in New Jersey (population 18), Teterboro has no fire department of its own. Instead, it relies on neighboring jurisdictions for fire-fighting and law enforcement services. That makes things complicated under the best of circumstances. However, the possibility that the crash might be a terrorist incident brought large numbers of police officers to the scene—and ratcheted up the tensions.

First, came the Port Authority police with their mobile command post. Local fire and police rebuffed their efforts to take charge, pointing out that the incident was not occurring on Port Authority property. Then the Bergen County police showed up with their command post. Then the Bergen County Sheriff's Department appeared with its command post. Then came the New Jersey state

From *Governing*, September 2005.

police with, yes, their own command post. None of them were working together. As a result, some local fire fighters who left the scene briefly found that when they attempted to return to their job, they were barred from "the crime scene" or asked to sign back in.

Miraculously, no one was killed in what turned out to be an ice-related accident, and Teterboro muddled through. But the uncertainty over lines of command and protocols for operations hardly reflected a coordinated response. At the heart of the difficulty that morning was an intractable problem—tension between fire fighters and law enforcement officers.

For more than a century, competitive, sometimes strained, relations between police and fire departments have been the norm in many American cities. Indeed, the rivalry between the two public safety entities is one of the most enduring fault-lines in municipal government. To some extent, such tension is unavoidable. At the policy level, police officers and fire fighters compete for the same municipal dollars. Higher wages for one profession (usually the police) often come at the expense of the other. "The system puts us in an adversarial position," says Phoenix Police Commander T. J. Martin, "and if you've got a culture that lets it flourish, it continues to go and go."

For the most part, police and fire agencies work through these tensions. But when police and fire are called upon to work together in a crisis, all too often coordination has broken down—and turf wars have broken out. Among the most innovative police and fire chiefs, there's a growing awareness that the status quo is unacceptable, even dangerous, in the event of a large-scale terrorist attack or natural catastrophe, and that tabletop drills and management protocols aren't enough to overcome the animosity. "If you think dropping a bomb on a city is going to get people to hug and kiss and get along, I don't think it is," says Phoenix Fire Chief Alan Brunacini.

What's needed, he and other officials say, is a concerted and ongoing effort to bridge the divide between the two professions. "Weapons-of-mass-destruction responses," Brunacini argues, "will emerge from everyday local responses." A look at the New York metropolitan area underscores the perils of the status quo and illustrates what more healthy relationships might look like in the future.

PAPER PLANS

The difficulty of coordinating emergency services operations is hardly an unrecognized problem. In recent years, the federal government has attempted to address the situation by requiring cities to manage emergencies using a management protocol called the Incident Command System. At the heart of ICS is the concept of a unified command where police, fire and other emergency services agencies meet to develop and oversee a coordinated response. By the end of this federal fiscal year, all cities will be required to have ICS plans in place before they can qualify for federal funds.

But formal agreements alone are not enough to overcome years of rivalry and distrust, as the experience of New York City has shown. The Big Apple is a singular place. No region of the country has been more affected by terrorism; none has a greater incentive to set fire and police relationships aright. With 36,000 police officers and 11,000 fire fighters, its scale and resources are unparalleled. However, greater resources have never meant better coordination. On the contrary, the NYPD and the FDNY have more overlapping services than most urban police and fire departments. Both are tradition-bound and aggressive about their turf. The result has been a uniquely tense relationship.

Since at least the late 1970s, New York's mayors have recognized that the strained relations between the two departments were a potentially serious problem and have tried but largely failed to rectify the situation. The administration of Mayor Rudolph Giuliani was more aggressive than most. In July 2001, Giuliani updated a directive called "The Direction and Control of Emergencies in New York City." Its purpose was "to eliminate conflict among responding agencies which may have areas of overlapping expertise and responsibility"—particularly the fire and police departments. The directive set forth a variety of scenarios and specified which agency would function as the "incident commander" in those circumstances. The Office of Emergency Management, itself created by Giuliani in 1996, was charged with serving as "the on-scene interagency coordinator." Two months later, on September 11, the new emergency management system got its first test.

By most accounts, cooperation was not as effective as it could have been. While noting that "to some degree the Mayor's directive for incident command was followed on 9/11," the 9/11 Commission nonetheless concluded that "response operations lacked the kind of integrated communications and unified response contemplated in the directive." An investigation by the National Institute for Standards and Technology found that FDNY and NYPD department chiefs "were not working together at the same command post, and that they did not formulate unified orders and directions for their departments."

The consequences of this failure in terms of lives lost have been hotly debated. In his memoirs, Giuliani defended establishing dual police-fire command posts to deal with the attack on the World Trade Center, asserting that given the circumstances there was no other practical course of action available. Many fire fighters believe that information from NYPD helicopters might have led to an earlier evacuation of fire fighters from the second tower. The 9/11 Commission itself concluded that the answer was ultimately unknowable. However, it left no doubt as the seriousness of the shortcoming: "If New York and other major cities are to be prepared for future terrorist attacks, different first-responder agencies must be fully coordinated," the commission report concluded.

Yet many experts believe the administration of current Mayor Michael Bloomberg has moved away from more effective coordination. In May 2004, the city adopted an emergency response plan that called for joint operations between police and fire departments rather than a unified command—a plan criticized by the 9/11 Commission. This April, the city unveiled its version of the ICS, dubbed the Citywide Incident Management system. CIMS shifted authority away from the fire department to the police department. Instead of entrusting police with responsibility for responding to crime scenes and vesting fire with responsibility for commanding response operations, CIMS allows the NYPD to make the initial determination on whether a hazardous materials incident involves a crime or terrorism. If it does, the NYPD is in charge. That decision angered the fire department and puzzled many fire experts. "I don't get it," says Glenn Corbett, a professor of fire science at the John Jay College of Criminal Justice. "They have now split hazmat function down the middle. The police are in charge of assessment; fire is in charge of life safety... The duplication not only didn't get better, it got worse."

The Bloomberg administration has rejected these criticisms. Indeed, it has rejected the notion that there's a systematic coordination problem between the police and fire department at all. "Realize this. Police and fire every day work an excess of 100 to 200 incidents," says Joseph Bruno, the head of New York's Office of Emergency Management and former FDNY fire commissioner. "The overall level of cooperation is outstanding." The only area where New York "has had problems," says Bruno, "is communications."

That's a claim that astonishes Councilwoman Yvette Clarke, who chairs the city's Fire and Criminal Justice Services Committee. "I share the belief that there were no coordination problems because there was no coordination," she says sarcastically.

BUILDING NEW RELATIONSHIPS

Thirty miles north of Manhattan, in a conference room at the White Plains public safety building, a very different kind of police-fire relationship is being built. It's 9:15 on a Monday morning and a group of 20 or so public safety officers are gathered for a weekly Compstat meeting. It's the kind of meeting that now plays out in any number of American cities but for one thing—this Compstat session includes both police and fire officers.

At the head of the table sits the architect of this unusual arrangement, Frank Straub, White Plains' commissioner for public safety. Straub's determination to bring White Plains' police and fire departments together on a regular basis reflects his experiences on September 11, 2001. At the time, Straub, a veteran of several federal law enforcement agencies, was serving as executive deputy inspector general in the New York State Inspector General's office. His offices were only three blocks south of the World Trade Center complex. When the first plane hit the north tower, he, like many other law enforcement officers, hurried to the scene.

"I was saved by a fire truck when the second tower came down," Straub says quietly. "For me, it's a very real thing. I saw an awful lot of people—police, fire and civilians—die that day, needlessly in many cases."

Two weeks after 9/11, Straub joined the NYPD as deputy commissioner for training. He stayed with the department—moving over to serve as assistant commissioner of internal training for the counterterrorism bureau when Ray Kelly took over as commissioner—until the summer of 2002, when he accepted the job of public safety commissioner in White Plains.

"I knew a lot about emergency services, and this was very personal for me," says Straub. "We all were saying we couldn't let it happen again. The biggest thing for me is that unless you have fire and police [working together], you're looking at a disaster. No one agency can do it themselves"—not even the 36,000-officer NYPD.

When Straub arrived in White Plains, however, he found a familiar tension. "I really had two separate and distinct departments," says Straub. "And very rarely did they talk." Indeed, fire fighters had become so estranged from the previous public safety commissioner that they were even seeking their own freestanding department.

Straub set out to find areas where police and fire could act together. First, he moved their respective chiefs onto the same floor and into offices that are next to each other. Then he required both to participate in a weekly Compstat meeting. Finally, in order to demonstrate his commitment to the fire department, Straub went through the training to be certified as a fire fighter. He also has made a point of going in person to most fire scenes.

All of Straub's actions have been aimed at one thing: persuading fire and police officers to work together on a routine basis. One such area concerns safe housing. Every spring, hundreds if not thousands of immigrants move into affluent Westchester County for seasonal jobs. Many of them crowd into run-down boarding houses, which often fail to meet code. At Straub's initiative, White Plains police answering calls in these areas learned how to identify problems and report them to the fire department. Likewise, fire fighters have received training in how to look for telltale signs of gang activity, such as graffiti tags, and report them to the police. The two bureaus' elite rescue and emergency services units also have trained together on an increasingly regular basis.

"Every opportunity we get we keep putting them in the room together and making them work together," says Police Chief James Bradley. The goal is routine interaction. "You can break out a protocol sheet and say we've agreed to do this or that," he says, "but unless you're used to doing it at the level of daily execution, it doesn't work."

"It's the day-to-day things: Compstat meetings, safe housing, bar and restaurant inspections, accident calls or doing rescue off the side of a building together," says Straub. "That's what builds collaboration and cooperation, and that's what tears down the traditional 'go to hell' mentality."

Straub worries that that is what New York City is neglecting. "Fundamentally the problem when you look at New York City and probably other cities is there's not that baseline coordination and cooperation. Places like New York need to find small areas where they can work together on a daily basis," says Straub.

OTHER MODELS

Straub's work in White Plains has been made easier by his organizational chart: As public safety commissioner, he has clear authority over both the fire and police bureaus. However, public safety departments of this sort are relatively uncommon. Nonetheless, other cities interested in improving police-fire relations have found ways to bridge bureaucratic divides.

Charlotte-Mecklenburg, the government in North Carolina's largest metropolitan area, has made a concerted effort to improve police-fire relations since the 1970s, when the county decided to situate its fire and police departments in the same building. That daily interaction, says Police Chief Darrell Stephens, "contributes a lot to what has happened on the street." The county also supports a special 90-person outfit—known as ALERT (Advanced Local Emergency Response Team)—that includes a mixture of fire fighters and police officers, as well as personnel from the FBI, EMS, the County Medical Examiner's Office and the Carolinas Medical Center. "We still have our moments," concedes Stephens, "but when they happen, we sit down and deal with it or develop a new protocol."

Phoenix has gone even further. There, in the months after 9/11, the police and fire departments teamed up to staff a unified Homeland Defense Bureau. It started out with six police officers and fire fighters. Today, it encompasses more than 100. A new utility tax will provide a dedicated source of funding for its operations. As in Charlotte, co-location is central to Phoenix's effort, although Police Commander T. J. Martin concedes that he took some flack from other officers when it was revealed that the bureau would be housed with the fire department.

"By virtue of co-locating, it's a lot easier to communicate," says Alan Brunacini, the fire chief. "It's a lot easier to use their expertise in a routine way. They see each other, go on calls. They like each other. I think there's a different dynamic when people are in a day-to-day way just closer."

"We train together, we eat together, we shoot the breeze. We play the 'what if' game a lot," adds Martin. In the process, the two departments have found that they rely on the integrated communications and operations of the Homeland Defense Bureau on a daily basis—and perform better as a result.

"When you start doing this, it's almost impossible to separate the two functions," says Brunacini. The goal, he notes, is not to combine functions but rather to make cooperation natural, almost reflexive. "There are things fire does best and another set of things police do best. When you can put those together, two and two is six."

31

Land Law

Alan Greenblatt

A Supreme Court win for a Connecticut city could end up curbing some uses of eminent domain.

The U.S. Supreme Court's recent decision on eminent domain, *Kelo v. New London,* has unleashed heavy political fallout—much of it negative—in the U.S. Congress and in the states.

On the surface, the ruling does appear to be a win for cities. Neighborhood homeowners could be forced to sell not just to a city but to private developers who want to build a project that would expand the city's tax base. The Court clearly indicated that localities have a legitimate role in planning and that economic development—and particularly, improving blighted areas—can't be halted simply because some property owner objects.

"In a political vacuum, the *Kelo* decision is very good for local governments," says Mark Flynn, director of legal services for the Virginia Municipal League. But the real political world is something else. The decision has some states rushing to curb local powers of eminent domain (an action that has the Court's blessing). The Texas House and Senate, meeting in special session in July, quickly approved competing bills to block local governments from taking private property for economic development projects.

There would have been much more legislative response if more state legislatures had been in session when the decision came down in June. In fact, in anticipation of the Court's ruling, a few states, including Utah and Nevada, passed new restrictions on eminent domain earlier this year.

More is certain to come. Indiana state Representative David Wolkins intends to introduce a bill next year that would narrow Indiana's definition of "blight" and would force redevelopment agencies to pay ousted owners 150 percent of the appraised value of a property, just to discourage them. "What I don't like is where somebody has a

From *Governing,*
August 2005.

162

higher and better use in their minds, and they give the land to a private developer," Wolkins says. His bill won't touch local governments' right to invoke eminent domain for clear public uses such as building roads or parks.

Redevelopment agencies are likely to serve as a prime target in other states as well. Eminent domain skeptics in states such as Colorado and Nevada have already found they couldn't muster the support for a broad attack on localities.

Not everyone is rushing to change the rules. The other political reality is that governments can't seize any land they'd like—the unpopularity of eminent domain serves as a curb on the practice even where it's perfectly legal. That was the case, for instance, in Cypress, California, where the political fallout from a decision to force a church out to make way for a Costco store led local officials to find a more expedient settlement.

"Elected officials rightly know that they cannot go around taking property at will," says Indianapolis Mayor Bart Peterson, who has taken the lead on this issue for the National League of Cities. Peterson argues that eminent domain remains a crucial tool for revitalizing neighborhoods, pursuing large economic development projects and fighting sprawl. As state legislatures debate the issue in the coming months, many local officials will be making those same points repeatedly—and are likely to keep their authority—despite the sudden distaste for the idea in the wake of the Court's decision.

32

Toil and Trouble

Jonathan Walters

Illegal immigrants working as day laborers present one of the toughest, most divisive issues to land on local government's doorstep in recent years.

From *Governing*, April 2006.

It's just after six o'clock on a crisp February morning in the Village of Brewster, New York, one of a string of small towns that dot a busy commuter rail line leading into Manhattan, 50 miles to the south. The dark outlines of Main Street's one- to three-story commercial buildings are silhouetted against a pink and purple dawn sky. Despite the early hour, there is a general stirring downtown. Descending from the hill above the village's commercial row is a steady stream of men in work clothes, hooded sweatshirts and ball caps pulled down to just above their eyes.

It's the beginning of the daily procession of immigrant workers—most of them from Guatemala and most of them undocumented—as they take their places along Main Street in clusters ranging from three to more than a dozen. They stand curbside waiting to be picked up by the small convoy of trucks and SUVs that circulates through Brewster seven mornings a week, contractors and home-owners looking for a day's work out of men willing to do dirty, hard jobs for wages that most American workers wouldn't even consider.

The scene that unfolds nearly every morning in Brewster is mirrored in hundreds of municipalities, both large and small, across the country. Groups of men—from places such as Mexico, Guatemala, Ecuador, Colombia and El Salvador—up early in the morning, gathering at casually established pickup points, hoping to make enough money to live and perhaps send to family back home. And while many Americans seem comfortable with the concept of cut-rate labor when it comes to home renovation or grounds-keeping, they seem decidedly less sanguine about the consequences of such economics, the most fundamental of which means playing host to a new and very different group of residents in and around their communities.

164

And so in villages, towns and cities from New York to California, the day labor phenomenon is bringing with it predictable tensions revolving around race and culture, and perceptions of poverty and crime. To date, local governments have been the front line in dealing with the issue. The ways they have managed it are as varied as the communities experiencing the phenomenon, but the approaches can be broken down into three general categories: ignore it, crack down, or adapt and manage.

OVERT CONFLICT

A quiet bedroom community of about 2,000 people, Brewster was one of those places that for a decade more or less ignored the issue. But as its undocumented day-laborer population began to swell (some estimate it to be as many as 600 to 1,000), tensions inevitably ratcheted up. Complaints about intimidating groups of strange men on the sidewalks watching women walk by, public drunkenness, homelessness and other objectionable behaviors simmered.

The situation heated up further last fall when a day laborer was found passed out on the grounds of a local elementary school. It boiled over in early January, when a Putnam County sheriff rounded up eight day laborers who were playing soccer on the grounds of the same elementary school during school hours. They were all arrested for trespassing. One was reported to federal immigration authorities and faces deportation. With the arrests, Brewster became one more pinpoint on the national map of places where the battle over day laborers had broken out into the open.

Why streams of immigrants have arrived in the United States to take jobs that most Americans don't seem to want isn't much of a mystery. Ask any day laborer why he's here and at least some part of the answer will include that work here pays incredibly well by the standards of their home countries. Eduardo, a 32-year-old, undocumented worker who first arrived in Brewster 11 years ago, and who now lives just to the south in the Village of Mount Kisco, says he has managed to carve out a specialty in tree work, which earns him as much as $25,000 per year, more than half of which he sends back to his family in Guatemala. He makes that much, he says, "because the work is very dangerous." While Eduardo says he now has a steady employer, initially he too was part of the small army of young men in Brewster standing on the sidewalk willing to take just about any work that came their way.

According to a recent study of the day-labor phenomenon, Brewster has its equivalent in more than 500 other communities nationwide—where roughly 120,000 laborers gather every day to try to find work—or, more accurately, where they hope work will find them. Three-quarters of those workers are here illegally. About half work directly for homeowners, and just over 43 percent for contractors. The jobs they do vary from as low-skill as washing dishes, to as high-skill as fine masonry, although most appear to be basic, hard and often dangerous.

The study documents a fairly high level of abuse of day laborers at the hands of employers—the most common form being failure to pay owed wages, but ranging up to outright neglect when it comes to workplace danger and on-the-job injuries. It also touches on some issues related to how day laborers are treated by the communities in which they live and work, noting frequent instances of hostility from both police and local merchants. Nonetheless, at least 63 communities have tried to defuse the tension by setting up organized sites where they can gather and wait for work.

The concept of day-labor centers isn't one that's quickly accepted by most communities. Many localities have resisted this approach, believing that it will only draw more illegal workers to their town. Other communities have decided (or have been compelled to decide, in part through legal action) that it makes more sense to at least create a safe place where workers can get a hot cup of coffee, use a bathroom and perhaps benefit from some other centralized services.

CENTRAL SITE

Port Chester, which sits on Long Island Sound just below the Connecticut border, is one of those places that decided on its own to deal with the growing problem of congregating day laborers. About a dozen years ago, day laborers discovered Port Chester as a handy jumping off point for work opportunities in affluent Westchester County, New York. And while a number of gathering points had been created informally by day laborers, one of the favorites was the centrally located and bustling commuter rail station downtown. It was a situation bound for trouble as it put heavy commuter traffic into direct conflict with heavy contractor traffic, and forced well-paid white-collar commuters to work their way through a small army of hard-looking Latino immigrants.

"We saw the need several years ago," says Port Chester Mayor Gerald Logan, a Republican who is in the middle of his third two-year term. "And I mentioned it in an article in the local newspaper." As it turned out, Logan wasn't the only one thinking about the issue. Tim Ploch, the pastor at the local Holy Rosary Catholic church, also noticed, and after reading the mayor's comments in the paper, stepped up to offer his parish as the site for a day-labor center. With an identified site on the table, the Westchester Hispanic Coalition agreed to help staff the center and coordinate programs.

In stark contrast to the situation in Brewster, day laborers in Port Chester now head for a single, central site where contractors know to go when they need help. The location is handy because it's within walking distance of where many day laborers live, and is also close to the train station—some day laborers take the train to Port Chester because it's known as a work center. Perhaps equally important, it's just down a main road from a Home Depot. "So contractors can swing over to Home Depot and then swing by here," says Soraya Principe, director of the center. (In many localities Home Depots have become ground zero for conflicts over the day-laborer issue. In fact, a handful of local governments are now demanding that Home Depots and other big-box construction supply outlets create day-labor shelters on site as a condition of site plan approval.)

The center at Holy Rosary, which gets no government money, is roomy, warm and well lit. At one end, hot coffee and pastries are being served. For those who don't get work on any given day, the center offers English classes taught by volunteers. Workers who use the center also have access to services offered by the Westchester Hispanic Coalition, including help with immigration authorities or in tracking down contractors who fail to pay promised wages. Principe says the coalition enjoys about a 50 percent recovery rate.

Port Chester, though, is the clear exception when it comes to how various communities have dealt with day laborers. The official reception has been rough in a lot of places. Last September, undercover police posing as contractors arrested 30 day laborers in Houston for violating a local ordinance against soliciting work in the roadway. Last November, police in Farmingville, New York, on Long Island, arrested several day laborers for trespassing

(Farmingville also has witnessed assaults on day laborers). Last December, Oconee County, Georgia, sheriff's deputies swept into a Home Depot parking lot and arrested 31 day laborers for loitering. And early in January, five day laborers were arrested in Cicero, Illinois, part of a group of 40 men in a Home Depot parking lot waiting for work. The same month, the new mayor of Morristown, New Jersey, Donald Cresitello, vowed to crack down on the overcrowding of illegal immigrants in local housing, a phenomenon known as "stacking."

Stacking is frequently citied as one of the most common and potentially dangerous public safety side effects of the day-laborer phenomenon. The high rents in Brewster (a small studio apartment goes for around $1,000 per month) make it tempting for landlords to carve houses and apartments into ever-smaller, more numerous units. Still, buildings that are carved up into multiple units can be firetraps, and also put a strain on local utilities. Some localities have beefed up inspections of properties where stacking is suspected. Others have passed local laws requiring landlords to regularly report on their tenant loads. Brewster has gone to a stricter monitoring of water use as a way to identify the practice.

While some localities try to crack down on day laborers, others are going after contractors, on the grounds that it's illegal under federal law to hire undocumented immigrants. In East Hampton Village, New York, police last fall started taking down the license plate numbers of vehicles picking up day laborers, threatening to report the contractors to federal authorities. In Riverside, California, police are enforcing "red curb" zones—where it is illegal to pull over and pick anybody up—at traditional day-labor gathering sites.

MILITANT RESPONSE

As the day-labor issue has seen increasing numbers of local flashpoints, there's also been a national backlash in the form of groups urging tough action against illegal immigrants, in general, and day laborers, in particular. Last January, immigration control activists organized "Stop the Invasion" day, which saw about 40 groups demonstrating in 20 states, from New Jersey to California.

Even some local officials are starting to lean toward the militant. "Mayors and County Executives for Immigration Reform," a coalition of local officials, is pressuring the federal government to act. "It's local governments that are experiencing the fallout of a failed federal policy," says one of the effort's founders, Mayor Mark Boughton of Danbury, Connecticut. "We're all left to our own devices to try and manage this flow of people without any support or backup from the feds, and you're seeing communities get into these bitter, divisive fights. Until we secure the borders, we're wasting our time. Things like hiring halls and day-laborer centers, that's just managing a policy and system that has spun out of control."

It is not hard to understand why there is so much tension—and even hostility—around the whole day-labor phenomenon. No local politician or chamber of commerce president would argue that groups of undocumented workers clustered along downtown sidewalks is a good thing for business, public safety or the civic image. Jane Neri, who runs a consignment shop on Main Street in Brewster, says she's seen a 70 percent decline in business over the past few years, as more day laborers have begun to congregate and then hang around downtown if not hired that morning.

Neri, who on this particular morning is complaining that she just had to clean vomit off her storefront window courtesy of a day laborer, says that her customers have told her they are afraid to run the gauntlet of men who now congregate on the sidewalks outside her shop. She doesn't blame all day laborers, just a hard-core group that seems uninterested in co-existing with the rest of the community, she says.

In talking to those on both sides of the issue, the operative emotion does seem to be fear. Mayra, who manages a laundromat on Brewster's Main Street, an unofficial gathering site for day laborers, says that the young men who frequent her place—virtually all of them undocumented—are afraid, too, especially in the wake of the school arrests. "They're afraid of immigration [officials]; they feel like"— and here she struggles for a word—"chickens."

When asked how such fear might be diffused in Brewster, Istebon Jiminez, who came to Brewster from Mexico about 10 years ago, gained citizenship and now runs a downtown Mexican restaurant, says "communication." Yet he admits to never having approached merchants just a few doors down the street, such as Jane Neri, to talk about dealing with what even he recognizes is a problem for local business people. One significant obstacle to such contact is obvious: Jiminez, a potentially powerful emissary to the local business community because of his background and his clear understanding of the

roots of tension in town, speaks very little English. Given their level of interaction, Jiminez and Neri might as well be living in different towns.

The other factor that's impossible to ignore is color. As some in Brewster point out, the village has a long history of accepting and assimilating immigrants. In the early 1900s, Irish and Italians arrived in Brewster to work at the thriving Borden condensed milk plant at the east end of Main Street and the quarries outside of town. But Brewster's liaison to the day-labor community, Victor Padilla, thinks this wave of immigrants is having a harder time of assimilating for the simple reason that "they may be a little too brown."

POLICY FAILURES

Whatever the roots of the problems, the clearest failure on the day-labor front is political and runs up and down the governmental food chain. Convoluted and complicated federal immigration laws inconsistently and sporadically applied haven't helped, nor has the fact that Congress is bitterly divided on immigration issues. States, meanwhile, are for the most part absent from the debate, as they neither have the authority to deal with immigration policy, nor suffer the consequences of local day-labor skirmishes. Counties have been a bit more involved. In fact, the Westchester County Legislature held the first of what will be a series of hearings on the day-labor issue in February, investigating how the county might step in to help.

But in the final analysis, the day-laborer conflicts continue to fall squarely in the laps of city and town governments, and most seem to experience bitter fights before things improve. The Village of Mount Kisco, a half-dozen stops south of Brewster on the same commuter rail line, is one of those places. Ten years ago, it was open warfare in the village. Mel Berger, a former local pharmacist, remembers fuming over the growing number of day laborers congregating around the village's downtown train station. "I even went as far as to call the U.S. Immigration and Naturalization Service in New York City," says Berger. "I said, 'Come up here and arrest these people!' The INS guy laughed and said, 'What are you kidding? I could walk out my door and go around the corner and arrest 100 people right here.'"

So Mount Kisco decided to take matters into its own hands. The town launched midnight housing raids looking for code violations in dwellings known to harbor day laborers, and also passed a law restricting public solicitation of work. The flurry of activity certainly got people's attention, but not the kind that the village wanted. The Westchester Hispanic Coalition brought a discrimination suit against the village. As part of the settlement, Mount Kisco agreed to stop openly harassing Latinos, to open up a local park to the day-laborer community and to be more bilingual in official postings and signage.

At the same time, a group led by a local Presbyterian church launched an effort to find a suitable site for a day-labor center as a further way to defuse community conflict. The search committee was led by, of all people, Mel Berger, who says his view began to shift as he got to know members of the Latino community and to understand what the day-laborer phenomenon was all about. While he says the search was an eye-opening exercise in NIMBYism, the center opened in 2000.

Located in a mini-industrial park, the center is spacious, with a front room lined on one wall with banks of computers. Volunteers teach everything from English to budgeting. Hiring is handled in two ways: Unskilled laborers are listed on a first-come, first-served basis on a board in the front room. Skilled laborers—painters or roofers, for example—are matched with employers looking for such skills. On busy days, as many as 60 to 80 laborers will circulate through the center. Its $410,000 budget is covered entirely by private contributions. When it comes to the immigration status of those who use the center, "We never ask," says executive director Carola Otero Bracco.

While the situation in Mount Kisco isn't perfect—there is still tension, and day laborers report that they continue to be hassled regularly by the police—the community has clearly made progress.

If Brewster has any advantage over the Mount Kisco of 10 years ago when it comes to working through the day-labor issue, it's that key political leaders understand what the village is up against by way of bringing together a divided community. Mayor John Degnan has no interest in touching off a Mount Kisco-like war as a prelude to working things out. "It is an evolution," says Degnan, "but we've seen the successes in other communities around us. The key is going to be community involvement. Even if you make progress with a brick-and-mortar day-labor center, you still have to do a lot better job of communication within the community."

Budgets and Taxes

The good news is that state governments have managed, fiscally speaking, to stop the bleeding. The bad news is that many of the patients now need transfusions.

Most states have managed to get past a disastrous few years that saw shrinking revenues and painful choices about program cuts and tax hikes. Overall, state budgets shrank in real (that is, inflation-adjusted) terms for three years running between 2002 and 2004. In the two years following, revenues rebounded and state spending ticked up.

While those increases are welcome news compared to decreases, this modest upward trend is not always enough to keep up with the fiscal pressures that continue to squeeze states. For example, while the average general fund budget increased by 6 percent in 2006, the costs associated with Medicaid went up 7.5 percent.[1] And those sorts of increases do not even account for the pressures created by spending deferred and delayed during the lean years. In other words, there are still some painful choices being made.

As the readings in this section make clear, states are in better financial shape than they have been in a while. Yet many face short- and long-term monetary pressures that suggest the good news about state and local government funding is likely to come in small doses for the foreseeable future.

RAISING AND SPENDING MONEY

According to the most recent estimate, state and local government expenditures total roughly $2 trillion, that's a 2 followed by 12 zeros, roughly $6,600 for every citizen of the United States.[2] By any measure, that's a lot of money. Where does it all come from?

State and local governments rely on six major sources of revenue: sales taxes, property taxes, income taxes, motor vehicle taxes, estate and gift taxes and grants and transfers from the federal government. Of the taxes state and local governments levy, the biggest revenue producers are sales taxes (about $324 billion), property taxes ($279 billion) and individual income taxes ($203 billion). Grants from the federal government add $360 billion to state and local coffers.[3] Other sources of revenue include everything from fees for licenses to hunt, fish, or marry to interest earned on bank deposits. There is enormous variation from state to state—and even locality to locality—in how governments raise their money. Some states (for example, Florida and Texas), have no individual income tax and rely more heavily on sales taxes.

There are pros and cons to employing different forms of taxation. Property taxes, for instance, are one of the most hated forms of taxation. They are typically levied as a portion of the assessed value of property, such as a house. They are most often paid in a lump sum once or twice a year, and thus tend to be stark reminders to taxpayers about how much government takes from them. For most homeowners, property taxes work out to be about 1.55 percent of their house's value. So someone who owns a house worth, say, $200,000, will pay about $3,100 a year in property taxes. Writing a check that big can be painful.

While property owners are never going to be enthusiastic about them, property taxes have clear advantages for state and local governments. Most importantly, they are a relatively stable form of income. Income and sales taxes will rise and fall with the ups and downs of the economy. Property values can fall too, of course, but they rarely fall much.

Much of the controversy surrounding state and local taxes comes from the perennial issues of fairness and who pays. The advantage of a sales tax, proponents argue, is that it is a fair tax. Technically it is a flat tax, meaning everyone pays the same rate, regardless of the ability to pay. It doesn't matter whether Bill Gates or a cash-strapped college student buys a book or a television or a car; if they buy that product or service in the same place, then they pay exactly the same tax.

Critics of the sales tax say that equity is what makes it so unfair. To be fair, the tax should take into account

ability to pay; taxes that do not take into account ability to pay are called regressive. In contrast, income taxes are typically progressive taxes, meaning that how much you pay is dependent upon how wealthy you are. The tax rate increases progressively with income; in short, richer people get hit with a higher tax than poor people. Critics of the income tax say that isn't fair—in effect a progressive tax punishes people for being successful. The arguments over sales versus income, and regressive versus progressive taxes, are neverending, and most states do not take an either/or approach. Most choose some mix of both, and generally speaking no one is happy with the result.

There is another prominent source of revenue governments can tap: borrowing. The federal government covers a significant chunk of its spending with deficient financing. In simple terms, the federal government covers the gap between revenue and expenditure with a credit card. State and local governments also borrow, primarily by issuing bonds. Bonds are nothing more than IOUs, certificates stating that the state or locality will pay the bearer of the bond a specified interest rate for a specified period of time and return the principle when the bond reaches maturity.

State and local governments, however, cannot engage in the same sort of "credit card" financing as the federal government. The vast majority of states are legally required to produce balanced budgets, that is, by law expenditures cannot exceed revenue. This is a major reason why state governments suffered so much a few years ago when a recession cut income and sales tax growth. States and localities simply have less wiggle room when times get fiscally tough—they are all but forced to raise taxes, cut spending, or do both. The only exception is Vermont, which alone among the states is free to run itself into debt in a similar fashion to the federal government.

What do states and localities spend their money on? Well, a big chunk goes to education, roughly $600 billion (about $411 billion on elementary and secondary education, the rest on higher education). Other big-ticket items include social welfare programs (about $280 billion) and roads ($115 billion). Some government expenditures, however, are less visible to citizens. State and local governments spend more than $100 billion annually on employee retirement benefits, and a further $75 billion paying interest on all those bonds.[4]

RECENT TRENDS

The most notable recent trend in budgets is the waning of the financial crisis that gripped many subnational governments during the past few years. The essay by Corina Eckl shows that state budgets are at a five-year high-water mark, thanks to an improving economy and some painful decisions. While budgets are sound, however, there are looming fiscal pressures that are going to make for tough debates during the next few years. Education demands are growing, and Medicaid costs are going nowhere but up. Even states that by most measures do a prudent job of fiscal planning find some spending is all but beyond their control.

The essays by Arturo Pérez and Alan Greenblatt show why this is the case. Pérez details the increasing costs associated with rising prison populations. Criminal justice budgets are growing by 10 percent or more in some states. These costs are exacerbated not just by a growing prison population, but also by an aging prison population. Health care costs for graying felons put an additional squeeze on corrections budgets already in an upward trend because of growing inmate populations. Greenblatt's essay takes a look at the financial implications of pension obligations to public employees. State pension funds are collectively $300 billion short of their future obligations. The money to pay such retired public workers as teachers has to be found somewhere. The question is, where?

Ellen Perlman's essay details the downside of one more attempt to create a painless tax. Pennsylvania, like a number of other states, has looked to gambling to provide a lucrative source of revenue, something that could ease property taxes. The "easy" money scheduled to come out of the state's slice of gambling proceeds, however, comes wrapped in a complex piece of legislation, and some question the program's ability to deliver on its promises of large injections of revenue to local governments.

1. National Association of State Budget Officers, "The Fiscal Survey of States 2005," www.nasbo.org/Publications/fiscalsurvey/fsfall2005.pdf (accessed April 27, 2006).

2. U.S. Census Bureau, *Statistical Abstract of the United States 2006*, Table 426, www.census.gov/prod/2005pubs/06statab/stlocgov.pdf (accessed April 29, 2006).

3. Ibid.

4. Ibid.

33

State Budgets: Bliss or Blues

Corina Eckl

With state revenue performance improving, states appear to have turned the corner on the latest national recession.

State budgets are healthier than they've been in five years, thanks to improving revenues and careful balancing of priorities. Although the downturn seemed to last forever, the turnaround has occurred quickly. While final numbers for fiscal year 2005 are still coming in, the news is surprisingly positive on several fronts. Revenue figures and year-end balances, in particular, stand out as noteworthy.

Part way into FY 2005, lawmakers learned that tax collections were outpacing projections, in some cases by substantial amounts. By March 2005, half the states reported that collections were exceeding forecasts for every major tax thanks largely to increasing employment and rising corporate profits. The reports were even better after April personal income taxes were tallied.

Although robust revenue collections were a welcome change from the situation of recent years, lawmakers were caught by surprise. When they were developing their FY 2005 budgets, states estimated revenues would grow 2.8 percent above FY 2004 levels. The final figure will be closer to 6 percent. Many states used unexpected revenue growth to support supplemental appropriations while others, either through deliberate action or because their legislative sessions already had concluded, left the funds unspent or deposited them into their rainy day funds.

Nationally, states expected to end FY 2005 with a collective balance of 3.6 percent of general fund spending. Estimates now place that figure at 7 percent—nearly twice as high as expected. Although balances are expected to drop by the end of the current fiscal year, they are still projected to reach 4.7 percent.

How long will this relative prosperity last? No one knows for certain, but budget insiders are wary. "Fiscal people never relax, we

From *State Legislatures,*
October/November 2005.

anguish over this stuff all the time," says Michael Calvert, director of Nebraska's Legislative Fiscal Office. "But as we look at the long-term trends, there are genuine reasons to be concerned."

Any discussion of state budgets and the pressures on them starts with the biggest cost drivers: elementary-secondary (K-12) education and Medicaid. Together, these programs account for nearly 50 percent of state general fund budgets, up from 42 percent a decade ago.

EDUCATION DEMANDS

State constitutions guarantee public education. And K-12 education also enjoys strong bipartisan and public support. It would be politically difficult, if not impossible, to shrink the K-12 share of the budget.

Various factors are propelling K-12 spending. The requirements of the federally mandated No Child Left Behind law are expensive: Experts estimate that the states are shouldering an extra $10 billion annually to comply with the law.

Other factors are fueling costs, too. For years, states have been struggling to address court rulings that their school funding systems are inadequate. Arkansas is one of the most recent states where the system was declared unconstitutional. Lawmakers responded by imposing a 0.875 percent increase in the sales tax and earmarking it for K-12 education.

Most other states are boosting K-12 funding, too. Even in bad times, education usually is spared the budget axe. And now that revenues are improving, K-12 is benefiting. States are raising teacher salaries, enhancing funding formulas, starting new programs or generally increasing their share of K-12 support.

A recent citizen initiative in Maine requires the state to provide a greater share of K-12 educational costs. The original proposal—which raises the state's share from 43 percent to 55 percent—called for the change to occur in FY 2006, but the Legislature is phasing in funding and will reach the target by FY 2009. Maryland is in the middle of a five-year state initiated plan to significantly increase its support for public education. The state has approved $1.3 billion in additional support, which will boost its share of total funding to 47.5 percent from the 40 percent level when the plan originally was approved. Under the current schedule, state aid will increase $500 million per year in the final two years of the program's phase-in.

New or expanding education programs also are raising costs. Delaware lawmakers appropriated $3 million in FY 2006 to continue pilot funding for full-day kindergarten. If the program is implemented statewide, the estimated annual cost is $20 million. Florida's current budget includes $388 million to phase in universal voluntary pre-kindergarten for four-year-olds, a program approved by voters in November 2002. Another voter mandate reduces public school class size by two students annually until constitutionally imposed targets are met. In Oklahoma, lawmakers are using new education trust fund lottery revenues to fund full-day kindergarten and third grade remediation.

Other recent increases in education spending have been driven in part by teacher pay raises or pension costs (Alaska, Mississippi, Oklahoma, Virginia), special education costs (Hawaii), increases in state base aid per pupil (Kansas, Kentucky, Louisiana, Minnesota, Montana, Nebraska, New York) and higher enrollment (Utah).

MEDICAID CONCERNS

Just as education spending is rising, so are Medicaid costs. And like K-12 education, they are difficult to contain. At their discretion, states may add optional populations and services to those that are mandated. But if they fail to provide the minimum levels, they loose the federal match.

Medicaid costs and other health expenses are in the national spotlight. Medicaid consumes 16 percent of state general fund budgets and is the fastest growing category of state spending. Although the national recession is behind us—which presumably means that caseloads are dropping or stabilizing—Medicaid costs are not leveling off. In fact, they are expected to rise as budgeters look at demographics.

More than 50 million Americans receive health services or long-term care through Medicaid. About three-fourths of them are adults and children who meet the income requirements to receive health care benefits. The remainder are individuals with disabilities and elderly people who depend on Medicaid for health services and long-term care benefits. Although these beneficiaries account for only 25 percent of the Medicaid population, they account for 70 percent of Medicaid expenses. With the graying of America, these costs are expected to skyrocket.

GASB 45 Raises Concerns

The Governmental Accounting Standards Board (GASB), as its name implies, sets accounting standards for state and local governments. In 2004 it issued a new rule that affects how state and local governments estimate and track health care and other benefit costs for retired employees.

The rule is known as Statement Number 45, Accounting and Financial Reporting by Employers for Postemployment Benefits Other Than Pension. The statement generally requires governments to estimate the eventual total costs of their health care programs for retired employees and report on their annual progress in funding the costs. A previous GASB standard already imposed similar reporting requirements for pensions.

The statement does not require a government to report its total liability for retiree health care costs. Instead, the requirement is for recognition of the annually accruing cost of future health benefits—the equivalent of the annual added cost of pension benefits that is reported to most legislatures. The government must report whether it has met that cost, and whether any part of its annual obligation is unfunded.

The GASB rule requires disclosure, not funding. In the past, governments rarely have required actuarial studies of the future cost of retiree health benefits. The numbers could be shocking. Standard & Poor's has commented that "The new reporting may reveal cases in which the actuarial funding of post-employment health benefits would seriously strain operations, or may uncover conditions under which employers are unable or unwilling to fulfill these obligations." Standard & Poor's suggests that some governments may choose to reduce or drop health care plans for future retirees, once the costs are known. Some private sector employers followed that course when a similar rule was applied to them in past years.

Governments with revenues of more than $100 million (all state governments and many large counties and cities) are subject to the new rule for fiscal years beginning after Dec. 15, 2005. The rule comes into effect later for smaller governments.

The new rule is beneficial in that policymakers will receive information on costs they have agreed to meet. The costs, however, could throw government budgets out of balance if it's not possible to cover them in any given year. To the many governments already hit with escalating retiree pension costs, the new accounting standard could come as very bad news.

—Ron Snell, NCSL

In their 2005 sessions, several state legislatures attempted to restrict the rate of spending growth for Medicaid. Maryland reduced the rate of increase for nursing home and managed care payments and bolstered efforts to reduce fraud and abuse. Mississippi changed its prescription drug policy, implemented some co-pays and modified eligibility consideration to save funds. Missouri made optional services subject to appropriation, eliminated the Medical Assistance for the Working Disabled program and changed certain income guidelines. New Hampshire authorized changes that involve long-term care services, estate recovery and asset transfers, all of which are expected to have an impact in the long run.

Ohio's actions included new cost sharing arrangements for dental and vision care, certain prescription drugs and non-emergency services. Pennsylvania's current budget reflects $350 million in savings from a number of cost containment measures. Tennessee's current Medicaid budget is constructed around the disenrollment of three optional adult categories so that the state can maintain funding for the medically needy (another optional adult category).

Despite these and other cost containment measures, Medicaid is still budgeted to grow 8.1 percent in FY 2006. Similar growth rates are anticipated for the future. At NCSL's Spring Forum last April, Secretary of Health and Human Services Michael Leavitt projected that Medicaid would "grow well north of 7 percent annually over the next 10 years."

State officials are very concerned about this trend. Vermont conducts five-year projections of Medicaid costs and the news is alarming. "We can squeak by until FY 2007, but there is darkness after that," says Stephen Klein, director of Vermont's Joint Fiscal Office.

Medicaid is not unique in experiencing rapid rate increases. Many of the same cost drivers are affecting other health care programs, such as those for state employees, retirees and prisoners. Private employer health plans are feeling the pinch, too, with costs escalating even more rapidly.

OTHER PRESSURES

Although K-12 education and Medicaid attract a lot of attention and get the lion's share of spending, there is the rest of the state budget to consider. As spending for these two programs has expanded, many other programs have shrunk, including higher education. Having weathered years of cuts or flat funding, higher education and most other programs now are exerting their own pressure on the budget.

"We have old obligations and new expectations, and we can't keep up," says Representative Maxine Bell, who chairs Idaho's House Appropriations Committee. "Right now we're even, but that's only for a brief moment."

Several states see the current prosperity as temporary because more and more demands are placed on the budget. Consider Maryland's situation. Although the state ended FY 2005 with a $1.2 billion closing balance, officials project a $1 billion deficit by FY 2008.

Are State Budgets Sound?

Budget experts point to a looming fiscal crisis driven by the persistent mismatch between growth rates in revenues and spending. Among state budget writers the lexicon now routinely includes terms like "antiquated tax systems," "structural deficits" and "unsustainable budgets." They all point to trouble.

States are required—either by statute or constitution— to balance their budgets. In recent years lawmakers closed budget gaps by cutting spending, raising revenues or tapping reserves. Some states even borrowed money. Nearly every state used one-time funds to keep budgets in the black.

Although temporary or one-time actions get the job done, they don't offer a long-term solution and eventually work to undermine budget stability. A structurally sound budget must be built on a revenue base that keeps pace with spending over the long term. If the two become misaligned, lawmakers must cut spending, raise taxes or implement some combination of these.

According to the Center on Budget and Policy Priorities, a state has a structural deficit when "the normal growth of revenues under existing tax policy is chronically inadequate to fund the normal growth of expenditures for current services, even at times of healthy economic growth."

The Center on Budget and Policy Priorities has identified 10 factors that place a state at risk for a structural deficit. Using these factors, the center found that 44 states faced five or more risk factors, with 11 states having nine or 10 risk factors. Most of the risk factors are associated with a state's tax structure.

Much has been written about the inadequacies of current state revenue systems (an excellent source is NCSL's book *New Realities in State Finance*). The bottom line is this: Without modernizing tax structures to fully capture growth in the economy, state collections will persistently lag behind spending growth. Cutting spending, raising taxes—or both—will become painful realities.

Although some states have attempted to restructure their tax systems, policymakers almost always encounter fierce resistance to change. Citizens are reluctant to accept new taxes even if others are lowered in the process. The old adage, "The devil you know is better than the one you don't," seems to prevail. As a result, most changes have been modest at best. At the same time, well-organized interest groups mobilize to oppose new taxes that might affect them. Louisiana Senator Russell Long's famous quip is apropos: "Don't tax you, don't tax me, tax that fellow behind the tree."

Nevada and Virginia modified their tax systems in recent years. In Nevada, the 2003 Legislature approved tax increases after completion of a study that reviewed and made recommendations to address the state's structural imbalance. In Virginia, the 2004 tax package was considered a key step in addressing the state's structural gap. The intention was to develop sustainable revenue streams that could support budget obligations rather than resorting to budget gimmicks.

Still other states are trying to address structural gaps by focusing on the spending side of the ledger. Several have reformed programs or modified services to slow spending growth. Some states have reformed Medicaid to rein in spending. Others have asked state employees to shoulder a greater share of health care insurance costs. Some states are moving from defined benefit plans to defined contribution plans to save on future pension costs. It is too soon to know if these actions or others ultimately will make a difference in closing structural gaps.

State efforts to realign long-term spending and revenue growth rates have been slow. Over the years, periodic bubbles in tax collections have masked underlying problems in state budgets, delaying the need for serious or immediate attention to structural imbalances. But the day of reckoning may be looming.

"We're living in a fiction," says Vermont's House Speaker Gaye Symington.

Number of Factors Contributing to a Structural Gap

Most at Risk ◄───────────────────────────────────────► Least at Risk

10 OR 9	8	7	6	5	4 OR 3
Alaska	Alabama	Arizona	Connecticut	Kansas	Minnesota
Arkansas	Georgia	California	Delaware	Louisiana	Nebraska
Colorado	Kentucky	Hawaii	Illinois	Maine	New Jersey
Florida	Missouri	Idaho	Iowa	Maryland	North Dakota
Nevada	Rhode Island	Indiana	Massachusetts	New York	Vermont
New Mexico	South Dakota	Michigan	Montana		Wisconsin
Pennsylvania	Washington	Mississippi	New Hampshire		
South Carolina		Oklahoma	North Carolina		
Tennessee		Virginia	Ohio		
Texas			Oregon		
Wyoming			Utah		
			West Virginia		

Source: Center on Budget & Policy Priorities, Washington, D.C., August 2005. The report, "Faulty Foundations: State Structural Problems and How to Fix Them," can be found at www.cbpp.org.

THE BEST LAID PLANS

Many unknowns can derail even the most carefully crafted budgets. Although most budgets contain some flexibility to adapt to changing circumstances, that latitude usually is minor. It certainly is insufficient to deal with significant events like natural disasters.

Hurricane Katrina—in addition to causing loss of life and property—is dramatically altering budgets in the Gulf Coast states. Although the federal government and charitable groups will contribute to the recovery, the affected states still will face enormous costs to aid victims and rebuild infrastructure.

With businesses and jobs lost, tax collections will suffer. Mississippi officials estimate the loss of tax revenue from Biloxi casinos alone will cost state coffers at least $500,000—every day. Last year, the coastal casinos contributed approximately $73 million to the general fund. Before Katrina hit, that figure was expected to rise to $84 million for FY 2006.

The losses are expected to be dramatically higher in Louisiana, where officials are in the process of developing new revenue forecasting models to adjust for the hurricane's effect. "A big chunk of our economy got turned off," says Greg Albrecht, chief economist in the Legisla-

tive Fiscal Office. "It'll take some time to get an actual assessment of the revenue impact, but it's going to be a lot of money. We've got a big problem here."

Although economists point out that the rebuilding process will be an eventual economic boost, that out-

Ten Risk Factors That Contribute to Structural Budget Problems

- Lack of services in the sales tax base
- Corporate income tax weakness
- Untaxed e-commerce
- Extensive tax preferences for the elderly
- Limited progressivity of the personal income tax
- Tax policy mix and choices that worsen structural gaps
- The growth of expenditure needs for residents
- Process barriers such as tax and expenditure limitations
- Failure to detach from federal policies that reduce state revenue
- Presence of structural gaps found by other studies

Source: Center on Budget & Policy Priorities, Washington, D.C., August 2005.

look is little consolation right now. "At some point we'll be adding money, but it will be from a very low trough," adds Albrecht.

Other looming factors can upset budget plans. What if the recovery stalls? David Wyss, chief economist for Standard & Poor's in New York, warns that today's energy prices pose a real risk to economic growth.

"Obviously, high energy prices are going to hurt, both because states have to buy gas and because of increased subsidies for the poor to keep the heat on. Most important, however, could be any revenue drop caused by resulting economic problems," says Wyss.

It's impossible to say how long oil prices will stay high—that depends in part on getting Gulf refineries and oil platforms back in operation. "At this time, I think the impact will be moderate, about 0.5 percent," says Wyss. "But if the outages last longer than a month, we may have to revise the national economic forecast down."

The Gulf states have been hardest hit physically and financially by the hurricane and its aftermath. But other states expect to feel the ripple effects as the economy absorbs the shock. The Creighton University Economic Forecasting Group already is predicting slowdowns in other regions of the country.

Notwithstanding the effects of Hurricane Katrina and high energy prices, most state budgets appear to be stable for the moment. But they face myriad challenges in the short and long term. How long the current prosperity will last is anybody's guess.

Stay tuned.

NALFO Speaks

What are the biggest fiscal issues in the coming legislative session and beyond? Members of the National Association of Legislative Fiscal Offices (NALFO) shared their projections during a roundtable discussion at NCSL's Strong States, Strong Nation meeting in Seattle.

✓ **MEDICAID:** Medicaid ranks as the fastest growing category of state spending. Despite many states' efforts to rein in costs, it is still budgeted to grow 8.1 percent in FY 2006.

✓ **OTHER HEALTH CARE COSTS:** Many of the same factors driving Medicaid are affecting other health care spending, too. State officials are seeking ways to manage growing health care costs for state employees and retirees, not to mention aging state prisoners.

✓ **K-12 EDUCATION:** Either through their own initiative, court order or constitutional mandates imposed by voters, state officials are boosting K-12 education spending.

✓ **FEDERAL COST SHIFTS:** Costly new programs like No Child Left Behind and REAL ID pose considerable expense for states. Congressional and administration efforts to balance the federal budget could mean even more cost shifts, along with reductions in federal aid to states.

✓ **PENSIONS:** Referred to as a stealth issue by many, state officials are concerned about unfunded pension obligations. Costs could reach billions of dollars.

✓ **PROPERTY TAX RELIEF:** The rapid rise of real estate values and the resulting increases in property taxes have generated renewed calls for property tax relief programs.

✓ **TAX AND EXPENDITURE LIMITS:** Advocates of smaller government are promoting limits modeled after Colorado's Taxpayer Bill of Rights, whose provisions include limiting allowable revenue growth to population growth plus inflation.

✓ **HIGH ENERGY PRICES:** States that don't benefit from severance taxes might be hit on two fronts: sales tax collections could fall as discretionary spending gets directed toward gasoline purchases and spending could grow to cover heating for state buildings and gasoline for state fleets.

✓ **YO-YO TAX POLICY:** The recovery of state revenues and the resulting reserves may exert pressure on lawmakers to cut taxes during their 2006 sessions.

✓ **GASB 45:** This one is too complicated for a brief summary. See the sidebar on page 174 for an explanation.

34

States Wrangle with Corrections Budgets

Arturo Pérez

Criminal justice budgets challenge states as costs and inmate populations increase.

Prisons are overcrowded, understaffed and aging. Add to that the rising costs of health care for prisoners, and it's no wonder that states are spending more and more on corrections.

California's 15.8 percent increase is way above average for FY 2004 to FY 2005, stemming from a new emphasis on segregating high risk prisoners, medical transportation costs and reforms to the probation process. And it could be worse. One-time federal fiscal assistance grants lowered its FY 2004 figures.

The average increase in corrections spending is 4.9 percent, but in some states, like California, it's much higher. Wyoming's increase, for example, is 13 percent, Maine and North Dakota have jumped more than 11 percent. Increases in Vermont and Minnesota are 10 percent.

States held 1.3 million inmates at the end of 2003, a 1.6 percent jump from 2002, according to the most recent Bureau of Justice statistics. For the past 20 years, the average annual growth rate is much higher—2.9 percent. Nationally, in 2003, the incarceration rate was 430 prisoners per 100,000 residents.

HEALTH CARE COSTS JUMP

Corrections ranks fourth in total allocations behind K-12 education, Medicaid and higher education. Corrections budgets in FY 2005 total $31.4 billion—6 percent of general fund spending, compared with 5.3 percent 10 years ago.

Increases are being driven by health care costs—more disease, mental illness, substance abuse and an aging inmate population. Inmates tend to have higher infection rates for HIV/AIDS, tuber-

From *State Legislatures,* May 2005.

178

Incarceration Rates (Per 100,000 Residents, 2003)	
Highest	**Lowest**
Louisiana (801)	Maine (149)
Mississippi (768)	Minnesota (155)
Texas (702)	North Dakota (181)
Oklahoma (636)	Rhode Island (184)
Alabama (635)	New Hampshire (188)

Idaho is keeping some offenders out of state prisons through the use of drug courts and mental health courts. "In addition to saving on the cost of incarceration," says Senator Denton Darrington, "these alternates give people the opportunity to turn their lives around."

Almost half of released prisoners are convicted of a new crime within three years. The Maryland legislature is trying to reduce the recidivism rate by rehabilitating offenders in custody. Pilot programs at two prison sites, one male and one female, addresses inmates' substance abuse, social and education needs and will support them as they reenter the community.

culosis and hepatitis C than the general population. Providing health care to its 164,000 inmates is the fastest growing expense in California's adult correctional system.

"California's prison population is graying like the prison walls," says Senator Gloria Romero. "Health care needs multiply as inmates grow older and develop more chronic illnesses. It's the biggest price tag in the staggering $5.6 billion corrections budget—almost 20 percent."

Arkansas is trying to keep health care costs down. Recently it imposed a $3 co-pay on inmates seeking health treatment in an attempt to control the number of clinic visits by inmates. "Inmate health care costs," says Senator Dave Bisbee, "are rising faster than any other part of the corrections budget but that mirrors the increases in other health related programs in our budget."

Pennsylvania's corrections department is attempting to save money by bidding out medical, mental health and pharmacy services. It has also consolidated four infirmaries at prison facilities that are close to each other.

Michigan moved to a managed care arrangement for specialty and hospital services and uses drug formularies and generic medicines whenever possible.

CONTROLLING OTHER EXPENSES

Building new prisons is another huge cost. But some states are exploring other options. Colorado, for example, is placing 11 percent of the inmate population in more affordable community corrections programs. The move saved the state $1.9 million in FY 2005.

Percentage Change in General Fund Appropriations for Corrections, FY 2004 to FY 2005

Alabama	0.2%	Montana	1.2%
Alaska	2.7%	Nebraska	6.0%
Arizona	2.3%	Nevada	4.0%
Arkansas	2.3%	New Hampshire	2.0%
California	15.8%	New Jersey	4.9%
Colorado	6.5%	New Mexico	1.2%
Connecticut	−2.4%	New York	4.5%
Delaware	2.8%	North Carolina	6.0%
Florida	5.1%	North Dakota	3.9%
Georgia	−2.6%	Ohio	2.4%
Hawaii	3.7%	Oklahoma	2.8%
Idaho	2.3%	Oregon	8.3%
Illinois	−2.9%	Pennsylvania	3.0%
Indiana	−3.9%	Rhode Island	1.5%
Iowa	2.1%	South Carolina	0.2%
Kansas	3.8%	South Dakota	8.4%
Kentucky	n.a.	Tennessee	1.4%
Louisiana	8.1%	Texas	0.0%
Maine	11.4%	Utah	4.0%
Maryland	1.7%	Vermont	10.0%
Massachusetts	1.6%	Virginia	8.7%
Michigan	6.1%	Washington	3.6%
Minnesota	0.9%	West Virginia	1.5%
Mississippi	1.0%	Wisconsin	0.7%
Missouri	6.3%	Wyoming	13.1%
Total			**4.9%**

Source: 2004 survey of National Association of Legislative Fiscal Offices, NCSL.

Delegate Joan Cadden has high hopes for the multi-faceted Restart program. "It touches on all aspects of rehabilitation," she says, "by including drug rehabilitation experts, along with psychiatrists, psychologists, and social workers." Cadden says the education portion of the program is much stronger than what was offered in the past.

In Texas, where the prison system is almost at capacity, lawmakers are looking at the probation system as a solution to higher costs and overcrowding. The average daily cost of incarcerating an inmate is $40.06. Probation costs $2.27 per day.

"We have a unique opportunity this session to alter the direction we have been traveling—building more and more prison units," says Senator John Whitmire, chair of the Texas Senate Criminal Justice Committee.

WHAT'S AHEAD

As lawmakers explore options for meeting the basic task of incarcerating criminal offenders and carrying out state criminal justice policies, they must not forget the rights of victims," says Darrington of Idaho. "Attempts to control corrections costs should not come at the expense of crime victims. Society would benefit more from emphasis on the old adage, "Don't do the crime and you won't do the time," he says.

35

Plight of the Benefits

Alan Greenblatt

Retiree costs are moving from the easy promise of a nest egg to the harshness of a political hot potato.

Colorado Governor Bill Owens hopes to get his state's fiscal house in order before leaving office in a few months, but he faces one particularly vexing problem. Colorado's pension funds are more than $11 billion short. There's still plenty of money in the system right now to keep paying annual stipends to retired teachers and bureaucrats, but not enough to satisfy Owens' concerns about adequate funding in the future. If legislators can't come up with a solution he can support by next month, Owens vows to call them back into special session.

Owens isn't the only state or local leader putting himself on the line over pension issues. So have such governors as California's Arnold Schwarzenegger and Illinois' Rod Blagojevich. For good reason: Collectively, states are close to $300 billion short of meeting future pension obligations. And now, with a new government accounting rule forcing states and localities to budget for future promises of retiree health care coverage, retirement benefits are quickly turning into a potential political crisis and a major budget-buster.

The ramifications trickle out everywhere. Pressures to cut spending on non-retiree programs are intense along with counter pressure to cut the benefits themselves. These twin strains may mark the beginning of a profound shift in public-sector employment. Governments have never paid as well as private companies but have usually offered their workers greater security and superior benefits. Now, states and localities might not be able to raise taxes to maintain the same level of promises in the future. "The fundamental principle," says Dan Pellisier, a top aide to California state Representative Keith Richman, who is sponsoring a bill to lower public pension benefits, "is that public employees should not be retiring

From *Governing*, April 2006.

181

early and relying on private-sector employees to work longer to pay for their retirements."

THE UNFEATHERED NEST

In Colorado, the pension fix will be a choice between Owens' preference to shore up the shortfall by diverting 1 percent of employee pay, taken out of future pay raises for the next three years, and the more traditional tax-based approach of plan officials. Because the Democrats, who control the legislature, don't particularly like Owens' solution, they'd probably be inclined to wait him out. But there's one other factor that's keeping them at the negotiating table.

An initiative is all set to go on this November's ballot, sponsored primarily by the anti-tax Americans for Prosperity Foundation. In place of today's "defined benefit" plans, in which Colorado teachers and state employees are paid a fixed amount each month from retirement until death, Colorado would move to a 401(k)-style "defined contribution" system. Every month, the state and its employees would each pay a certain percentage of the workers' salaries into the retirement plan to be invested in funds of the employee's choosing. When they retire, employees would take their accumulated assets with them. At that point, the state's financial obligation to them would be at an end.

This would line Colorado up with what's been happening in the private sector: Companies have been turning their defined-benefit plans into defined-contribution systems for years. The decline of big pension plans run by struggling companies such as United Airlines and General Motors has gotten lots of attention of late, but even healthy employers such as IBM, Verizon and Hewlett-Packard are now getting out of the old-fashioned "until death do us part" plans. Today, only 17 percent of employers still provide defined-benefit pensions, reasoning that they represent too much risk when people are living so much longer than they did just decades ago. Defined-contribution plans may or may not require more employer contributions up front, but they put an end to open-ended obligations once the employee retires.

In the public sector, defined-benefit plans still dominate. Some states and localities have experimented with defined contribution—offering employees a choice or shepherding new employees into the new plan. Alaska became the first state last year to set up a defined-contribution plan to cover all employees. Nonetheless, 90 percent of state and local government employees are covered by defined-benefit plans. That is a discrepancy that some lawmakers believe is unsustainable.

Many state and local leaders are looking to defined contribution and other approaches for answers. And they see public opinion swinging their way. "Pension plans are, to put it bluntly, a ticking time bomb set to explode," says Dave Owen, who is carrying Bill Owens' pension package in the Colorado Senate. "Ninety-five percent of the people in this state aren't in PERA"—the Colorado Public Employees' Retirement Association. "They're in some other plan that's going down the tubes."

But the plans may not be as imminently threatened as Owen believes. It's the public employees whose benefits are on the line that can make a strong case that sways public opinion. Last year, Governor Schwarzenegger came to grief when he backed a plan to move California state employees into a redesign of their pension systems, a design that, unfortunately for Schwarzenegger's political health, appeared to cut off funds from widows and orphans left behind by police and fire fighters.

BIG NUMBERS

The fiscal instability of public retirement systems is widespread. Just a few weeks ago, Oklahoma became the latest state to announce a huge shortfall—more than $10 billion in unfunded pension liabilities. With an overall state budget of $6.6 billion, that $10 billion looms especially large. Meanwhile, many municipalities' plans can rival those of the states in per-employee shortfalls.

It's worth bearing in mind that we've been here before. Public pensions were running similar deficits, on a percentage basis, back in the 1980s. At that point, they became more aggressive in their investing—they turned to the stock market to earn healthier returns—and were able to lower the amount of money a state or locality had to put into the plan to keep liabilities in check. Today, about two-thirds of incoming pension monies come from investment returns, with governments putting up 25 percent and employees 12 percent.

Of course, aggressive investment policies have their downside. During the bear market of the early 2000s, investment returns declined precipitously—creating immense pressure on state and local governments to shore up their pension funds. Several states, suffering their own budget shortfalls, turned to the bond market to fund pension needs. More recently, states have been enjoying double-digit returns. However, since they average returns over periods of time, they are still feeling the effects of the earlier bear-market losses.

Investment returns in the exuberant 1990s had an unfortunate effect. Governments grew lazy about making their regular contributions. And that's a big reason that they're in so much trouble now. "Defined-benefit plans have been victims of their own success," says Steve Kreisberg, AFSCME's collective bargaining director. "They've been so successful that some politicians decided that the benefits are free and stopped contributing to the plans."

BENEFIT MANIA

Pensions are both complicated and lacking in sex appeal. Few people without a direct interest pay much attention to them. It's easy to punt the problems into the future, if only by fudging out-year numbers. "Who's going to protest?" wonders Peter Ricchiuti, Louisiana's former chief investment officer. "It's not like you have people on the steps of the capitol saying, 'Don't raise the actuarial assumptions!'"

Despite the problems, states and cities kept adding to the benefits offered to their employees. But the years of neglected contributions and generous benefit add-ons have finally come home to roost. San Diego has become notorious for just this problem. City officials conspired with pension board members to hike up benefits even as the city failed to put more money into its stagnant fund.

In Colorado, at least some of Bill Owens' pension problem was self-inflicted, the result of his pressuring PERA to sell discounted "service credits" to public employees, allowing them to buy more time on the job. A 15-year employee, for example, could buy enough service credits to retire and collect the amount of pension due someone with 20 years on the job. Owens hoped that state employees would retire early, helping his efforts to streamline government. Many rushed to take advantage of the offer; in 2002 and 2003, PERA members bought 128,133 years worth of credit toward their pension service time. The result is that more employees are retiring earlier at greater expense to the state.

Other governments have had a hard time in recent years resisting the temptation to give their workers souped-up benefits—benefits that they are now having a hard time paying for. It was easy for governments that couldn't afford raises for workers to promise better pensions, which didn't cost much at first.

Because pensions are, by their nature, a long-term problem, it's difficult to get public officials—classic short-term thinkers—to pay them serious attention even when the bills are coming due. That's well illustrated by the situation in Illinois. When he took office in 2003, Governor Blagojevich inherited the nation's largest pension deficit—a massive $43 billion. The state hadn't paid its full share of pension contributions for 30 years. Illinois had come up with a plan to deal with it in 1995, but in the usual fashion, the pain of repayment was put off.

Blagojevich has taken a more serious swing at the problem, issuing $10 billion worth of pension bonds to help close the gap. His administration has also reduced state employment ranks by 13,000, which among other things reduced long-term pension liabilities by $5 billion. Blagojevich made some changes in pension rules as well. The end result is that pension fund assets should cover 60 percent of liabilities—a far from robust ratio but better than the 2003 ratio of 48 percent. That may be progress but, as budget director John Filan concedes, pensions remain "a long-term problem that will take continued discipline."

Blagojevich and his team weren't able to summon up quite as much discipline as was required during last year's budget process, in which they finally closed a deal with legislators by agreeing to spend $2.2 billion scheduled for pension repayment for other purposes. Other programs, Filan says, such as education and health care, felt more "urgent and immediate."

That is also the case in Omaha. Each year that city waits to fill its $235 million police and fire pension deficit, the cost of the fix increases by more than $400,000. The city is negotiating with those unions for workers and the city to each make a contribution into the system. But during the last budget season, pension fixes ran into the usual wall. "Of all the things we were trying to accomplish," says Paul Landow, chief aide to Mayor Mike Fahey, "dealing with an underfunded pension was not a high priority. It's not something you have to deal with the day after tomorrow. Omaha's not going out of business."

Paying In

Employee contributions to state and local retirement systems as a percentage of total receipts, 2003-04

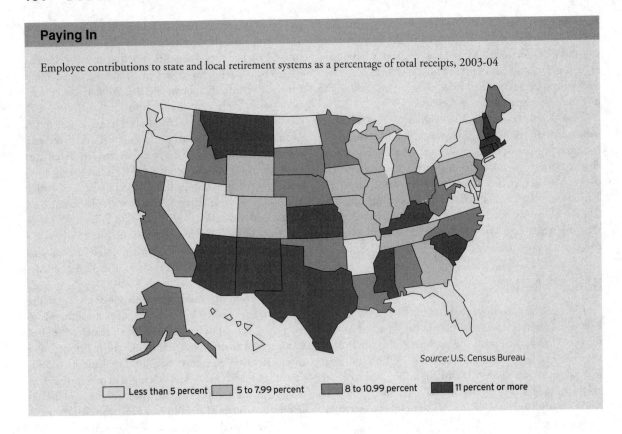

Source: U.S. Census Bureau

Less than 5 percent ☐ 5 to 7.99 percent ☐ 8 to 10.99 percent ☐ 11 percent or more ■

THE OTHER SHOE

Policy makers will soon have to grapple with another set of figures that could be even more daunting than pension shortfalls. Because of a new rule put forward by the Governmental Accounting Standards Board, all states, cities and counties will have to declare the amount they expect to pay out for retiree health benefits over the next 30 years.

Most states have no idea what their 30-year projected cost is going to look like, but the early returns are sobering: California, $36 billion; Alabama, $11 billion; Maryland, $20 billion.

Currently, governments typically pay retiree health costs on an ongoing, annual basis. GASB won't require them to change this or declare how they intend to pay these bills in the future. But bond-rating agencies are on the case. "Obviously, Wall Street doesn't care whether you reduce benefits or whether you provide the necessary funding," says Robert Mears, finance director in Fairfax County, Virginia. "But Wall Street has made it pretty clear that they are looking for the well-managed jurisdictions to deal with this one way or the other."

Unlike pensions, which are pretty well guaranteed once a worker is vested, retiree health benefits can be altered—or eliminated. Some places are doing just that, whether it's changing the age at which full benefits kick in or requiring higher copayments. "Employers don't like to use their compensation money for people who don't work there anymore," says John McFadden, a benefits and compensation expert at the American College.

Some governments are considering issuing bonds to cover their expected retiree health costs. The city of Gainesville has already done so, while Rhode Island Governor Don Carcieri wants to establish a trust using tobacco bond money. Such moves guarantee financing but would also cap benefits.

Mayor Michael Bloomberg, presumably one of the best financial minds in government, is looking to put $2 billion in city money into a trust as earnest money in

Big Soulders

Beneficiaries of state and local retirement systems as a percentage of total state populations, 2003-04

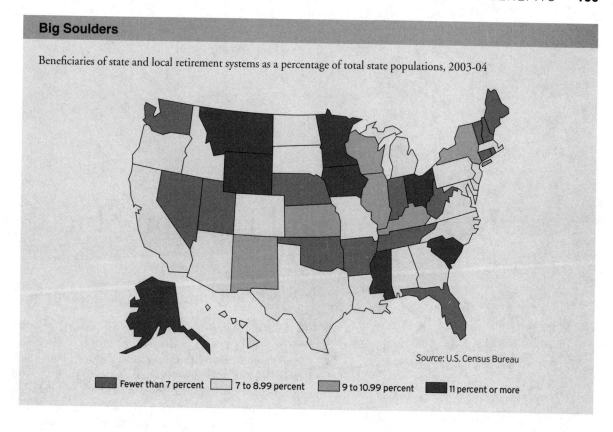

Source: U.S. Census Bureau

| ▇ Fewer than 7 percent | ▢ 7 to 8.99 percent | ▇ 9 to 10.99 percent | ▇ 11 percent or more |

New York City. Mears is leaning toward a trust for Fairfax County. The earnings on the money, he says, will ultimately mean the trust will cost the county millions of dollars less than a pay-as-you-go approach.

Such trusts require putting the money aside. That's the tricky part. Maryland state Senator Patrick Hogan led a task force on the GASB issue that has recommended putting aside $100 million in the coming fiscal year and $300 million in 2008, while creating a commission to decide how to address the state's projected $20 billion retiree health bill over the long haul. "The good news of the new GASB rule is that it has forced us to quantify our problem, face and pay for it," he says.

"We don't have any choice." Hogan also thinks that proper planning will save Maryland money over time, as opposed to staying on a pay-as-you-go footing. But he admits that some colleagues, who have not yet fully focused on the issue, may be tempted to spend the proposed $100 million down payment on other things.

"To fund it for the long term means hitting today's taxpayers for future costs," says David Wyss, chief economist for Standard and Poor's. "The longer you can put it off, the less likely it is to affect your reelection. My feeling is that nothing will change until it's a crisis on both GASB and the pension plans."

But that's a crisis that is moving closer.

36

Hard Luck on Slots

Ellen Perlman

Pennsylvania's plan to use gambling revenue for property tax relief has turned into a political lemon.

The residents of Pottstown, Pennsylvania, would like nothing better than to get a little bit of property tax relief. Bethlehem Steel and Firestone closed down plants there in the late 1970s, and Mrs. Smith's Pies, another longtime local enterprise, left town in 1998. All told, in the past two decades, more than 5,000 local manufacturing jobs have been lost. While the borough, 35 miles northwest of Philadelphia, has many historic buildings and new retail is slowly coming in, the depleted industrial base has saddled citizens with the bulk of the tax burden.

Yet a few weeks ago, when the state dangled a plan before local officials that could have provided eligible homeowners with an annual tax break of $217 apiece, Pottstown opted out. School boards across the state were given until May 30 to decide whether to take a share of the revenue from the introduction of slot machines and levy a small income tax on residents in exchange for the tax-relief program. Board members in Pottstown called the legislation "seriously defective."

Pottstown was hardly alone. Similarly anxious and uncertain school districts sued for more time to make a decision. But the deadline stood firm, so rejection seemed the safest bet. In the end, only 111 of 501 school districts opted into the program. Many of those did so reluctantly. The fiscal and political repercussions are being felt from Erie to Easton. For the rest of the country, the Keystone State's recent fiasco offers a cautionary tale about trying to do too much at once, and using a revenue source many consider unseemly to solve an entrenched tax policy problem.

From *Governing,* July 2005.

TWO-PRONGED APPROACH

Pennsylvania's Edward Rendell was one of several East Coast governors who rode to victory in 2002 on a pro-gambling platform, determined to ease budget problems, or tax burdens, with "easy" money: as in, revenue generated without drastically raising taxes or cutting spending. Rendell took office pumped up about his two-pronged plan for bringing in slot machines and using the proceeds to offer residents relief from skyrocketing property taxes. But if the governor expected this to be the signature program of his first term, it's now clear he will have to look elsewhere.

Starting up gambling in a state is never easy, as Governor Robert Ehrlich in neighboring Maryland also discovered this year when he watched his plan to put slots at racetracks fail. Perhaps Rendell and Pennsylvania lawmakers believed that linking slots to desperately needed property tax relief would ensure widespread support. Evidently not. It now appears that the complexity of this coupling was largely the cause of the plan's downfall.

The legislation that flummoxed so many came in two parts. Act 71, passed in July 2004, created a gaming control board and set up the framework for allowing 61,000 slot machines in 14 locations around the commonwealth. Seven of the licenses would go to horse tracks; the other half to stand-alone sites.

When Pennsylvania was painting the financial picture for supporting slots, officials proffered studies that showed that slots could generate about $3 billion in gross revenue a year. That would net the commonwealth somewhere as much as half a billion to a billion dollars. Ten percent would go specifically to the horse racing industry. "It's geared to make racing more attractive in Pennsylvania, create and keep more jobs, and bring more people here," says Nick Hays, spokesman for the Pennsylvania Gaming Control Board.

More than 50 percent of all slots revenue, however, is slated to go to programs. The biggest chunk—34 percent—would be devoted to property tax relief. The second piece of legislation, Act 72, covers how the money that comes ringing in from those machines will be doled out to school districts.

Act 72 has proved to be the really complicated one. First, it required homeowners in school districts to apply for property tax reduction. Then, if their school district opted in for a share of the gambling pot, it would impose a one-tenth of 1 percent income tax on all wage earners in the district, even those who do not qualify for tax relief, such as renters. Those benefiting from property tax relief would get a bite taken out of that amount through the increase in their income tax. (Philadelphia is an exception. There, all residents receive a wage-tax cut but no property tax relief.)

School districts that opted in also would lose some control over their budgets and taxing powers. Anytime their budgets contain a tax increase that exceeds an inflationary index, residents could nix it through a referendum. "There are a lot of problems school districts have with this," says Jon Rupert, business manager for the Highlands School District. "Why do you want your hands tied like that?"

Nevertheless, Highlands School District opted in because the district is heavily populated with senior citizens who would benefit from a property tax reduction. "The board wanted to give any type of relief it could, even though every one of them had reservations," says Rupert.

Last year, health insurance alone went up 40 percent in the Highlands School District, to more than $1 million. That, and the other state education mandates the district is required to meet, forced the school board to increase taxes by more than the rate of inflation. In the future, such an increase will have to go to referendum. Rupert is concerned about how such a vote would turn out. "They might say, 'To heck with your health insurance.' Then what happens?"

The choice was not an easy one for most districts. Those that turned down the opportunity to get in on the deal not only would get no gambling money but would not be given another chance to opt in. "It was, 'If you don't get in now, you'll never get in,'" says Rupert. "It was crazy." And given the time it will take to get slots up and running, those that opted in are not likely to see any of the money until at least 2007. To add to all the uncertainty, there is a lawsuit pending over the Act 71 legislation that created the gaming control board and gambling structure to bring in slot machines.

School board after school board wrestled with the matter throughout the month of May. Most of them went down to the wire—and ultimately turned a cold shoulder on the deal. They had myriad reasons for doing so. For communities with a high percentage of renters, property tax relief offered no value to a large segment of constituents. Some school board members weren't happy about the need to prepare school budgets months earlier than previously. Many also were skeptical about whether the gambling proceeds would add up to what was promised. And others didn't like the link between gambling and education for moral reasons.

"It was touted as a way to get property taxes down," says Rob Morgan, one of nine school board members in Pottstown. "Really, it's about gambling." People will have to lose an awful lot of money in the slot machines for people to get their couple of hundred bucks, he points out. Morgan calculates that every adult in Pennsylvania would have to lose $314 a year to produce the tax reduction promised. If only 10 percent of people gambled, they'd each have to lose $3,140 to produce the same amount of revenue.

A HEAVY LIFT

Meanwhile, back in Harrisburg, a governor who had expected that all districts would opt in was stunned and embarrassed. Rendell "never thought it would be so difficult to give money away," says press secretary Kate Philips, adding that the plan represented the largest property tax reduction in Pennsylvania history.

Legislators, too, are second-guessing whether they should have made it mandatory for school districts to participate. And with such a lopsided result, everyone is wondering how the gambling money will be dispensed. If doled out as written in the law, only one-fifth of the commonwealth's school districts would get the hoped-for tax relief. Not exactly the intended result.

School board members and Pennsylvania residents who have followed the issue are scratching their heads and wondering why policy makers didn't choose to take the proceeds from gambling and send them directly to homeowners for tax relief, without putting the school boards in the middle of things. That's what Rendell originally had proposed, but negotiations with the legislature resulted in the enactment of Act 72.

With the benefit of hindsight in the days following the May massacre, politicos and others were saying it is simply against human nature to vote for putting limits on your own power. "Voting for Act 72 was probably a heavy lift," Philips acknowledges. "It was probably not the easiest way to get school districts to opt in." But it did represent a balance between the school boards' ability to do their jobs and properly build their budgets, and the taxpayers' right not to have "arbitrary and burdensome tax increases," she says.

School districts bristle at the idea that they made imperialistic decisions to protect their turf. Board members approached their decision-making based on whether the tax-relief plan was appropriate, says Scott Shewell, spokesman for the Pennsylvania School Boards Association. They considered how the plan would affect their local districts and had open meetings to seek input from district residents. I certainly hope the legislature and the government respect the decisions school boards made, Shewell says."

It likely will take until the fall to enact legislation addressing property tax relief for the people living in the 390 school districts that opted out. At least five legislative proposals are on the table. A couple of them give voters the opportunity to opt in to the plan via a referendum in November. Another requires all school districts to opt in. Another not only requires participation in Act 72 but seems to punish those that did not opt in voluntarily by imposing far more restrictive referendum provisions.

While lawmakers attempt to deal with the mess they have made, property owners in Pottstown and other municipalities will continue to pay their onerous tax bills.

PART

X

Policy Challenges

If the readings in this book make only one thing clear, it should be this: state and local governments are expected to do a lot. Subnational governments deal with everything from filling potholes to locking up potheads, educating citizens to addressing illegal immigration.

Indeed, state and local governments wrestle with such a broad spectrum of issues that their most important policy challenges are hard to identify. Regardless of what the issue is, some state or local government is dealing with it somewhere. Generally, this can be thought of as a good thing. One of the big advantages of a federal system is that regional governments can experiment with different approaches to similar problems, and the most successful and effective can be adopted by all.

In fact, many major national policies and programs have their genesis in the states. State legislatures created pensions for the elderly long before the federal government created Social Security. States also were ahead of the federal government in such areas as worker compensation laws, and recent federal reforms in everything from health care and environmental policy have their genesis in state innovation.[1] As the readings in the section will show, states are currently busy experimenting with everything from energy policies to programs designed to mitigate the impact of a flu pandemic.

The sheer number of issues state and local governments must face make it hard to pick out a handful to highlight as the most prominent challenges of the immediate future. Yet governments are like people in general; they have a limited amount of time, attention and money. Those limits mean that while state and local governments will be asked to do, well, just about everything, a limited number of issues will get a disproportionate slice of that limited amount of time, attention and money. What will they be?

TRENDS

One way to answer this question is to take a look at where state and local governments spend their money. A general rule of thumb in politics is that budgets reveal policy priorities. That being the case, there are a couple of easy calls: education and health care. These two areas consume a large portion of state and local spending, their costs are growing, and these are areas considered primary responsibilities of subnational governments.

Health care is both a fiscal and a welfare issue for the states. Rising health care costs outstrip inflation and growth in state revenues by a considerable margin, and this puts considerable financial pressure on states. Idaho's Medicaid program, for example, has averaged annual growth of 15 percent for two decades. A decade ago Medicaid accounted for 12 percent of state general fund expenditures. Today it's up to 17.6 percent of general fund expenditures, and growing fast.[2] Millions of Americans have no health insurance at all, and their health care costs often end up being paid for with public funds.

How can states ensure that their citizens have access to good health care without breaking the bank? Massachusetts recently passed a law that requires all citizens to get health insurance—an approach similar to that adopted by most states towards automobile insurance. Will this help hold down government spending while helping the less fortunate maintain access to health care? No one is certain. What is certain is that other states will be watching the Massachusetts approach carefully. If it works as planned, look for other states to try similar approaches.

Like health care, education is an issue that mixes money and values into an often volatile political cocktail. State and local authorities fund, govern and regulate K-12 schools and public colleges and universities. They set grade school curricular requirements, hire and fire teachers, and generally handle the myriad logistical and administrative details that come along with doing everything from teaching calculus to fielding a football team.

In recent years, the federal government has made significant regulatory inroads into public education, often in ways that state and local governments do not appre-

ciate. This is best exemplified by the No Child Left Behind (NCLB) Act. The signature education initiative of the Bush administration, the basic idea behind NCLB is to mandate a set of performance and accountability standards. The law requires states to set and achieve these standards, mostly through a series of standardized testing schemes. States have often resented these mandates, which can be expensive to implement and have been criticized for being needlessly complicated. Some have estimated that implementing NCLB will cost state governments billions more than the financial support they get from the federal government for the program.[3]

It's not just the costs for K-12 education, and not just conflict with the federal government over what is best for students, however, that is going to challenge states and localities in the next year or two. Some of the biggest fights in education are within states and have nothing to do with money. A prime example is the conflict over teaching evolution in public schools. This issue has generated considerable controversy. Georgia, Kansas, and Pennsylvania have attracted national and even international attention as state or local authorities seek to shape how evolution is—or is not—taught in the classroom. These controversies show that schools are important not just because they constitute the biggest line item on state and local budgets, and not just because they are responsible for teaching reading, writing, and arithmetic. Public schools are viewed by many as repositories of values; conflicts over values can become more intense than conflicts over money.

Higher education suffered considerably during the past four or five years as states struggled to balance their budgets. Historically, appropriations from state legislatures have been the central revenue sources for public colleges and universities. For many public institutions of higher learning, this is no longer the case. Some universities now get less than one fifth—sometimes less than one tenth—of their revenue as appropriations from state government. This raises the question of when a public university stops being a public university, which in turns raises issues of governance and control.

The readings in this section highlight these issues and more. The essay by Josh Goodman takes a tour of the key issues that state and local governments are currently grappling. This grab bag includes everything from health care to eminent domain to property taxes, from immigration to pension plans.

The rest of the essays focus on specific issues: energy, avian flu, and education. The essay by Matthew H. Brown (on energy) and Amy Winterfeld (preparing for the avian flu) were chosen because they highlight two issues typically thought of as national-level policy concerns. As these essays make clear, however, state and local governments are at the forefront, not just of implementing programs to deal with these problems, but in formulating the programs themselves.

The essays by Stanley Ikenberry and Sara Vitaska provide a more in-depth look at the higher education and teaching evolution issues briefly discussed earlier. As these essays demonstrate, education is at the forefront of state and local policy challenges because of dollars and cents, and also because they are institutions that play a significant role in shaping the values and opportunities for society.

Notes

1. Ed Fouhy. 2005. "Strong States Strong Nation." *State Legislatures.* July/August, 16–17.

2. Arturo Pérez. 2005. "The Medicaid Spending Morass." *State Legislatures.* March, 19–21.

3. William J. Mathis. 2004. "No Child Left Behind Act: What Will It Cost the States?" *Spectrum: The Journal of State Government.* Spring, 8–14.

37

Issues to Watch

Josh Goodman

State legislatures face a slate of intergovernmental challenges.

As legislatures in most states come back into session this month, their members will be spending an unusual amount of time dealing with issues that involve other levels of government.

Congress, for example, voted to add a prescription drug benefit to Medicare in 2003, but gave states a large role in implementating the program. As a result, legislators will be fine-tuning the benefit, which went into effect on January 1. State action in other areas, such as immigration and eminent domain, may hinge on how—if at all—Congress addresses these issues this year.

While legislators keep an eye on the feds, they will have to lend an ear to local governments. Municipal officials are concerned that state and federal action will deprive them of powers and revenue sources they currently enjoy. They will lobby states not to restrict their eminent domain powers or undermine their ability to offer franchises to companies that provide video services. City and county governments will also be major stakeholders in debates over whether to cut property taxes.

The private sector, of course, is hardly a bystander in the legislative arena. Bills under consideration in many states would prod businesses to offer health care coverage to more of their workers, something many companies oppose. Business groups are also fearful that if states crack down on illegal immigrants, as many legislatures are considering, they will be deprived of a source of cheap workers. Organized labor, meanwhile, will fight efforts to make pensions for state employees less generous.

How lawmakers will address important issues in 2006 is anyone's guess. But one thing is clear: As policy makers weigh their choices,

From *Governing*, January 2006.

they will be keenly aware of their constituents' views. After all, more than 80 percent of legislators will be up for reelection this year.

EMINENT DOMAIN

As a result of the U.S. Supreme Court's landmark decision in *Kelo v. New London,* which affirmed the use of eminent domain for economic development, more than 20 state legislatures are likely to consider bills restricting eminent domain this year. Last fall's ruling generated an immediate backlash among both conservative property-rights advocates and liberal critics of big business. "To have a private group come in and say, 'We want this just because we think we can make more money off of it,' and to have the local government help, that is just wrong," says Oklahoma state Senator Daisy Lawler. A few states, including Alabama, Delaware, Ohio and Texas, have already passed measures restricting eminent domain.

Legislative action will not happen without a fight, however. Municipalities and redevelopment authorities are lobbying legislators not to curtail their use of eminent domain. They argue that sweeping eminent domain restrictions could undermine widely accepted local government goals, such as redevelopment of blighted areas and brownfields.

Business groups, on the other hand, have largely stayed on the sidelines or are advocating for limits on the use of eminent domain for economic development. The National Association of Realtors is backing restrictions in state legislatures. "A lot of small businesses could be gobbled up by big competitors," says Maryland Delegate Anthony J. O'Donnell, a supporter of eminent domain restrictions.

Even without the help of the business community, municipal representatives seem to be getting through to some legislators. Although many lawmakers remain convinced that action is necessary, they speak of hearing from different stakeholders and balancing competing interests. Just how extensively legislators decide to restrict eminent domain will hinge on the details of the bills they consider—how they define terms such as "economic development" or "blight" or "public purpose." In some states, lawmakers will also be deciding between statutory and constitutional approaches.

Municipal representatives are having a tougher time selling their perspective to federal lawmakers. Last year, the U.S. House of Representatives voted 376 to 38 to withhold federal funds from governments that use eminent domain for economic development. "We've had conversations with members of Congress that will talk to us," says Don Borut, executive director of the National League of Cities, "but they are not willing to go out front." Federal legislation could supersede state laws, but irrespective of what Congress decides, legislators have vowed to act on the issue.

HEALTH INSURANCE

Legislators will grapple with conflicting impulses when considering health care issues this year. Many want to expand coverage to the nation's 45 million uninsured and improve the quality of care for everyone else, but at the same time, Medicaid expenses represent ever-larger shares of state budgets, leading to a desire to cut costs. In the face of this conundrum, an increasing number of policy makers are looking to the private sector to shoulder more of the burden, either willingly or forcibly.

Last year, for example, Maryland's legislature passed a bill requiring businesses with 10,000 or more employees in the state to dedicate at least 8 percent of their payroll to health care costs. Although Governor Robert Ehrlich vetoed the bill, supporters are optimistic they can override his veto this year. At least a half dozen states, including Michigan, New Jersey and Pennsylvania, will consider similar legislation this year. Others, such as Massachusetts, will mull requiring businesses to pay a tax if they do not offer health insurance. Some states will consider requiring businesses to report how many of their employees are on Medicaid or other government-funded health care programs, a possible precursor to laws akin to the bills under consideration in Maryland and Massachusetts.

Supporters of these measures say that because states end up footing the bills for employees who do not get health coverage at work, taxpayers ultimately bear the costs. They also argue that if businesses can get away with not offering health insurance, then companies that do offer coverage will be hurt. "We have to pick up the costs when the employers are not doing so," says Delegate Anne Healey, sponsor of the Maryland legislation. "It puts the employers who are doing the right thing at a competitive disadvantage."

While Democrats generally support these efforts, most Republicans and business groups oppose them. They argue that such requirements would harm the business climates of their states and lead to higher prices for consumers. Fearing a national trend, Wal-Mart—the only company that currently would be affected by Maryland's bill—has deployed 12 lobbyists to the state to try to defeat the legislation.

Other states will consider a more conciliatory approach. Iowa Governor Tom Vilsack has identified assisting small businesses in providing health coverage as a legislative priority. Montana approved legislation with the same goal last year. "If you give them the tools to get things done," says Vilsack spokesperson Jennifer Mullin, "they will take the high road."

TELECOM REGULATION

A variety of telecom issues are on the legislative agenda. In addition to continuing efforts to limit the ability of municipalities to offer broadband, a new issue is coming to the fore in statehouses nationwide: Many states—likely including California, Connecticut, Michigan, Minnesota, Missouri, New Jersey, North Carolina and Virginia—will consider bills that would allow companies to receive statewide franchises to provide video service.

Currently, to offer video service, companies have to apply for franchises at the local level, deals that typically require them to pay fees and be subject to local regulation. Phone companies would like to break into the cable business, but, with so many local governments involved, they have struggled to do so. Thus, phone companies are leading this year's legislative push in the hopes of obtaining franchises for entire states in one fell swoop.

Predictably, the biggest opponents of statewide franchise bills are cable companies, the sworn enemies of the phone companies, who plan to jealously guard their turf against encroachment. Municipalities also are concerned with the legislative push, worrying that they could lose out on franchise fees and regulatory authority if such bills pass. On the other hand, advocates of the measures argue that they will increase competition and lower prices for consumers.

Texas was the only state to approve a statewide franchise last year. The Texas legislation may represent a model for others to imitate in order to win broad-based support. Initially, municipal representatives were deadset against the bill, but lawmakers offered concessions, grandfathering in existing franchises and ensuring that fees from statewide franchises would be redirected to local governments. The result was that although big cities still opposed the final bill, the Texas Municipal League stayed neutral, and the legislation passed.

Congress may also get involved in the debate. Phone companies will seek a law to allow for federal video franchises. If approved, the legislation would render local or state franchises unnecessary, a possibility that has municipalities concerned. "It's an onslaught against the local franchising authority," says Marilyn Mohrman-Gillis, director of the National League of Cities' Center for Policy and Federal Relations.

PROPERTY TAXES

With rapidly rising real estate values hitting homeowners with higher taxes, legislatures across the country will consider cutting property taxes this year. But the impetus behind the bills will have as much to do with school funding and a desire to shift certain taxes from the local level to the state level as it will with any property tax revolt. States that will likely discuss property tax cuts include Alabama, Idaho, Indiana, Nevada, New Jersey, North Dakota, Pennsylvania, South Carolina and Texas.

Since property taxes generally are levied at the local level and often fund public school systems, any discussion of property taxes almost inevitably links to school funding. Texas will reconsider its property tax system because the state Supreme Court deemed the present system unconstitutional last year, while North Dakota's lawmakers, who do not go into regular session until 2007, are mulling changes to their system amid the backdrop of a similar suit. Even in states such as New Jersey and South Carolina, where the property tax debate is largely motivated by a desire to lower taxes, school funding issues also come into play.

Most of the bills being proposed will strive to replace property tax revenue with increases in other taxes. Many states are running surpluses and could—at least temporarily—direct their extra revenue to localities to compensate for property tax cuts. But, with fresh memories of tough fiscal times, most legislators will be reluctant to do so. "Whether that is going to be ongoing is a big question," says North Dakota Representative C. B. "Buck" Haas of his state's surplus. "It might be just a little blip."

A few states may also mull measures to cut property taxes indirectly, by limiting increases in real estate assessments or the frequency of assessments. Discussions in Alabama have centered on shifting from annual to quadrennial assessments, while a Nevada legislator is proposing a ballot measure to cap assessment increases at 2 percent or the rate of inflation, whichever is less.

Supporters of property taxes tout the stable revenue stream they provide and worry that their removal could lead to boom-and-bust cycles in state government. "The problem is doing something with the property tax and replacing it with a volatile tax, like the income tax," says Brigham Young University Professor Gary Cornia, former president of the National Tax Association. Although some legislators think property taxes are more volatile than experts acknowledge, many also recognize the importance of property taxes, in addition to sales and income taxes. "People will argue that you need all three and probably you do, but at what share?" says Haas. "That's the question we're wrestling with."

IMMIGRATION

With immigration issues roiling all levels of government, legislatures will host a variety of spirited immigration-related policy debates. To proponents of stricter enforcement of immigration laws, the increasing focus on illegal immigrants is the result of lawmakers' finally paying attention to the concerns of their constituents. "The grass roots are finally connecting to the elites," says George Grayson, a former Virginia legislator and professor at the College of William and Mary. In contrast, opponents of tougher laws or tougher enforcement smell rank political opportunism in election year anti-immigration talk.

Regardless of the motives involved, legislators will consider a number of approaches to address the 10 million or more illegal immigrants in this country. A handful of states will consider measures that would require individuals seeking state services to offer proof that they are legal residents. Arizona moved in this direction by passing Proposition 200 in 2004, and at least seven states considered similar legislation last year. Such an approach may gain traction this year in Georgia, where Republicans control the legislature and will pursue a bill akin to Proposition 200. "It's actually patterned after the federal law that is already in existence," says Georgia state

Senator Chip Rogers, wryly noting the lack of enforcement of federal immigration laws.

Although a flurry of immigration-related bills will be introduced, in recent years the vast majority that were introduced did not pass. One reason for the low success rate is that businesses benefit from cheap immigrant labor, so they tend to oppose stricter immigration laws. That is especially true when states propose bills to deny state contracts to businesses that employ illegal immigrants or punish businesses that employ undocumented workers, as more than 10 states did last year.

While most of the immigration legislation in statehouses this year will seek to get tough on illegal immigrants, some bills will attempt to expand benefits and services. For example, a Massachusetts bill would make illegal immigrants eligible for in-state tuition rates—a benefit they already enjoy in nine states—and legislation in Nebraska and Indiana would offer driving certificates to members of the undocumented community. "State and local governments have an opportunity to do something positive in not just welcoming but integrating immigrants into their communities," says Tanya Broder, a staff attorney with the National Immigration Law Center.

The situation is further complicated by the possibility of federal action. The congressional picture is murky, with a number of bills under consideration that would dedicate more resources to border enforcement or offer undocumented immigrants a way to legalize their residency status.

PENSION PLANS

Many legislatures will have little choice this year but to invest large sums of new money in state pension systems or to pursue overhauls to make them less generous. In terms of the sheer amount of money involved, no fiscal challenge is more daunting than unfunded pension liabilities. Even many small states have long-term liabilities in excess of a billion dollars and in many larger states the totals come to tens of billions. "We have postponed the day of reckoning in every way imaginable, but it's here now," says New Jersey Assemblyman Richard Merkt.

Pensions became a common trouble spot through the confluence of legislative misjudgments and national economic conditions. Many states offered generous new retiree benefits to their employees in the 1990s or failed to invest adequately in their pension systems. Then, the economy weakened at the beginning of this decade, and the stock market turned more bearish as well. As a result, state pension systems took a sizable hit, and massive unfunded liabilities emerged.

The silver lining is that for the first time in five years, many legislators will be working with sizable budget surpluses. States including Tennessee, Washington and West Virginia will consider investing part of their surpluses into their pensions. In December, Montana Governor Brian Schweitzer called lawmakers into a special session to tackle the issue. The surplus cash available is a pittance compared with the unfunded liabilities, but since the pension bills are due over the course of decades, an immediate infusion of cash could be enough to bring some states back onto solid financial footing—at least temporarily.

Other states will seek to cut into unfunded liabilities by reducing their pension spending for future state employees. In this regard, the most controversial approach will be switching from defined-benefit pensions to 401(k)-style defined-contribution plans. Alaska shifted to a defined-contribution system last year and legislators in other states such as New Jersey may contemplate a similar change this year.

Public employee unions will fight any move away from defined benefits. They argue that defined-contribution systems are less efficient and that legislators should do what in some cases they did not do in the 1990s: make adequate funding of state pension systems a priority. Due to the pushback from unions, legislatures will also contemplate less dramatic changes to state retirement systems, such as requiring employees to contribute more money to their pensions or having benefits start at a later age. Legislators in Colorado, New Jersey and New Mexico will be looking at those options.

MEDICARE PART D

With the Medicare prescription drug benefit having gone into effect the first of January, state lawmakers are watching closely to see how well it works and whether new legislation might be needed. "There is some concern that problems will surface that nobody has anticipated," says Ed Dale, senior legislative representative for AARP's State Affairs Department. Congress passed the Medicare Modernization Act in 2003, which included the "Part D"

drug benefit, but states have much of the responsibility for implementing the program.

In particular, legislators will be listening for complaints from beneficiaries that they are confused by their plans or are not eligible for the drugs they need. If that occurs, at least two ideas may gain traction in more statehouses. One is for states to simplify the daunting array of choices available to Part D participants by designating a few preferred plans and then allowing beneficiaries to opt into other plans if they so choose. The federal Centers for Medicare & Medicaid Services (CMS) must sign off on these proposals and, according to AARP's Dale, may be increasingly willing to do so in order to get more people enrolled in Part D. Last year, CMS signed off on preferred-plan proposals in Massachusetts, Pennsylvania and Vermont. Other states have passed legislation but have not yet won approval from CMS.

If beneficiaries find Part D inadequate, another option is to supplement it with additional assistance. Many states have already moved in this direction, passing "wrap-around" legislation to merge State Pharmaceutical Assistance Programs (SPAPs) with the Medicare drug program. As a result, participants can continue to enjoy the often-superior benefits offered by SPAPs, even as they sign up for Part D. Last year, at least 17 states passed wrap-around legislation. At least four of those did not have existing SPAPs and instead created new programs to supplement Part D. States such as California and North Carolina are likely to consider wrap-around bills this year.

Another issue that's likely to cause plenty of consternation is the "clawback" provision of Part D. Under the clawback, states must make monthly payments to the federal government that are intended to compensate the feds for taking on prescription drug costs previously borne by the states. But lawmakers have argued that states will lose money overall and some, such as Kentucky, New York and Texas, may pursue legal action. Legislators, however, cannot do much for now, except perhaps to take a stance similar to what New Hampshire adopted last year: refusing to make clawback payments while litigation is pending.

EMERGENCY PLANNING

Driven by Hurricane Katrina and fears of avian flu, not to mention ongoing homeland security concerns, legislatures will consider a variety of measures related to emergency planning. "Katrina clearly propelled us in a broader, new direction," says Maine state Senator Ethan Strimling, co-chairman of the state's homeland security task force.

Improving communication among local governments and between state and local governments will be a top area of concern. In Maine, the legislature will consider upgrading the state's communications technology. New Hampshire lawmakers will attend an educational meeting on emergency preparedness. The goal is for the state's 424 legislators to serve as liaisons to their local communities. "Most reaction has to come at the local level," says state Representative Peter Batula. Along the same lines, Tennessee will consider a bill that would require state emergency management officials to provide annual disaster-preparedness training to legislators and to every member of a municipal legislative body.

Utah will debate legislation to make it easier for the state to quarantine large groups of people. Elsewhere, notably in Hawaii and California, infrastructure is the priority. Governor Arnold Schwarzenegger will push the California legislature to authorize billions of dollars in bonds for infrastructure improvements, including a major upgrade of the state's levees, which became a concern after the catastrophic flooding in New Orleans.

Last year's hurricane season is reframing discussions of emergency planning, even in places where new legislation is not imminent. For example, after observing the strain Katrina's evacuees placed on governments throughout a broad geographic area, legislators in states bordering large metropolitan areas are mulling how they can be prepared if victims flee to their states. "Another person's disaster could be our disaster," says Nevada state Senator Bob Coffin.

38

Energy Crisis Déjà Vu

Matthew H. Brown

The U.S. energy needs—and the world's—are changing fast. Are we prepared?

I s the United States at the beginning of another energy crisis? Oil prices surged past $50 a barrel in late 2004, bumping heating oil and gasoline to the highest prices in years. Natural gas jumped to around $6 per million Btu after having spent most of the late 1990s at one-third that price. The power transmission system failed in eight eastern and Midwestern states in the summer of 2003—and some of the fundamental flaws that caused the failure have yet to be fixed. And the nation continues not only to import more than half of all the oil it uses, but is now beginning to import more natural gas to make up for its falling gas production. Whether or not these diverse factors add up to a crisis might not matter. The fact is that the energy system is changing fast, and not all of those changes have been easy. Federal energy legislation is stuck in partisan wrangling, so most of the action to address energy is at the state level.

UNDERSTANDING THE CHANGES

Representative Carl Holmes, a Republican, who chairs the Kansas House Energy Committee, suggests that legislators need to understand the fundamental changes at work in the energy system. "Kansas is ninth in oil production in the country," he says. "Oil used to be a big part of the economy in the state, but now our oil and gas production is declining. We're using our energy resources up fast."

Democratic Representative Terry Backer, who chairs the Connecticut House Energy Committee, agrees. "Not only are we using

From *State Legislatures*, February 2005.

more and more energy, but we are starting to import more and more of it from outside the country. We're starting to expose ourselves to new risks," he says.

Both Holmes and Backer suggest that legislators need to be aware of some big shifts in the way we get our energy, and that we need to think hard about more efficiently using what we have while exploring all the alternatives that will give us new supplies, like renewable energy, along with the fossil fuels we know so well.

The United States is likely to import more and more oil and gas, at the same time other countries are beginning to need a lot more. China's appetite for oil and gas will double every five years at its current 14 percent growth rate. Tom Hewson of Energy Ventures Analysis says the United States is now exporting coal to China. China is on track to add 562 coal-fired power plants over the next eight years. For the first time, China's billion-plus population is starting to affect what we pay for energy, and that's not likely to change any time soon.

Tom Markin, a vice president with BP, observes that at the same time other countries like China are increasing their energy consumption, North America is the only major region showing a decline in gas production. The United States' need for energy just seems to grow and grow.

COMPETITION = HIGHER PRICES

What does this mean for states? It means the states that now see their gas prices set by domestic factors will suddenly start to see their gas prices set by international factors. When Japan was forced to shut down several of its nuclear facilities for an extended period in 2003 it switched to natural gas fired power plants. Since Japan imports almost all of its natural gas, the demand affected international gas prices. If the United States had been importing a lot of natural gas, as it now does with oil, it would have seen its own gas prices go up because power plants went down in Japan.

"Is gas the next oil? Will we be as dependent on imports of gas 20 years from now as we now are on oil?" asks Kansas Representative Holmes.

He has a point. Gas production in the United States and Canada has been declining over the past several years. The country is at least going to have to give a lot of thought to putting up some large new natural gas

import terminals, yet hardly anybody likes to see a big industrial facility built nearby.

"People worry about these big import terminals," Representative Backer says about proposed liquefied natural gas terminals in New England. "But the fact is that we have to do something to meet our energy needs."

The fact that these import terminals are even being considered is one among several indications that some big changes in our energy policy may be ahead. Once again, states are taking the lead in thinking about these new energy policies.

THERE ARE SOLUTIONS

"States need a comprehensive energy policy," says Utah Representative Sheryl Allen. "An energy policy is something that states can refer to when they are developing other pieces of energy legislation." Utah is going to spend a good portion of the year developing just such a policy, she says. So is Kentucky.

Given Kentucky's large reserves of coal, Representative Tanya Pullin, who chairs the House Energy Committee, says her state's plan is likely to focus on finding ways to develop new markets. "One thing I'm very interested in is the new clean coal technology," she says.

Clean coal technology vastly reduces [the] amount of sulfur dioxide and nitrogen oxides that a power plant releases. Clean coal refers to many things. But frequently it means using technology to turn coal into a gas, and then to run that gas through a standard combustion turbine to generate electricity. Although it's not the cheapest way to generate power and is still a new technology, two first-of-their-kind plants in Indiana and Florida have been using this clean coal technology for years and several others will soon be built.

Dave Hadley, who serves on the Indiana Utility Regulatory Commission is a big proponent of investing in clean coal. "Every utility regulator should ask their utilities to consider an investment in clean coal technology before they make the investment in a conventional facility."

Renewable energy offers a lot of promise, and it costs a lot less than it used to. In 1979, wind energy cost 40 cents per kilowatt hour. Today it costs between 3.5 to 5 cents per kilowatt hour before some federal tax credits.

Almost every state in the West is planning to build some wind projects, and 18 states around the country require their utilities to get some of their power from renewable energy. Colorado's voters passed a ballot initiative in November that requires the state's largest utilities to get 10 percent of the power they generate from renewable sources like wind power.

Representative Jeff Morris, chair of the Washington Science Technology and Energy Committee, suggested that part of the answer may lie in new technology. "Smart electrical meters and distributed generation [small scale power plants often located on a customer's premises] can actually make the power system more secure and can make it run smarter," he says. Morris says it's important for states to remember the role new technologies can play in using the existing system efficiently, and in the end reducing our dependence on big power plants and power lines.

Senator Harris McDowell of Delaware looks at the problem a little differently. He believes the nation's energy system needs to invest in efficiency before building new power plants.

"The cheapest and cleanest kilowatt hour of electricity is the kilowatt hour you never generate," he says.

BEING EFFICIENT

Most energy efficiency programs come from states. Fourteen now have a "system benefit fund" which is a small charge on electricity customers' bills. Utilities and the state (or another organization the legislature designates) can spend the accumulated funds on energy efficient measures—subsidizing efficient air conditioners or light bulbs for instance. States use other methods, too. When Colorado's utility proposed to build a 500 MW coal plant in Pueblo, environmental organizations objected, but agreed to support the construction when the state's major utility agreed to fund large energy efficiency programs.

So is there a silver bullet that can solve this quiet energy crisis? Maybe not, but perhaps that silver bullet needs to fit in the cartridge of a six-shooter. The nation's need for energy is growing so fast, and the world's need for energy is growing even faster. We're going to need it all—whether it be using energy as efficiently as possible, introducing new sources of energy, finding ways to make use of our coal resources within constraints of today's and tomorrow's environmental regulations, or stretching the most out of domestic and imported natural gas and oil.

With the deadlock in Washington, D.C., on any major new energy legislation, it is once again up to the states to find solutions that work for them.

Renewable Energy Standards

Eighteen states require their utilities to get a percentage of their power from renewable energy by a target year.

States	Requirements	Target Year
Arizona	1.1% (60% solar)	2007
California	20%	2017
Colorado	10%	2015
Connecticut	10%	2010
Hawaii	20%	2020
Iowa	2%	1999
Maine	30%	2000
Maryland	7.5%	2019
Massachusetts	4%	2009
Minnesota*	19%	2015
Nevada	15% (5% solar)	2013
New Jersey	6.5%	2008
New Mexico	10%	2011
New York	24%	2013
Pennsylvania	8%	2020
Rhode Island	16%	2019
Texas	2.7%	2009
Wisconsin	2.2%	2011

*Includes minimum requirements adopted for one utility.

System Benefit Funds for Renewable Energy
(Cumulative between 1998–2017)

Fifteen states place a surcharge on consumers' bills to fund renewable energy development.

States	Fund Amount by 2017 (in millions)
Arizona	$234
California	$2,048
Connecticut	$248
Delaware	$18
Illinois	$114
Massachusetts	$494
Minnesota	$200
Montana	$14
New Jersey	$286
New York	$89
Ohio	$25
Oregon	$95
Pennsylvania	$67
Rhode Island	$30
Wisconsin	$21

Unfinished Business

The 109th Congress must deal with a long list of unfinished business left over from 2004. One long-standing issue is the energy bill, which narrowly failed in a November 2003 Senate filibuster vote.

The filibuster targeted a contentious safe-harbor provision for producers of methyl tertiary-butyl ether (MTBE), a fuel additive whose use in recent years has become controversial because of incidents of water contamination.

In an attempt to prevent another deadlock between the chambers, House Energy and Commerce Committee Chairman Joe Barton of Texas says he will wait for Senate Energy and Natural Resources Committee Chairman Pete Domenici of New Mexico to take the lead. Domenici already has laid the groundwork to reopen natural gas discussions. In December, he issued a request for proposals on natural gas issues and was to have held a conference on natural gas production and demand issues late in January.

Other issues of importance to states are also likely to come up this session. One would remove much of the authority for permitting construction of certain power transmission lines from the states and place it instead with the Federal Energy Regulatory Commission. Another major provision would convert some voluntary standards that keep the power system running reliably to enforceable mandatory standards. Finally, it is likely that Congress will attempt to repeal the Public Utilities Regulatory Policies Act, which many states rely on to encourage renewable energy production in their states.

—Tamra Spielvogel, NCSL

39

Preparing for a Pandemic

Amy Winterfeld*

Concern over a possible avian flu pandemic is moving states, communities and the federal government to action.

Pandemic. It's a word of horrific implications. In the past, millions of people have died from flu viruses that swept through a less populated, less well-traveled world than the one we know today. So the idea that the avian flu, a bird virus that has killed some 100 people in Asia, may be the precursor of the next pandemic has started a national dialogue about how prepared we are and where responsibility lies.

And much of it lies with the states.

"It is states and communities that will be on the front lines," says Health and Human Services Secretary Mike Leavitt. "While the federal government is stockpiling antivirals, success will be determined by whether state and local officials can put pills in people's hands everywhere they are needed within a short time.

"Actions at the state and local level will define victory."

Preparation seems wise. The H5N1 strain of the avian flu virus has infected 173 people in Asia, including the Near East. As of mid-March, 98 of them have died, according to the World Health Organization.

In poultry or wild birds, the virus has spread into Europe and Africa. Human-to-human transmission of the virus is rare—but there are a handful of cases, the result, apparently, of close and prolonged contact. Most infections in humans are believed to occur from direct contact with infected poultry or contaminated surfaces.

From *State Legislatures,* April 2006.

* Amy Winterfeld tracks flu for states. Rachel Morgan, who follows the issue in NCSL's D.C., office also contributed to this piece.

But fears that the virus could eventually mutate and be easily passed between humans, as viruses have in the last hundred years, make avian flu big news.

THE FACTS

Avian flu is an infection caused by a bird virus. All avian flu strains originate in migratory waterfowl, which carry the virus in their intestines usually without becoming sick. The virus is very contagious and can sicken domesticated birds, including chickens, ducks and turkeys, and kill them in large numbers.

The flu strain that's concerning health officials today is the Avian Influenza A (H5N1) virus. In late 2003 and early 2004, outbreaks in poultry resulted in the death or destruction of more than 100 million birds in eight Asian countries (Cambodia, China, Indonesia, Japan, Laos, South Korea, Thailand and Vietnam).

In 2005, the H5N1 strain was detected in domestic poultry in Turkey and Romania and in wild birds in Croatia. Active outbreaks have continued in 2006, mostly following wild bird migratory routes into Europe. In early March a dead cat in Germany tested positive for H5N1, probably the result of eating infected birds.

THE FEARS

A flu pandemic occurs when a new type of virus emerges for which there is little or no immunity in humans. It causes serious illness and spreads easily person to person worldwide.

At least three human influenza pandemics have occurred in the 20th century. In the most deadly of these, the 1918 Spanish Flu, a virus that probably began in the United States killed an estimated 20 million to 50 million people worldwide. The virus evolved into a virulent form easily transmitted between humans and circulated on the crowded battlefields of World War I. In 1957, a flu strain from China caused 70,000 deaths in the United States. The most recent influenza pandemic occurred in 1968 with the Hong Kong flu outbreak, which resulted in nearly 34,000 U.S. deaths.

"It will happen again," says John Barry, distinguished visiting scholar at the Center for Bioenvironmental Research at Tulane and Xavier Universities and author

---

Tracking Avian Flu

Nations with confirmed cases of H5N1 avian flu in poultry or wild birds from 2003 through mid-March include:

Austria	Japan
Azerbaijan	Kazakhstan
Bulgaria	Laos
Bosnia and	Malaysia
Herzegovina	Mongolia
Cambodia*	Myanmar
Cameroon	Niger
China*	Nigeria
Croatia	Poland
Denmark	Romania
Egypt	Russia
France	Serbia and
Georgia	Montenegro
Germany	Slovenia
Greece	Slovakia
Hungary	South Korea
Hong Kong	Sweden
Italy	Switzerland
India	Thailand*
Indonesia*	Turkey*
Iran	Ukraine
Iraq*	Vietnam*

*Countries with confirmed human cases.

The United States bans poultry and bird imports from countries with confirmed avian flu.

---

of a book on the 1918 Spanish Flu. He points out that the longest gap between human influenza pandemics was 42 years and "right now we're at 37 years and counting."

"I am not alone in saying that another pandemic is going to happen," Barry says. "Everybody, the WHO, CDC, says this is going to happen. It may not be H5N1. It may not come for 30 years." But, he says, "when there's enough exposure, it's going to jump species. We must prepare and we are not yet adequately prepared."

Today, unlike 1918, people frequently travel around the world in packed airplanes. An easily transmittable avian flu virus will inevitably spread around the globe. The entire world will be susceptible.

THE CHALLENGES

The challenges of a pandemic are enormous. A rapidly spreading virus, an overloaded health care system, a need for vaccine that is likely to outstrip the supply, a shortage of antiviral drugs that will force decisions about who will receive them. Travel bans, school closings and cancellation of public events might help slow the spread of the virus. Widespread economic and social disruptions—affecting everything from grocery stores to gas stations to transportation—will snowball as workers succumb to the flu or stay home to care for others or because they are afraid of catching the disease.

Barry says that governments "should be thinking hard about how they sustain the society during an enormous outbreak of disease and what that does to the economy. How to keep people and government supplied with things like water. Most treatment facilities don't have more than a few days of chlorine. We've gone to a 'just-in-time' society."

PREVENTION AND RESPONSE

Are we prepared? Many people cite the lack of a coordinated federal response to Hurricane Katrina as proof we're not.

"I tend to think back to Katrina and what didn't happen," says Iowa Representative Linda Upmeyer, a nurse practitioner. "The bottom line is that you have to be prepared at the local level." She and her staff have organized local preparedness meetings in every legislative district after hearing from U.S. Department of Health and Human Services Secretary Mike Leavitt who is going state to state urging local readiness.

State and local governments are scheduled to receive $100 million through HHS to strengthen preparedness efforts. The allocation is a portion of a $350 million emergency appropriations package passed by Congress in December and intended to supplement state activities. The remaining $250 million will be allocated sometime before August and will focus on specific objectives, which are being developed.

Each state will initially get $500,000, plus more based on population. New York City, Chicago and Los Angeles County will get separate grants. Money is to be used for practical, community-based procedures that could prevent or delay the spread of influenza, and help reduce the burden of illness during an outbreak.

Federal Funds for State and Local Pandemic Planning

Money is to be used for practical, community-based procedures that could prevent or delay the spread of influenza, and help reduce the burden of illness during an outbreak.

Alabama	$1,595,205
Alaska	657,647
Arizona	1,856,742
Arkansas	1,163,333
California	6,723,207
LA County	2,900,529
Colorado	1,605,882
Connecticut	1,347,950
Delaware	698,960
D.C. Region	635,601
Florida	4,633,819
Georgia	2,609,920
Hawaii	803,669
Idaho	832,432
Illinois	2,878,268
Chicago	1,197,706
Indiana	2,007,596
Iowa	1,215,422
Kansas	1,162,607
Kentucky	1,501,451
Louisiana	1,592,758
Maine	818,369
Maryland	1,840,470
Massachusetts	2,061,287
Michigan	2,951,805
Minnesota	1,731,493
Mississippi	1,200,982
Missouri	1,890,782
Montana	723,275
Nebraska	922,515
Nevada	1,045,254
New Hampshire	813,384
New Jersey	2,601,641
New Mexico	956,824
New York	3,205,759
New York City	2,466,271
North Carolina	2,547,844
North Dakota	654,029
Ohio	3,281,387
Oklahoma	1,352,695

(continued)

Federal Funds for State and Local Pandemic Planning *(continued)*

Money is to be used for practical, community-based procedures that could prevent or delay the spread of influenza, and help reduce the burden of illness during an outbreak.

Oregon	1,366,765
Pennsylvania	3,508,291
Rhode Island	761,679
South Carolina	1,508,881
South Dakota	686,008
Tennessee	1,921,423
Texas	5,875,044
Utah	1,071,983
Vermont	650,610
Virginia	2,291,072
Washington	1,990,994
West Virginia	940,502
Wisconsin	1,831,224
Wyoming	622,102
Total	**$97,713,349**
Puerto Rico	1,443,014
American Samoa	114,066
Guam	139,782
N. Marianas Islands	118,513
Virgin Islands	126,461
Micronesia	126,298
Marshall Islands	113,722
Palau	104,795
Total	$2,286,651
Grand Total	**$100,000,000**

So far, there is no vaccine to protect humans from a potential pandemic, but researchers are working on it. The National Institute of Allergy and Infectious Diseases, part of the National Institutes of Health, has been conducting a clinical trial for nearly a year on an experimental vaccine based on the H5N1 virus. While there is no way for scientists to know exactly what a pandemic virus will look like, research focuses on the bird flu virus that has infected people in Asia.

There is $3 billion in the Department of Defense Appropriations Act for the development of vaccines, antivirals and other necessary supplies to respond to a possible outbreak as well as for the improvement of current laboratories, and for more research at the Centers for Disease Control.

State officials are still concerned about being able to afford vaccines and antivirals if there should be a pandemic. In late February they didn't yet know how the purchase arrangements would be set up. All state officials do know at this point is that the federal government will pay 25 percent of the cost of antivirals, whatever that is. They also know there will be a limited number of doses available for all the states and territories. The federal government only plans for 20 million doses as recommended by WHO. States may purchase antivirals outside of the negotiated agreement with the feds but they are taking a risk of paying a great deal more.

States in Motion

California legislators are acutely aware of the potential impact of an avian-borne illness. In 2002–03, the Exotic Newcastle Disease forced the slaughter of more than 3 million birds in Southern California. It cost the federal government more than $160 million to purchase and destroy the birds to prevent a national outbreak. In 2005, the Legislature directed the state's Department of Food and Agriculture to cooperate with other states and the U.S. Department of Agriculture in planning a program to protect poultry from an avian influenza outbreak, and in turn to keep the flu from spreading to humans.

More legislation is planned this year. Assemblywoman Lois Wolk wants to establish a task force in consultation with the University of California that would develop a plan for surveillance, monitoring, sampling, diagnostic testing and reporting of avian influenza in wild birds and animals.

Other legislation is being developed by Assembly Member Lori Saldaña who worries about agricultural workers handling infected poultry. "Doctors and nurses are on the front line of treating people who are sick," she says. "Agricultural workers are on the front line of dealing with infected birds."

In Illinois, proposed legislation would use federal funding to help local health departments prepare. Hawaii legislators, noting that about half of U.S. deaths in the 1918 pandemic were due to secondary pneumonia infections, are considering a $1 million appropriation for free vaccinations for people over 65 and those with weakened immune systems.

(continued)

States in Motion *(continued)*

Washington state lawmakers are proposing a surcharge of $2 per homeowner's policy and $4 for every commercial and business policy to pay for strengthening coordination between local and state emergency management. Other proposed legislation would require local public health officials to develop pandemic flu preparedness plans that include public information in various languages, responder training drills, disease surveillance, and coordination and communications systems for responding agencies.

At least 10 other states (Georgia, Illinois, Indiana, Massachusetts, Michigan, New Hampshire, Oklahoma, Pennsylvania, Rhode Island and Tennessee) are also considering avian flu legislation.

medications, encourages research and has distribution systems in place. This is the federal role.

"A pandemic, unlike other disasters, can happen in a thousand different places all at the same time," Secretary Leavitt says. "States and communities will be the ones making decisions about whether to close schools or cancel public events. They will also be deciding how to handle the influx of patients at local hospitals and how to distribute medicines."

The states are key in the fight against a pandemic. But avian flu is just one example of an outbreak that poses a statewide health hazard. Preparing for a pandemic now will help state public health officials respond to other emergencies that may occur as well.

THINKING AHEAD

Being ready for any kind of catastrophe requires a public health infrastructure that is equipped to survey and quickly assess the magnitude of the event [and] effectively communicate risk and response through government agencies to the public. This, according to Leavitt, is the state and local role.

"I've had people say, it will never happen," says Representative Upmeyer. "But if we do nothing to be prepared, how will we look to the world? We don't need to panic. We just need to think ahead."

Preparing for infectious diseases or deliberate bioterrorism requires a public health system that supports vaccine development and production, stockpiles of antiviral

More Resources

NCSL on public health preparedness:
 www.ncsl.org/statefed/health/PubPrep.htm
World Health Organization up-to-date information:
 www.who.int/csr/disease/avian_influenza/en/
Centers for Disease Control:
 www.cdc.gov/flu/avian/index.htm
State and Local Planning Checklist:
 www.pandemicflu.gov/plan/pdf/Checklist.pdf
State plans currently online:
 www.pandemicflu.gov/plan/stateplans.html
Health and Human Services:
 www.hhs.gov/news/press/2006press/20060112.html

40

Higher Ed: Dangers of an Unplanned Future

Stanley Ikenberry

This education expert believes we need to engage in a national dialogue to discuss funding, pricing, governance and society's expectations for public colleges and universities.

From *State Legislatures,* September 2005.

There is cause for concern about the future of public higher education. The unease is driven in part by the recent cuts in state funding of most public universities and by the harsh reality that today's strains are merely a continuation of a three decades-long trend driven by systemic tensions in state budgets.

The apparent transformation of public higher education is occurring piecemeal, campus by campus, state by state, absent any overarching design, significant national debate, or studied assessment of the broader implications. As Penn State University President Graham Spanier commented recently: "The privatization of public higher education is not related to any political party, any governor, or any legislative leader. But it is happening, nonetheless."

The precise circumstances vary from campus to campus, but the overall picture is disturbingly consistent. For the University of Michigan, the decline in state dollars as a percentage of the total budget went from roughly one-third of the total some 20 years ago to 18 percent now. The picture for the University of Illinois shows a comparable decline in state support, from 47 percent of the total two decades ago to 25 percent today. At the University of Colorado, state funding has dropped below 10 percent.

Compounding the pressures from Medicaid, corrections and other sectors of the state budget, states have yielded to the temptation in good years to create new and expanded obligations and to enact tax cuts. As state support for public institutions has been squeezed, tuition and other charges have escalated as campuses have attempted to replace lost state revenue. Hikes in tuition and fees have outpaced inflation, growth in personal income, and virtually every available benchmark.

As tuition and other college costs have grown, states and institutions have increased need-based financial aid, though such efforts too often have proved to be inadequate. In the face of an economic downturn, even state funding for need-based aid is not immune to cuts.

CONFRONTING REALITY

America is not likely to return to an earlier, simpler vision of the public university. It is time to confront reality and explore new options and approaches that will preserve the "public essence" of the public university while empowering these institutions to be more responsive to changed circumstances.

To address this challenge, we must confront at least four central issues.

1. The social contract—the public essence—that binds public universities, the states and society must be refined. At the time of the passage of the 1862 Morrill Act, the broad outlines of the social contract were fairly clear: Create a broader curriculum aligned with the changing needs of the new industrial society; expand access for the middle class; and apply knowledge to the broader welfare of the society.

Throughout the 20th century, the public university mission focused on teaching and on discovering and sharing knowledge. After World War II, however, the environment began to shift. As recently as 1960, the University of Illinois, like most other public universities, was a near-open-admissions institution. And while not free, it was relatively inexpensive.

Today, the university where I work is far from free, and admission is highly competitive. Sons and daughters of farmers and factory workers can still be found, but so too can the high-achieving children of surgeons and stockbrokers. The question that needs asking in Illinois and every state is this: What does the public want and require from public universities and colleges? In other words, what are the central interests of the state and the public, and what values underpin them?

> *"The privatization of public higher education is not related to any political party, any governor, or any legislative leader. But it is happening, nonetheless."*
>
> —Graham Spanier

In today's world, open and affordable access to high-quality education is crucial in every state. Research, innovation and the capacity to tackle the core challenges confronting society are no less important, as most state policymakers have known for years.

But how are these needs and values to be expressed in the expectations and commitments between public universities, governments and the many others with a stake in the outcome? Ultimately we must ask: What new policies and approaches can reconcile forces now threatening both the public interest and public colleges and universities? The answers should form the backbone of a new social contract defining the relationship between public higher education and society.

2. Prices at public universities must be set more rationally. More than any other factor, changes in tuition-pricing policies have set off alarm bells and triggered questions about the future of public higher education. Tuition increases alone, however, are not responsible. Novel actions taken in several states are setting fresh precedents—and raising new questions.

In 2003, Miami University of Ohio gained approval from the governor and legislature to increase tuition for all students, resident and nonresident, to the full-cost, non-Ohio-resident level. In return, the university shifted its total state appropriation from campus operations to student financial aid, some based on financial need and some based on merit and other factors.

Colorado is alive with pricing experiments and debates. Its university sought and received "enterprise" status that would have given it authority to set tuition. Then the legislature enacted a proposal backed by University of Colorado leaders to eliminate all direct state support and to adopt a quasi-voucher system coupled with contractual agreements with each institution.

While different in concept, the plans of Colorado and Miami of Ohio are similar in effect. And in some respects the pushback has been similar: In 2005 the Ohio legislature re-imposed a 6 percent tuition cap—and

Colorado's governor and legislative leaders this year successfully encouraged the University of Colorado to scale back its planned tuition hikes.

In Virginia, the leaders of the College of William and Mary, Virginia Tech and the University of Virginia backed legislation to trade some state support for greater independence from state control, including tuition-setting authority. The final bill adopted in 2005—while eliminating the tuition proposal and other items on the schools' wish list—still offered new institutional autonomy on matters ranging from capital construction projects to personnel and procurement. The level of autonomy an institution attains will depend on its financial and management capacity, as well as an explicit agreement to meet specific state policy goals such as increased access and affordability.

In Illinois, the legislature enacted a bill guaranteeing incoming students a relatively stable tuition level for the four years of undergraduate enrollment while giving institutions an implied nod to raise tuition for each incoming freshmen class.

Other examples could be cited. But it is obvious that present efforts are piecemeal, fraught with risk, and lacking in context against which the public interest can be gauged.

3. A more diversified funding base for public universities is essential. Thomas Kane and Peter Orszag in their Brookings Institution report, "Funding Restrictions at Public Universities," estimate that state appropriations for public higher education would be about $13 billion higher—roughly 20 percent above current levels—were the fraction of personal income devoted to public higher education in 1977 to prevail today. That lost ground is unlikely to be regained. More ominously, there is scant reason to believe the trend toward diminishing state government funding will be reversed in the foreseeable future.

As a consequence, public institutions rely to an increasing extent on tuition income and contributions from alumni and friends, and federal grant and contract support is essential for major research universities. Corporate partnerships, economic development, the exploitation of intellectual property and other points of contact between public universities and society will continue to be a central and unapologetic part of any strategy for public higher education.

On the other hand, the capacity of public universities and colleges to tap these alternative sources of revenue varies widely. What are the societal and institutional consequences, and how should these be addressed?

4. It is time for governance reform. Most public university boards are too small and are not reflective of the diverse mission and lines of accountability found in most major public universities. Most governing boards were shaped long ago, when tuition was relatively low, private gifts were rare, and links with the federal government and the business community were modest. Then and now, the state—often through the office of the governor—held all or nearly all of the seats on the governing board.

Times have changed. We need to craft new governing structures consistent with the broader public interests, the emergence of new stakeholders, and a clarified "state-public-university partnership" or "social contract."

The current path to the public university boardroom is treacherous. Quality of appointments varies from state to state and governor to governor.

Although recent corporate governance scandals and ethical lapses have placed the spotlight on governance reform in publicly held companies, no comparable wave of reform has touched public higher education. Who are the shareholders and stakeholders of public universities not now at the board table? What about independence, conflicts of interest and stakeholder accountability?

Governing structures of public universities and colleges need to be reexamined and reformed. The size of some boards needs to be increased. Sources of appointment or election must be diversified. No single governor, legislative committee, or party caucus should control the composition of public university governing boards. Alumni, donors, the business community, agriculture and other segments of society should be more directly and independently represented than they are at present.

TALKS ARE VITAL

Some will say this path toward a stronger future for public colleges and universities is too ambitious, that we are unlikely to clarify the social contract, create a more rational pricing policy, diversify the financial base, and reform governance structures anytime soon.

Others will argue the agenda misses the need for internal academic reform, for public universities to focus more sharply on core priorities, to increase efficiency and contain costs, to become more accountable and engaged. Such criticisms may be on target. Still, the day-to-day internal academic agenda of public universities and colleges will not move forward as it should until the "public essence" of these institutions has been reaffirmed.

In the end, the issue is not just about the future of public higher education. Given the changing nature of society and the economy, American public universities and colleges represent the crucial and indispensable means toward more compelling ends: a healthy, vital democratic society; satisfying, meaningful life chances for citizens; and survival in a rapidly changing, increasingly competitive, and uncertain world.

It is an unthinkable mistake for society to take the future of public higher education for granted. Institutions, missions, policies and programs are shifting in response to powerful forces, and the implications remain largely unexamined. The silos separating state policymakers, business and civic leaders, academics and the public must be deconstructed and a national conversation on the future of public higher education begun.

Piecemeal, campus-by-campus, state-by-state solutions may be inevitable, but when weighed against the broader public interest and the needs of the nation as a whole, they offer little comfort that public higher education will be all it needs to be in the future.

41

Revolution in Evolution?

Sara Vitaska

The evolution vs. creationism controversy continues to influence public school curriculum.

Forty-five percent of Americans believe that God created human beings, close to their present day form, approximately 10,000 years ago. A third of Americans believe that Charles Darwin's theory of evolution is a well-supported scientific theory. And a third of Americans consider themselves biblical literalists who believe that the Bible is the actual word of God and is to be taken literally, word for word, according to a 2004 Gallup Poll.

The famous "Monkey Trial" in 1925, ignited the modern day debate of teaching evolution in public schools. In a Tennessee courtroom, teacher John T. Scopes was convicted of teaching evolution in the classroom, then a violation of state law. The contentious value-ridden debate lay practically dormant, however, until the 1987 U.S. Supreme Court ruling that creationism is a religious belief and cannot be taught in public schools alongside evolution.

That historic ruling, stemming from a court case in Louisiana, subsequently paved the way for adopting new evolution-based science curriculum policies across the nation. Two states recently received national attention when their local school boards voted to modify their science curriculum to offer an alternative explanation to the scientific theory of evolution. Consequently, both the Cobb County School District in Georgia and the Dover Area School District in Pennsylvania are battling it out in court.

COBB COUNTY, GEORGIA

In 2002, the Cobb County School District, nestled in the suburbs of Atlanta, adopted the policy of placing disclaimer stickers in 13 middle and high school science textbooks. The disclaimers read:

From *State Legislatures,* May 2005.

"This textbook contains material on evolution. Evolution is a theory, not a fact, regarding the origin of living things. This material should be approached with an open mind, studied carefully and critically considered."

The stickers originated from Marjorie Rogers, a creationist who collected more than 2,000 signatures that led the school board to adopt the policy.

In response, a handful of parents, along with the American Civil Liberties Union, sued the school district arguing that the stickers promoted religion in public schools and therefore violated the U.S. Constitution's principle of separation of church and state. District Court Judge Clarence Cooper ruled in January that the disclaimers are unconstitutional and ordered the stickers removed at the end of this school year. The judge said that although the disclaimers do not directly mention or support religion, a reasonable person would interpret its message as endorsing religion. He said the religiously motivated stickers imply that the school board condones the beliefs of Christian fundamentalists and creationists. Furthermore, Judge Cooper wrote that muddying the definition of "theory" is dangerous as it misleads students into thinking that the theory of evolution is based on a "hunch" rather than a well-substantiated explanation of some aspect of the natural world.

The legal battle over the stickers continues as the Cobb County school board decided, by a vote of 5-to-2, to appeal Judge Cooper's ruling to the 11th Circuit Court of Appeals in Atlanta. The school board claims that it is not endorsing religion, but instead encouraging students to think critically in all subject areas.

DOVER, PENNSYLVANIA

The Dover Area School District, located in rural south-central Pennsylvania, is thought to be the first school district in the nation to require teachers to read a statement about intelligent design to their high school biology students. Intelligent design is a concept that holds that the universe is so complex, it had to be created by an unspecified guiding force. A portion of the statement reads: *Because Darwin's Theory is a theory, it continues to be tested as new evidence is discovered. The Theory is not a fact. Gaps in the Theory exist for which there is no evidence. A theory is defined as a well-tested explanation that unifies a broad range of observations. Intelligent Design is an explanation of the origin of life that differs from Darwin's view. The reference book,* Of Pandas and People, *is available for students who might be interested in gaining an understanding of what Intelligent Design actually involves. With respect to any theory, students are encouraged to keep an open mind. The school leaves the discussion of the Origins of Life to individual students and their families. As a Standards-driven district, class instruction focuses upon preparing students to achieve proficiency on Standards-based assessments.*

The controversy stems from the school board's 6-3 vote last fall to include an alternative to the theory of evolution in the science curriculum.

Two board members resigned and a half dozen families, the American Civil Liberties Union and Americans United for Separation of Church and State filed a lawsuit against the school district. They alleged that presenting the concept of intelligent design in public school science classrooms violated their religious rights by promoting particular religious beliefs to their children under the guise of science education.

Similar to the lawsuit filed against Cobb County, the lawsuit against the Dover district argues that teaching students that there are gaps or problems in the scientific theory of evolution, while failing to present any such gaps in the concept of intelligent design, would ultimately lead students to believe that the theory of evolution is false while implying that the truth lies in the religious beliefs advocated through intelligent design. The lawsuit cites violations to the Establishment Clause of the First Amendment, which calls for the separation of church and state.

The district has run into resistance among teachers and parents alike. Seven teachers signed a letter objecting to the policy on grounds that it violates the professional standards and practices code for teachers. Consequently, the district has agreed to temporarily exempt science teachers from reading the statement. Instead, administrators are reading it to ninth grade biology classes.

Additionally, the district has allowed students whose parents object to the policy to be excused from listening to the statement. The Dover Area School District maintains that the adopted biology curriculum policy does not advance religion, but instead informs students about the existing scientific controversy surrounding the theory of evolution.

Like it or not, public school science curriculum standards are changing. Proponents cite a national trend in restoring moral values and view the evolution-based science curriculum as biased. Critics cite a growing presence of religious voters in politics as the catalyst to placing creationism back into public school science curricula.

RECENT POLICY TRENDS

In Kansas, those who favor changing the state's science curriculum to include an alternative to evolution, have won a majority on the state Board of Education, again. Kansas reignited the evolution debate when, in 1999, the state Board of Education voted 6–4 to reject evolution as a scientific principle, virtually removing all references to it from the state's science curriculum. The board reversed the policy in 2001, when the membership changed.

With the verdicts from two of the nation's most recent court battles still out, other states are re-examining their science curricula to expose questions about evolution and alternative views. In 1995, Alabama's state board of education approved the nation's first state-sanctioned sticker to be placed in biology textbooks, warning students that evolution is a "controversial theory" that should be questioned. There seems to be no organized effort to oppose the curriculum, which has been revised by a committee of mostly science educators over the past year.

The Ohio Department of Education passed a measure encouraging teachers to hold classes that question the theory of evolution. In Grantsburg, Wis., the school

---

Bills in Discussion

Legislators in at least nine states this session have been looking at legislation that relates to teaching evolution in public schools.

- **Alabama:** Would allow teachers to challenge the scientific validity of the theory of evolution.
- **Georgia:** Would require teachers to present scientific evidence challenging evolution.
- **Kansas:** Would promote objectivity in science education.
- **Missouri:** Would require public school textbooks to have one or more chapters containing critical analysis of origins.
- **Pennsylvania:** Would allow school boards to add "intelligent design" to any curriculum containing evolution and allow teachers, subject to board approval, to present "supporting evidence deemed necessary for instruction on the theory of intelligent design."
- **South Carolina:** Would revise how the state selects textbooks and establishes a committee to study the origins of species and determine whether alternatives to evolution should be offered.

Bills in Arkansas, Mississippi and Montana died in committee or were not formally introduced.

---

board voted to incorporate a critical approach to evolution, without identifying specific alternatives.

And in legislatures this session, at least nine states have been discussing how to teach evolution in public schools.

Text Credits

Page	Credit
77	Reprinted with permission from *State Legislatures* magazine, the National Conference of State Legislatures, copyrighted 2005–2006.
86	Reprinted with authors' permission.
91	Reprinted with the permission of the National Governors Association. New edition will be published in 2007.
97	This information has been reprinted with the permission of the Council of State Governments.
111	Mathew Manweller. 2005. The "Angriest Crocodile": Information Costs, Direct Democracy Activists, and the Politicization of State Judicial Elections." *State and Local Government Review* 37:2:86–102. With permission of Carl Vinson Institute of Government, University of Georgia (www.vinsoninstitute.org).
127	"Courts are Different" was written for the League of Women Voters of the United States (LWVUS) and was first published on the League Web site (www.lwv.org). Permission for publication here is granted by the LWVUS.
145	This information has been reprinted with the permission of the Council of State Governments.

Page	Credit
152	Reprinted with authors' permission.
164	Reprinted with authors' permission.
172	Reprinted with permission from *State Legislatures* magazine, the National Council of State Legislatures, copyrighted 2005–2006.
178	Reprinted with permission from *State Legislatures* magazine, the National Council of State Legislatures, copyrighted 2005–2006.
198	Reprinted with permission from *State Legislatures* magazine, the National Conference of State Legislatures, copyrighted 2005–2006.
202	Reprinted with permission from *State Legislatures* magazine, the National Conference of State Legislatures copyrighted 2005–2006.
207	Reprinted with permission from *State Legislatures* magazine, the National Conference of State Legislatures copyrighted 2005–2006.
211	Reprinted with permission from *State Legislatures* magazine, the National Council of State Legislatures copyrighted 2005–2006.